Eixample
Pages 72–85

0 metres 750
0 yards 750

Eixample

Catalonia
Pages 110–131

Further Afield
Pages 94–101

Catalonia

Barcelona

0 km 50
0 miles 50

EYEWIT

BARCELONA
& CATALONIA

EYEWITNESS TRAVEL

BARCELONA & CATALONIA

Main Contributor **Roger Williams**

DK

LONDON, NEW YORK,
MELBOURNE, MUNICH AND DELHI
www.dk.com

Project Editor Catherine Day
Art Editors Carolyn Hewitson, Marisa Renzullo
Editors Elizabeth Atherton, Felicity Crowe
Designer Suzanne Metcalfe-Megginson
Map Co-ordinator David Pugh
Picture Research Monica Allende
DTP Designers Samantha Borland, Lee Redmond, Pamela Shiels

Main Contributor Roger Williams

Maps Jane Hanson, Phil Rose, Jennifer Skelley (Lovell Jones Ltd), Gary Bowes, Richard Toomey (ERA-Maptec Ltd)

Photographers Max Alexander, Mike Dunning, Heidi Grassley, Alan Keohane

Illustrators Stephen Conlin, Isidoro González-Adalid Cabezas (Acanto Arquitectura y Urbanismo S.L.), Claire Littlejohn, Maltings Partnership, John Woodcock

Printed and bound in China

First American Edition, 1999
16 17 18 10 9 8 7 6 5 4 3 2

Published in the United States by DK Publishing, 345 Hudson Street, New York, NY 10014

Reprinted with revisions 2000, 2001, 2002, 2003, 2004, 2005, 2006, 2008, 2009, 2010, 2011, 2013, 2014, 2015

Copyright 1999, 2015 © Dorling Kindersley Limited, London
A Penguin Random House Company

Published in the UK by Dorling Kindersley Limited.

A catalog record for this book is available from the Library of Congress.

ISSN 1542-1554
ISBN 978-1-4654-3754-9

Throughout this book, floors are numbered in accordance with local Catalan usage.

MIX
Paper from
responsible sources
FSC™ C018179
www.fsc.org

The information in this DK Eyewitness Travel Guide is checked regularly.
Every effort has been made to ensure that this book is as up-to-date as possible at the time of going to press. Some details, however, such as telephone numbers, opening hours, prices, gallery hanging arrangements and travel information are liable to change. The publishers cannot accept responsibility for any consequences arising from the use of this book, nor for any material on third party websites, and cannot guarantee that any website address in this book will be a suitable source of travel information. We value the views and suggestions of our readers very highly. Please write to: Publisher, DK Eyewitness Travel Guides, Dorling Kindersley, 80 Strand, London, WC2R 0RL, UK, or email: travelguides@dk.com.

Front cover main image: Sagrada Família by architect Antonio Gaudi, Barcelona

◀ Previous pages: The quayside at Cadaqués, on the Costa Brava

Contents

How to Use this Guide **6**

Jaume I, "El Conquistador", ruler of Catalonia 1213–76

Introducing Barcelona and Catalonia

Great Days in
Barcelona **10**

Putting Barcelona and
Catalonia on the Map **14**

A Portrait of Catalonia **18**

Catalonia Through
the Year **36**

The History of
Catalonia **42**

One of the many popular cafés in Barcelona's redeveloped Old Port

Barcelona Area by Area

Barcelona at a Glance **50**

The small, whitewashed town of Cadaqués on the Costa Brava

Old Town **54**

Eixample **72**

Montjuïc **86**

Further Afield **94**

Three Guided Walks **102**

Travellers' Needs

Where to Stay **134**

Where to
Eat and Drink **140**

Shopping in
Barcelona **154**

Entertainment in
Barcelona **162**

Outdoor Activities **170**

Survival Guide

Practical Information **174**

Travel Information **182**

Street Finder **188**

General Index **198**

Acknowledgments **205**

Catalan Phrase
Book **207**

Pa amb tomàquet – bread rubbed with
tomato, garlic and olive oil

Barcelona Metro and
Train Routes
Inside back cover

Barcelona Cathedral, in the heart of the city's
extensive and well-preserved Gothic Quarter

Spectacular stained-glass roof of
the Palau de la Música Catalana

Catalonia

Lleida, Andorra, Girona,
Barcelona Province,
Tarragona **110**

HOW TO USE THIS GUIDE

This guide has expert recommendations and detailed practical information that will enrich any visit to Barcelona and Catalonia. *Introducing Barcelona and Catalonia* puts the area in geographical, historical and cultural context. *Barcelona and Catalonia* is a six-chapter guide to important sights: *Barcelona at a Glance* highlights the city's top attractions; *Old Town, Eixample* and *Montjuïc* explore Barcelona's central districts in more detail; *Further Afield* profiles sights that are outside the city centre; and *Catalonia* delves into the surrounding region's four provinces. *Travellers' Needs* covers hotels, restaurants and entertainment. The *Survival Guide* provides vital practical information.

Barcelona and Catalonia

The region is divided into five sightseeing areas – the central districts of Barcelona, sights outside the centre, and those beyond the city. Each area chapter opens with an introduction and a list of sights covered. Central districts have a Street-by-Street map of a particularly interesting part of the area. The sights further afield have a regional map.

Locator maps show where you are in relation to other parts of Barcelona or Spain.

Each chapter of *Barcelona and Catalonia* has a different colour-coded thumb tab.

Sights at a Glance lists the area's key sights (great buildings, art galleries, museums and churches) by category.

1 Area Map of the City
Sights are numbered and located on a map, with Metro stations where helpful. The sights are also shown on the *Barcelona Street Finder* on pp188–97.

2 Street-by-Street Map
The area shaded pink on the *Area Map* is shown here in greater detail, with accurate drawings of all the buildings.

A suggested route for a walk covers the more interesting streets in the area.

3 Detailed Information on each Sight The sights listed at the start of the section are described individually and follow the numbering on the *Area Map*. A key to symbols summarizing practical information is shown on the back flap.

CATALONIA

Lleida · Andorra · Girona · Barcelona Province · Tarragona

There is a wealth of natural beauty in Catalonia's four provinces, plus the small Catalan-speaking country of Andorra; they unite rocky coasts and mountains, fertile plains and sandy shores. Many who visit don't stray far from the coast, but the rewards for venturing further afield are immense.

Lying beyond the constant bustle of Barcelona, Catalonia is essentially a rural region, with no large cities and few industrial blights. Of the four provinces, all named after their principal city, Lleida is the largest and least populated. Among its jewels are the Romanesque churches of the Boí valley and the Aigüestortes National Park.

The province of Girona is blessed with mountains and sea. This eastern end of the Pyrenees has the magical Cerdanya valley and the ancient monasteries of Ripoll and Sant Joan de les Abadesses, as well as medieval villages and a handsome and low-slung mountainseed capital city. Its coast, the Costa Brava, is rocky and full of delights.

Barcelona province has its own coast, the Maresme to the north is rather spoiled by the railway running beside the sea, but the Garraf to the south is more exciting – Sitges is a highly fashionable spot. Inland are the Holy Mountain of Montserrat (Catalonia's spiritual heart), the Penedès winelands, and the country town of Vic.

Tarragona, the most southerly of the provinces, has one of the peninsula's former Roman capitals. Here the land rolls more gently, supporting fruit and nut orchards and the romantic communities of Poblet and Santes Creus, before falling away towards the rice lands of the Ebro. The coastline is more gentle, too, with long, sandy beaches.

4 **Introduction to Catalonia** The chapter on *Catalonia* has its own introduction, providing an overview of the history and character of the region. The area covered is highlighted on the map of Spain shown on pages 112–13. The chapter explores Catalonia's rich historical, cultural and natural heritage, from the monasteries of Montserrat and Poblet to Tarragona's *casteller* festivals, from the sandy beaches of the Costa Daurada to the snowy peaks of the Pyrenees.

Exploring Catalonia

Catalonia includes a long stretch of the Spanish Pyrenees, whose green, flower-filled valleys hide picturesque villages with Romanesque churches. The Parc Nacional d'Aigüestortes and Vall d'Aran are paradises for naturalists, while Baixa beaches offers does reliable views. Sun-lovers can choose between the rugged Costa Brava or the long, sandy stretches of the Costa Daurada. Tarragona is rich in Roman monuments. Inland are the monasteries of Poblet and Santes Creus and the well-known vineyards of Penedès.

5 **Pictorial Map** This gives an illustrated overview of the whole region. All the sights covered in this chapter are numbered, and the network of major roads is marked. There are also useful tips on getting around the region by bus and train.

6 **Detailed Sight Information** All the important cities, towns and other places to visit are described individually. They are listed in order following the numbering given on the *Pictorial Map*. Within each town or city there is detailed information on important buildings and other sights.

Stars indicate the best features and works of art.

Monestir de Poblet

The Visitors' Checklist provides a summary of the practical information you will need to plan your visit.

7 **The Top Sights** These are given two or more full pages. Historic buildings are dissected to reveal their interiors. For larger historic sites, all the important buildings are labelled to help you locate those that most interest you.

INTRODUCING BARCELONA AND CATALONIA

Great Days in Barcelona   10–13

Putting Barcelona and
    Catalonia on the Map   14–17

A Portrait of Catalonia   18–35

Catalonia Through the Year   36–39

The History of Catalonia   42–49

GREAT DAYS IN BARCELONA

Days are long in Barcelona; morning extends until well after midday, with lunch starting around 2pm, and late opening hours mean that afternoon merges into evening. With so much time at your disposal, you'll want to make the most of your stay. Over the following pages, you'll find itineraries for some of the best attractions the city has to offer, from themed days to five-day sightseeing extravaganzas. All sights are cross-referenced so it is possible to look up more information and tailor the day to suit your needs. Price guides on these pages show the cost for two adults, or a family of four, excluding meals.

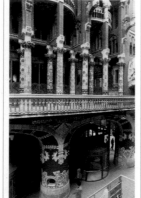

La Rambla, an exciting avenue for a stroll at any time

Historic Treasures

Two adults allow at least €100

- A stroll round the Gothic quarter and museums
- A Modernista concert hall
- Non-stop life on Spain's most famous street

Morning

Barcelona's preserved medieval centre is the **Barri Gòtic** (see pp56–7), a warren of streets where it is easy to get lost. You can happily spend the morning here without walking great distances. The focal point is the **Cathedral** (see pp60–61). Next to it is the **Palau Reial** (Royal Palace), part of which is now the **Museu d'Història de la Ciutat** (see pp58–9), where you can take a fascinating subterranean stroll over the excavated ruins of Roman Barcelona. The palace also houses what is perhaps Barcelona's most fascinating museum, the eclectic **Museu Frederic Marès** (see p58). There are plenty of places for a budget lunch in this area.

Afternoon

After lunch, take a guided tour of the **Palau de la Música Catalana** (see pp64–5) and its dazzling Modernista interior. After that, plunge into the atmospheric **El Born district** (see pp104–5), with its trendy shops. Take a look in the **Museu Picasso** (see pp66–7), then wander to **La Rambla**, a busy street where there is always plenty of activity.

Richly ornamental interior of Palau de la Música Catalana

Gaudí Greats

Two adults allow at least €120

- **Casa Batlló's organic forms**
- Gaudí's extraordinary church, Sagrada Família
- An evening's shopping in style in Passeig de Gràcia

Morning

For many visitors, Barcelona is synonymous with the unique architecture of Antoni Gaudí. He created many great buildings, all of which are worth visiting, but here are two places to make a start. Begin your day with a visit to Gaudí's most colourful and eccentric house, **Casa Batlló** (see pp78–9). Discover its fantastic organic forms and be sure to make your way up to the roof terrace to see the remarkable chimneys and "dragon's back". A little further up the road is the equally renowned **La Pedrera**, also known as Casa Milà (see p81). This can also be visited, but if you're short of time its remarkable façade can be admired from the outside. For lunch, you'll find there are several budget-priced restaurants in the streets near and parallel to Passeig de Gràcia.

Afternoon/Evening

Visit Gaudí's greatest, unfinished work, the **Sagrada Família** (see pp82–5). Allow plenty of time to make sense of the dense detail on the two façades of this extraordinary church – the Passion façade and the Nativity façade – and also to explore the vertigo-inducing fantasy towers (you

Casa Batlló, a house in an alternative architectural universe

go up by lift and return to ground level by stairs). Coming back down to reality, return to the **Passeig de Gràcia** and browse in its stylish shops. Look out for the design emporium **Vinçon** (see p155).

Museu d'Art Contemporani façade

Art for Art's Sake

Two adults allow at least €70

- Romanesque marvels on Montjuïc hill
- Contemporary works of art
- Collection of Old Masters

Morning
The number of great galleries you can cram into a day depends on your appetite and stamina, but here are five to give you a taster. Start at 10am when the **Museu Nacional d'Art de Catalunya (MNAC)** (see p91) opens on Montjuïc hill. Here, you'll see arguably the best collection of Romanesque art in any museum. Close by is the city's latest contemporary art gallery, **CaixaForum** (see p92), situated in a Modernista factory. Lunch in a local café.

Afternoon
For a change of pace, head to the **Monestir de Pedralbes** (see p97), a lovely 14th-century monastery with numerous religious objects and works of art on display. Back in the city centre, visit the **Museu d'Art Contemporani** (see p64), where you can be sure of something surprising, or visit the temporary exhibitions at the adjacent **Centre de Cultura Contemporània de Barcelona (CCCB)** (see p164).

Family Fun

Family of 4 allow at least €120

- A trip to the funfair
- A harbour cruise
- Sharks at the aquarium
- Exploring the museum

Morning
Tibidabo Amusement Park (see p100), on the highest hill behind Barcelona, is a family day out in itself - the trip up there by tram and funicular is half the fun. But if you don't want to go that far, stroll down La Rambla and take the lift up the **Monument a Colom** (see p71) for a good view of this part of the city. From the nearby quayside, board a **Golondrina** (see p71) for a cruise round the harbour. Then cross the wavy footbridge for the Maremagnum shopping centre, also the best place to grab a bite to eat.

Afternoon/Evening
Attractions that are specifically for children can, if you want to extend the day, be saved until after dark. The **Aquarium** (see p70) offers several activities for kids, as well as a fantastic, enormous central tank, which you pass through on a moving walkway to get a fish-eye view of the swirling shoals of sharks and other creatures. A short walk away is the relaxing, child-friendly **Museu d'Història de Catalunya** (see pp70 71), with exhibits on daily life in earlier times that include plenty of hands-on activities.

Barcelona's Aquàrium, a wonderful experience for children

2 Days in Barcelona

- Admire Gaudí's unfinished masterpiece, the Sagrada Família
- Get lost in the medieval warren of the Barri Gòtic (Gothic Quarter)
- Tuck into a paella by the beach in Barceloneta

A beautiful view of the city from the roof terraces of Gaudí's La Pedrera

Day 1

Morning Explore one of the largest and best-preserved medieval neighbourhoods in Europe, the **Barri Gòtic** (see pp56–7). Admire the stunning **Cathedral** (see pp60–61), particularly the enchanting cloister, and visit the remnants of the ancient Roman settlement in the **Museu d'Història de Barcelona** (Barcelona History Museum) (see pp58–9). Have lunch in one of the area's many restaurants and cafés.

Afternoon Stroll down **La Rambla** (see pp62–3) to **Port Vell** (see p70), where yachts bob in the harbour. Then visit **Barceloneta** (see p69), the fascinating fishing neighbourhood (perhaps grabbing some picnic supplies at the fantastic market on the Plaça de la Font), before hitting the beaches. Finish the day with paella on the seafront.

Day 2

Morning Jump on the Metro to reach Gaudí's extraordinary **Sagrada Família** (see pp82–5), its towers visible across the city, yet still awaiting completion. There's another Modernista

Barceloneta beach, one of the best urban beaches in the world

masterpiece very close by in the fairy-tale **Hospital de la Santa Creu i de Sant Pau** (see p81). Head back to have lunch in the Eixample neighbourhood.

Afternoon Wander along the **Passeig de Gràcia** (see p74), Barcelona's most fashionable street, perhaps doing a bit of shopping at one of the chic boutiques. This street is home to two of Gaudí's most spectacular domestic buildings: **La Pedrera** (see p81) and **Casa Batlló** (see pp78–9). Both are open to visitors, or you could just admire the stunning façades. Go for tapas in the Eixample district.

3 Days in Barcelona

- Be amazed by Gaudí's "Dragon House", Casa Batlló
- Visit the fantastic Picasso Museum
- Admire the stunning Romanesque mosaics in MNAC

Day 1

Morning Amble down the famous promenade, **La Rambla** (see pp62–3), then dive into the stone warren of the **Barri Gòtic** (Gothic Quarter) (see pp56–7). Take a peek at the **Casa de la Ciutat** (see p59), the **Palau de la Generalitat** (see p59), and perhaps visit the fascinating **Museu d'Història de Barcelona** (Barcelona History Museum) (see pp58–9), and the sublime Gothic **Cathedral** (see pp60–61). Tuck into lunch in one of

the neighbourhood's great old-fashioned taverns.

Afternoon Hang out in the trendy **Born** neighbourhood (see pp104–105), where the narrow streets are lined with boho-chic boutiques. Visit the **Museu Picasso** (see p66) and the city's most beautiful Gothic church, the **Basílica de Santa Maria del Mar** (see p66–7), before enjoying a stroll around the **Parc de la Ciutadella** (see p67). Enjoy some tapas at one of El Born's stylish eateries.

Day 2

Morning Devote the day to Gaudí. Spend the morning at the **Sagrada Família** (see pp82–5), perhaps taking a lift up one of the enormous towers, and then wander up to the nearby **Hospital de la Santa Creu i de Sant Pau** (see p81), built by another Modernista master, Domènech i Montaner. Take the Metro to the Eixample neighbourhood for lunch.

Afternoon Visit **Casa Batlló** (see pp78–9), one of Gaudí's most magical creations, and compare it with buildings by two other great Modernista architects that occupy the same block, known as the **Illa de la Discòrdia** (see p80). If you've got time, perhaps also take in **La Pedrera** (see p81), with its undulating roof terrace. You might also drop in to the **Fundació Antoni Tàpies** (see p80), where contemporary artworks are displayed in an early Modernista building.

Day 3

Morning Spend the morning at the **Museu Nacional d'Art de Catalunya (MNAC)** *(see p91)*, admiring the superb medieval frescoes that once adorned isolated Pyrenean churches. Then amble up through lovely gardens to reach the **Castell de Montjuïc** *(see p93)* on top of the hill, to enjoy spectacular views. Sway across the harbour on the cable car to **Barceloneta** *(see p69)* and enjoy some freshly prepared seafood by the beach.

Afternoon Stroll through the salty old fishermen's *barrí* of Barceloneta up to **Port Vell** *(see p70)*, where fancy yachts have now taken the place of fishing boats. Say hello to Columbus, atop the **Monument a Colom** *(see p71)*, then tour the harbour in one of the pretty, old-fashioned "swallow boats" called *golondrinas* *(see p71)*, or visit the superb **Museu Marítim** *(see p71)*, set in medieval shipyards.

Delicacies on display at the Boqueria market

Isabella and Ferdinand once greeted Columbus. Visit the beautiful Gothic **Cathedral** *(see pp60–61)*, before enjoying delicious tapas nearby.

Day 2

Morning Head into the multi-cultural **El Raval** neighbourhood *(see p64)*, beginning with a tour of Gaudí's **Palau Güell** *(see p64)*, one of his earliest commissions. Then head up to the dazzling, light-filled **Museu d'Art Contemporani** *(see p64)* for a shot of contemporary culture, and have lunch on the huge square in front of the museum.

Afternoon Wander along the **Passeig de Gràcia** *(see p106)*, where fancy shops rub shoulders with spectacular Modernista buildings, such as the trio of superb mansions including Gaudí's **Casa Batlló** in the Illa de la Discòrdia *(see pp78–9)*. Then head up to the **Park Güell** *(see pp98–9)* for spectacular, city-wide views.

Day 3

Morning Chic shops and arty cafés await you in the **Born** district *(see pp104–105)*, where you'll also find the **Museu Picasso** *(see p66)*, the **Basílica de Santa Maria** *(see pp66–7)*, and the extraordinary **Palau de la Música Catalana** *(see p65)*, a lavish Modernista concert hall. Stop for lunch at Els Quatre Gats, once patronized by Picasso.

Afternoon Spend the afternoon in **Barceloneta** *(see p69)*, the old fishing district, which has a great market. Take a long

walk along the spectacular city beaches, and follow it up with a well-deserved seafood dinner.

Day 4

Morning Spend the morning at the **Sagrada Familia** *(see pp82–5)*, Gaudí's vast and still unfinished temple, and the nearby **Hospital de la Santa Creu i de Sant Pau** *(see p81)* designed by Domènech i Muntaner, another leading light of the Modernista movement.

Afternoon Walk out onto the pitch and imagine the crowds roaring on the **Camp Nou Tour** of FC Barcelona's legendary stadium and its museum of trophies and memorabilia *(see p96)*. Then go back in time at the **Monestir Maria de Pedralbes** *(see p97)*, an enchanting Gothic church and cloister, now part of the city's history museum.

Day 5

Morning Head to Montjuïc to visit the sublime Romanesque artworks in the **Museu Nacional d'Art de Catalunya (MNAC)** *(see p91)* and, if time allows, pop into the nearby **Museu Aqueològic** *(see p91)*. Picnic in one of the lovely gardens nearby, or have lunch in the museum café.

Afternoon Visit the **Fundació Joan Miró** *(see p90)*, set in a stunning contemporary building with wonderful views over the city, then stroll back downhill to enjoy the enchanting spectacle of the **Font Màgica** fountain *(see p92)*.

---

5 Days in Barcelona

- Picnic in Gaudí's Park Güell
- Tour the fabled Camp Nou stadium and visit the Museu del FC Barcelona
- Admire the opulence of the Modernista Palau de la Música Catalana

Day 1

Morning Wander down **La Rambla** *(see pp62–3)*, popping in to La Boqueria Market to be dazzled by the array of produce, before arriving at **Port Vell** *(see p70)*, the city's spruced-up harbour. Admire the **Monument a Colom** *(see p71)* or visit the **Maremagnum** shopping and entertainment centre *(see p70)*, also home to the city's wonderful **Aquàrium** *(see p70)*.

Afternoon Get lost in the narrow lanes and squares of the atmospheric **Barri Gòtic** (Gothic Quarter) *(see pp56–7)*, dropping in at the **Museu d'Història de Barcelona** (Barcelona History Museum) *(see pp58–9)* to admire the grand throne room where

Palau de la Música Catalana, a Modernista palace with a spectacular interior

Putting Barcelona and Catalonia on the Map

Catalonia lies in the northeastern corner of the Iberian Peninsula and occupies six percent of Spain. Barcelona, its capital, lies almost exactly halfway along its coastline, which in turn stretches a quarter of the way down Spain's Mediterranean seaboard. Barcelona is the main point of departure for the Catalan-speaking Balearic Islands.

Key

— Motorway (highway)

— Major road

— International border

— Regional border

For keys to symbols *see back flap*

Canary Islands

Melilla

*See inset map
on next page*

Genoa, Livorno,
Civitavecchia

0 kilometres   100
0 miles   50

Europe and
North Africa

Barcelona City Centre

Set between the mountains and the sea, which still play an integral part in city life, Barcelona is a rare city, a patchwork of distinctive districts telling the story of its growth from a medieval core to the 19th-century expansion to today's ultra-modern showpieces. The three main sightseeing areas described in this guide illustrate this startling diversity. The hill of Montjuïc, abutting the sea, forms the southwestern end of an arc of steep hills that almost completely encloses the city. It is a district of monumental buildings and open spaces. The Old Town has a superb Gothic heart, with a myriad of narrow streets twisting among ancient houses. The densely populated Eixample, in contrast, is a district of immensely long, straight streets and superb Modernista architecture.

Montjuïc

There are wonderful views from the top of this large hill. Several of Barcelona's best museums are here, including the Museu Arqueològic (see p91) which displays this Roman mosaic.

0 kilometres 1
0 miles 0.5

Eixample

This area covers the most interesting part of the city's 19th-century expansion. Walks along its streets will reveal countless details of the Modernista style, such as this ornate doorway of Casa Comalat *(see p29)* in Avinguda Diagonal.

Old Town

This area includes all the oldest districts of Barcelona and its port, the 18th-century fishing "village" of Barceloneta and the new waterside developments. This new swing bridge is in the Old Port *(see p69)*.

Catalonia

Much of Catalonia is mountainous, with Barcelona sited on a narrow coastal plain. The beaches of nearby Sitges (see p130) are popular with city dwellers.

Key

☐ Barcelona and environs	▬ Main road
▬ Motorways (highways)	▭ Other road
▬ Dual carriageway	▬ International border
	▬ Regional border

A PORTRAIT
OF CATALONIA

Barcelona is one of the great Mediterranean cities. Few places are so redolent with history, few so boldly modern. Animated and inspired, it is a city that sparkles as much at night-time as in the full light of day. It is famous for its main avenue, La Rambla, for its bars, its museums and its enthusiasm for life.

Barcelona is the capital of the autonomous region of Catalonia, the most northeasterly corner of Spain, bordering France. The region is divided into four provinces, named after their provincial capitals: Barcelona, Girona, Lleida and Tarragona.

The city of Barcelona lies between two rivers, the Llobregat and the Besòs, and is backed by the Collserola hills, which rise to a 512 m (1,680 ft) peak at the Tibidabo amusement park. The city grew up as the industrial sweatshop of Spain, though the shunting yards and seaside warehouses have now gone. Around five million people live in Barcelona and its suburbs – about half the population of Catalonia. It is Spain's second city after its old rival, Madrid.

Politics and Society

Catalonia is governed by the Generalitat, housed in the Palau de la Generalitat in the heart of the Old Town and on the site of the Roman forum. The region's parliament is located in the Parc de la Ciutadella. The city of Barcelona has a separate administration, and its town hall, the Casa de la Ciutat, faces the Generalitat across the Plaça de Sant Jaume. Catalonia has developed its own police force, which has now taken over from Spain's national police in most of Catalonia.

Catalans are progressive but, as in many other countries, people in rural areas are more conservative than those in the cities. For 23 years after Franco's death, the Generalitat was run by the conservative Convergència i Unió under Jordi Pujol, while the city council was run by socialists. In modern times, however, the movement calling for full independence for Catalonia has proved a uniting force, with some four out of five Catalans voting for self-rule in a symbolic "referendum" held in 2014.

Strolling on La Rambla, Barcelona's tree-lined, traffic-free main avenue

◄ Mask-like balconies ornament the façade of Antoni Gaudí's astonishing Casa Batlló

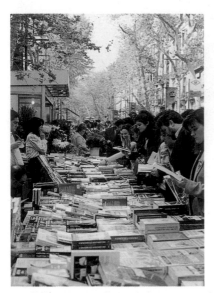

St George's Day in April – the day for giving books

Catalans, who banned bullfighting in 2012 and whose sedate national dance, the *sardana,* is unruffled by passion, are a serious, hardworking people. Some would rather be associated with northern Europeans than with other Spaniards, whom they regard as indolent. Part of their complaint against Madrid has been that, as one of the richest regions of Spain, they put more into the national coffers than they take out.

Two emotions are said to guide Catalans: *seny,* which means solid common sense, and *rauxa,* a creative chaos. A bourgeois, conservative element of Barcelona society can be seen at concerts and in pastry shops, but a certain surreal air is often evident, on La Rambla, for instance, where sometimes it seems that anything goes. The two elements are mixed in each person, and even the most staid may have the occasional *cop de rauxa,* or moment of chaotic ecstasy.

Catalans are not burdened with self-doubt. The vigour with which they have rebuilt parts of their capital since the early 1980s shows flair and a firm hand. Places of great sentimental value, such as Barceloneta's beachside restaurant shacks,

were torn down. Stunning new buildings such as the Museu d'Art Contemporani were put up in the Old Town, and old buildings such as the Café Zurich, a famous rendezvous for writers, artists and intellectuals on La Rambla, were rebuilt without hesitation.

Language and Culture

A Romance language similar to the old Langue d'Oc, or Provençal, once used in France, Catalan is Catalonia's official language, spoken by some 11 million people. It has always been a living language and it continued to be spoken in the home even when it was banned by Franco. Catalans do not think it rude to talk to each other in Catalan in front of someone who speaks only Spanish. All public signs and official documents in Catalonia are in Spanish and Catalan.

Street performer on La Rambla

If *rauxa* fuels the creative spirit as claimed, then Catalonia has been blessed with an abundance. Modernisme, led by Antoni Gaudí, is the region's gift to world architecture. Painters Joan Miró,

Poster for a Pedro Almodóvar film

Beach at Tossa de Mar on the Costa Brava

Salvador Dalí and Antoni Tàpies were born here, while Pablo Picasso spent his formative years in Barcelona. Designs by Javier Mariscal, creator of the 1992 Olympic motifs and Cobi, the mascot, furniture by Oscar Tusquets and fashion by Toni Miró help make Barcelona a city of great style. Bigas Luna, locally born director of *Jamón Jamón*, Pedro Almodóvar, whose film *All About My Mother* was shot in Barcelona and Woody Allen's *Vicky, Cristina, Barcelona* have raised the area's profile in the cinema.

Over the last 150 years, some outstanding musicians have emerged from Catalonia. Composers Isaac Albéniz (1860–1909), Enric Granados (1867–1916) and Frederic Mompou (1893–1987) brought music imbued with a true Iberian idiom into the classical mainstream. Pau Casals (1876–1973) ranked among the greatest of all cellists; Jordi Savall is an international figure in early music; and Montserrat Caballé and Josep Carreras can fill opera houses worldwide. New Catalan writing has burgeoned since the 1970s and there are many literary prizes; the most remarkable global success has been *The Shadow of the Wind* by Carlos Ruiz Zafón (English translation published in 2004).

Work and Leisure

Catalans stay true to their traditions and their families. Sunday lunch is a time to get together, although even during the week, most people who can do so return home for lunch. This creates a rush hour four times a day, with a lull in the early afternoon. Shops close around 8:30pm, and between 6pm and 8:30pm the streets are crowded. Dinner or entertainment starts around 9pm.

Allegiance to the local football team, Barça, is a matter of national pride for its supporters. Meals out, concerts and the cinema are popular activities. The week begins quietly but, as the weekend approaches, streets fill and visitors leaving La Rambla at midnight to go to bed may feel they are leaving a good party too soon.

Demonstration for Catalan independence

Flowers of the Matollar

The *matollar* is the distinctive landscape of Spain's eastern Mediterranean coast. This scrubland, rich in wild flowers, is the result of centuries of woodland clearance, during which the native holm oak was felled for timber and to provide land for grazing and cultivation. Many colourful plants have adapted to the extremes of climate here. Most flower in spring, when hillsides are daubed with yellow broom and pink and white cistuses, and the air is perfumed by aromatic herbs such as rosemary, lavender and thyme. Buzzing insects feed on the abundance of nectar and pollen.

Spanish broom is a small bush with yellow flowers on slender branches. The black seed pods split when dry, scattering the seeds on the ground.

The century plant's flower stalk can reach 10 m (32 ft).

Aleppo pine   Rosemary

Jerusalem sage, an attractive shrub that is often grown in gardens, has tall stems surrounded by bunches of showy yellow flowers. Its leaves are greyish-white and woolly.

Rose garlic has round clusters of violet or pink flowers at the end of a single stalk. It survives the summer as the bulb familiar to all cooks.

Common thyme is a low-growing aromatic herb that is widely cultivated for use in the kitchen.

Foreign Invaders

Several plants from the New World have managed to colonize the bare ground of the *matollar*.

The prickly pear, thought to have been brought back by Christopher Columbus, produces a delicious fruit that can be picked only with thickly gloved hands. The rapidly growing century plant, a native of Mexico that has tough, spiny leaves, sends up a tall flower shoot only when it is 10–15 years old, after which it dies.

Prickly pear in bloom

Flowering shoots of the century plant

The mirror orchid, a small plant that grows on grassy sites, is easily distinguished from other orchids by the brilliant metallic-blue patch inside the lip, fringed by brown hairs.

Climate Chart

Most plants found in the *matollar* come into bloom in the warm, moist spring. The plants protect themselves from losing water during the dry summer heat with thick leaves or waxy secretions, or by storing moisture in bulbs or tubers.

Temp (ºC) / Rainfall (mm)

J F M A M J J A S O N D

— Temperature   ▮ Rainfall

Wildlife of the Matollar

The animals that live in the *matollar* are most often seen early in the morning, before the temperature is high. Countless insects fly from flower to flower, providing a source of food for birds. Smaller mammals, such as mice and voles, are active only at night, when it is cooler and there are few predators around.

Ladder snakes feed on small mammals, birds and insects. The young are identified by a black pattern like the rungs of a ladder, but adults are marked with two simple stripes.

Scorpions hide under rocks or wood by day. When disturbed, the tail is curled quickly over the body in a threatening gesture. The sting, lethal to small animals, can cause some irritation to humans.

The Dartford warbler, a skulking bird that has dark plumage and a cocked tail, sings melodiously during its mating display. Males are more vividly coloured than females.

The swallow-tail butterfly is one of the most conspicuous of the great many insects living in the *matollar*. Bees, ants and grasshoppers are also extremely common.

Holm oaks are very common in eastern Spain. The leaves are tough and rubbery to prevent water loss.

The strawberry tree is an evergreen shrub with glossy serrated leaves. Its inedible strawberry-like fruit turns red when ripe.

Tree heather

Grey-leaved cistus, growing on sunny sites, has crumpled petals and bright yellow anthers.

Narrow-leaved cistus exudes a sticky aromatic gum used in perfumes.

Star clover is a low-growing annual whose fruit develops into a star-shaped seed head. Its flowers are often pale pink.

Romanesque Art and Architecture

Catalonia has an exceptional collection of medieval buildings constructed between the 11th and 13th centuries in a distinctive local Romanesque style. There are more than 2,000 examples, most of them churches. Those in the Pyrenees, which have largely escaped both attack and modernization, have survived particularly well. Churches had lofty bell towers, barrel-vaulted naves, rounded arches and imaginative sculpture, as well as remarkable wall paintings. Some frescoes and furniture have come to rest in the Museu Nacional d'Art de Catalunya *(see p91)* in Barcelona, which has the largest Romanesque collection in the world.

Sant Jaume de Frontanyà
(see p116) is a former Augustinian canonry with typical 11th-century features, such as the Lombard bands below the roofs of the three apses. The large octagonal central lantern is, however, unusual.

Vielha • Arties

• Esterri d'Àneu

• Boí

Llavorsí •

Sort • La Seu Puigcerdà •
• Pont de Suert d'Urgell •

Martinet • Ribes de
Frese

• La Pobla de Segur Bagà •

Coll de Nargó • Ripe

Tremp • Berga •

Isona •

Gironella •

Solsona •

El Segre • Ponts

Sant Climent de Taüll, an exemplary church in the Vall de Boí *(see p115)*, was consecrated in 1123. Its frescoes, including a *Christ in Majesty (see p91)*, are replicas, but the originals, which are now in Barcelona, are among the best in Catalonia.

Monestir de Santa Maria de Ripoll

The saints

The story of Solomon

The Old Testament

David and his musicians

The story of Moses

Christ with historical figures

The visions of Daniel

Plinth with patterns

The portal of the church of the former Benedictine monastery at Ripoll is known as "The Ripoll Bible" for its allegorical carvings. Although the church was founded in 879 and rebuilt under Abbot Oliva in 1032, the portal was added only in the late 12th century. In this fine piece of Romanesque decoration Christ sits above the doorway amid the beasts symbolizing the Apostles, and the monthly agricultural occupations are represented on the doorway pillars. There are seven biblical friezes running the length of the wall. The top frieze *(see p116)* over the tympanum represents the old men of the Apocalypse; the others are described in the captions above.

0 kilometres 30

0 miles 15

Sant Pere de Camprodon *(see p117)*, consecrated in 1169, is a monastery church in mature Romanesque style with five square apses. The slightly pointed barrel vault over the nave hints at the Gothic style to come.

Area of Major Romanesque Interest

Sant Cristòfol de Beget *(see p117)* is a beautiful church in a picturesque hamlet hidden deep in a valley. It has a uniquely preserved interior that includes a Romanesque baptismal font and this famous 12th-century crucifix – the *Majestat*.

Sant Pere de Rodes, situated at 600 m (1,968 ft) above sea level, was a Benedictine monastery. In its church's nave are the pillars of a Roman temple once on this site.

Portbou
• La Jonquera
Llançà
Camprodon
Figueres • Roses
Besalú
Golf de Roses
Olot
Bàscara • L'Escala
Banyoles
L'Estartit
Manlleu
Parlavà
Anglès • Girona
Vic
Santa Coloma
de Farners
Palafrugell
na
Palamós
Sant Feliu
de Guíxols

Sant Pere de Besalú *(see p117)* is the 12th-century church of an earlier Benedictine monastery. Stone lions guard this window over the portal. Inside, the ambulatory has finely carved capitals.

The Museu Episcopal de Vic *(see p126)*, adjacent to the cathedral, has an exquisite collection of Romanesque art. It includes this richly coloured and moving portrayal of the Visitation, which was originally an altar decoration in Lluçà monastery.

Sant Pere de Galligants *(see p118)*, a former Benedictine abbey, captures the very essence of Romanesque style. It has an 11th-century portal with a rose window, three naves and an octagonal bell tower. The cloister capitals are carved with biblical scenes. It now houses Girona's archaeology museum.

Gaudí and Modernisme

Towards the end of the 19th century, a new style of art and architecture, Modernisme, a variant of Art Nouveau, was born in Barcelona. It became a means of expression for Catalan nationalism and counted Josep Puig i Cadafalch, Lluís Domènech i Montaner and, above all, Antoni Gaudí i Cornet *(see p80)* among its major exponents. Barcelona's Eixample district *(see pp72–85)* is full of the highly original buildings that they created for their wealthy clients.

All aspects of decoration in a Modernista building, even interior design, were planned by the architect. This door and tiled surround are in Gaudí's 1906 Casa Batlló *(see pp78–9)*.

A dramatic cupola covers the central salon, which rises through three floors. It is pierced by small round holes, inspired by Islamic architecture, giving the illusion of stars.

Upper galleries are richly decorated with carved wood and cofferwork.

The spiral carriage ramp is an early sign of Gaudí's predilection for curved lines. He would later exploit this to the full in the wavy façade of his masterpiece, La Pedrera *(see p81)*.

The Evolution of Modernisme

1859 Civil engineer Ildefons Cerdà i Sunyer submits proposals for expansion of Barcelona

1878 Gaudí graduates as an architect

1900 Josep Puig i Cadafalch builds Casa Amatller *(see p80)*

1903 Lluís Domènech i Montaner builds Hospital de la Santa Creu i de Sant Pau *(see p81)*

Hospital detail

1850	1865	1880	1895	1910	1925

1883 Gaudí takes over design of Neo-Gothic Sagrada Família *(see pp82–3)*

Detail of Sagrada Família

1888 Barcelona Universal Exhibition gives impetus to Modernisme

1910 La Pedrera completed

1905 Domènech i Montaner builds Casa Lleó Morera *(see p80)*. Puig i Cadafalch builds Casa Terrades *(see p81)*

1926 Gaudí dies

Bizarrely decorated chimneys became one of the trademarks of Gaudí's later work. They reach a fantastic extreme on the gleaming, humpbacked roof of Casa Batlló.

Elaborate wrought iron lamps light the grand hall.

Ceramic tiles decorate the chimneys.

Gaudí's Materials

Gaudí designed, or collaborated on designs, for almost every known medium. He combined bare, undecorated materials – wood, rough-hewn stone, rubble and brickwork – with meticulous craftwork in wrought iron and stained glass. Mosaics of ceramic tiles were used to cover his fluid, uneven forms.

Stained-glass window in the Sagrada Família

Detail of iron gate, Casa Vicens (see pp28–9)

Mosaic of ceramic tiles, Park Güell (see p98)

Tiles on El Capricho in Comillas, Cantabria

Parabolic arches, used extensively by Gaudí, beginning in the Palau Güell, show his interest in Gothic architecture. These arches form a corridor in his 1890 Col.legi de les Teresianes, a convent school in the west of Barcelona.

Escutcheon alludes to the Catalan coat of arms.

Palau Güell

Gaudí's first major building in the centre of the city, on La Rambla (see p62), established his international reputation for outstanding, original architecture. Built in 1889 for his lifelong patron, the industrialist Eusebi Güell, the mansion stands on a small plot of land in a narrow street, making the façade difficult to see. Inside, Gaudí creates a sense of space by using carved screens, recesses and galleries.

Organic forms inspired the wrought iron around the gates to the palace. Gaudí's later work teems with wildlife, such as this dragon, covered with brightly coloured tiles, which guards the steps in the Park Güell.

La Ruta del Modernisme

The examples of Modernista architecture in Barcelona mapped here lie along a route designed by the city's tourist office. A *Guidebook*, available from Catalunya's tourist office *(see p175)*, the Hospital de Sant Pau, the Güell Pavillions on Avinguda Pedralbes and some bookshops, provides up to a 50 percent discount on admission charges and gives you the freedom to plan your own itinerary. Guided tours offered include the Casa Batlló and Lleó Morera, Palau Güell and Palau de la Música Catalana, among others, and entry is discounted at the selected museums. Many of the other premises, however, are privately owned houses, shops, cafés and hotels.

㊽ Casa Vicens
This bright, angular, turreted building by Antoni Gaudí, with ceramic mosaics and patterned brickwork, shows Moorish influence. The iron gate and fencing are hallmarks of his work.

㊶ Palau Baró de Quadras
Built in 1906, this handsome house is by Josep Puig i Cadafalch. The intricate, sculptured frieze above the first-floor windows has close affinities to early Renaissance Plateresque style.

⑲ Casa Lleó Morera
The first-floor dining room of this house is one of Barcelona's most stunning interiors. The stained-glass windows are by Lluís Rigalt and the eight ceramic mosaic wall panels, depicting idyllic country scenes, are by Gaspar Homar.

⑦ Antiga Casa Figueres
The mosaic, stained-glass and wrought-iron decoration of this, the most famous of the city's Modernista stores, was carried out in 1902 by Antoni Ros i Güell. It is today the elegant Pastisseria Escribà.

Key

···· Walking route
···· Bus route
···· Metro route

0 kilometres   500
0 miles   500

For map symbols *see back flap*

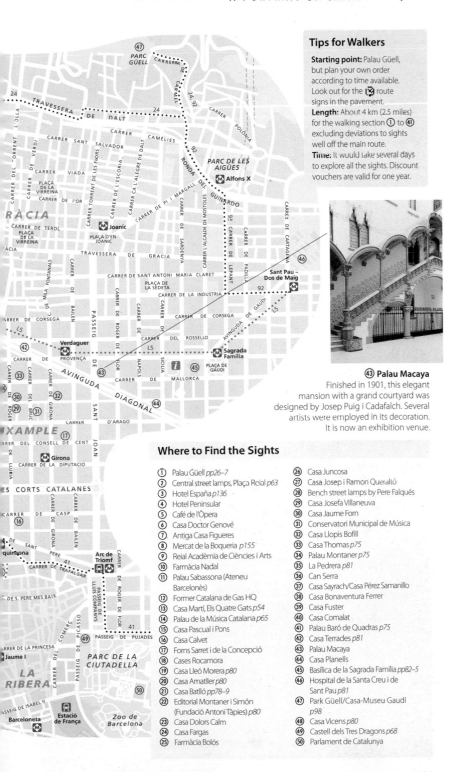

Tips for Walkers

Starting point: Palau Güell, but plan your own order according to time available. Look out for the 🚶 route signs in the pavement.
Length: About 4 km (2.5 miles) for the walking section ① to ④ excluding deviations to sights well off the main route.
Time: It would take several days to explore all the sights. Discount vouchers are valid for one year.

㊸ Palau Macaya
Finished in 1901, this elegant mansion with a grand courtyard was designed by Josep Puig i Cadafalch. Several artists were employed in its decoration. It is now an exhibition venue.

Where to Find the Sights

① Palau Güell pp26–7
② Central street lamps, Plaça Reial p63
③ Hotel España p136
④ Hotel Peninsular
⑤ Café de l'Òpera
⑥ Casa Doctor Genové
⑦ Antiga Casa Figueres
⑧ Mercat de la Boqueria p155
⑨ Reial Acadèmia de Ciències i Arts
⑩ Farmàcia Nadal
⑪ Palau Sabassona (Ateneu Barcelonès)
⑫ Former Catalana de Gas HQ
⑬ Casa Martí, Els Quatre Gats p54
⑭ Palau de la Música Catalana p65
⑮ Casa Pascual i Pons
⑯ Casa Calvet
⑰ Forns Sarret i de la Concepció
⑱ Cases Rocamora
⑲ Casa Lleó Morera p80
⑳ Casa Amatller p80
㉑ Casa Batlló pp78–9
㉒ Editorial Montaner i Simón (Fundació Antoni Tàpies) p80
㉓ Casa Dolors Calm
㉔ Casa Fargas
㉕ Farmàcia Bolós

㉖ Casa Juncosa
㉗ Casa Josep i Ramon Queraltó
㉘ Bench street lamps by Pere Falqués
㉙ Casa Josefa Villaneuva
㉚ Casa Jaume Forn
㉛ Conservatori Municipal de Música
㉜ Casa Llopis Bofill
㉝ Casa Thomas p75
㉞ Palau Montaner p75
㉟ La Pedrera p81
㊱ Can Serra
㊲ Casa Sayrach/Casa Pérez Samanillo
㊳ Casa Bonaventura Ferrer
㊴ Casa Fuster
㊵ Casa Comalat
㊶ Palau Baró de Quadras p75
㊷ Casa Terrades p81
㊸ Palau Macaya
㊹ Casa Planells
㊺ Basílica de la Sagrada Família pp82–5
㊻ Hospital de la Santa Creu i de Sant Pau p81
㊼ Park Güell/Casa-Museu Gaudí p98
㊽ Casa Vicens p80
㊾ Castell dels Tres Dragons p68
㊿ Parlament de Catalunya

Catalan Painting

Catalonia has a fine, if uneven, painterly tradition. It began where Spanish medieval painting was born – in the Pyrenees, where Romanesque churches were brightened by bold frescoes full of imagination *(see pp24–5)*. The subsequent Gothic period, which represented Catalonia at the height of its powers, was followed by a long period of lesser artistic achievement until the wealth of the 19th century revived the creative spirit. This fostered some of Europe's great 20th-century painters, all of whom, as Catalans, felt a close affinity to the spirit of Catalonia's incomparable Romanesque art.

St George and the Princess (late 15th century) by Jaume Huguet

Gothic

One of the first named artists in Catalonia was Ferrer Bassa (1285–1348), court painter to Jaume II. Bassa's exquisite decoration in the chapel of the Monestir de Pedralbes *(see p97)* constitutes the first known example of oil-painted murals, a style undoubtedly influenced by contemporary Italian painting.

In sculpture, Catalan Gothic begins with the work of Mestre Bartomeu (1250–1300), whose extraordinary, Oriental-looking *Calvary* is in the fine Gothic collection of Girona's Museu d'Art *(see p119)*.

There are also Gothic collections in Vic and Solsona *(see p126)* and particularly Barcelona, where the Museu Nacional d'Art de Catalunya, or MNAC *(see p91)*, has the most impressive. Important works include those by Lluís Borrassà (1365–1425), who painted

Tarragona cathedral's altarpiece, and Lluís Dalmau (d.1463), who visited Bruges and studied under Jan van Eyck. A feature of Catalan Gothic is *esgrafiat*, a process of gilding haloes, garments and backgrounds, which was favoured by one of the greatest Catalan Gothic artists, Jaume Huguet (1415–92). His *St George and the Princess* seems to capture the full majesty of a cultured and prosperous nation.

Renaissance to Neo-Classical

Artistically, Catalonia languished from the 16th to the 18th century, a period dominated by great masters from elsewhere in Spain: El Greco in Toledo, Murillo and Zurbarán in Seville, Ribera in Valencia, and Velázquez and later Goya in Madrid. A few of their works can be seen at the Museu Nacional d'Art de

Catalunya *(see p91)* alongside Catalonia's only two distinguished artists of the period – Francesc Pla and Antoni Viladomat.

Procession outside Santa Maria del Mar (c.1898) by Ramon Casas

The 19th Century

Barcelona's art school opened above La Llotja *(see p65)* in 1849 and new patrons of the arts appeared with wealth generated by the industrial revolution. Industry had, however, already begun to train its own artists. In 1783, a school was founded in Olot *(see p117)* to train designers for local textile firms. An Olot School of artists developed; its main figures were Josep Berga i Boix (1837–1914) and Joaquim Vayreda i Vila (1843–94), who also founded the Art Cristià (Christian Art) workshops that today still produce church statuary.

The greens and browns of the Olot landscape artists were countered by the pale blues and pinks of the Sitges Luminists – Arcadi Mas i Font-devila (1852–1943) and Joan Roig i Soler (1852–1909).

The Gardens at Aranjuez (1907) by Santiago Rusiñol

They were influenced by Marià Fortuny, who was born in Reus in 1838 and had lived in Rome and Paris. He was commissioned by Barcelona's city council to paint a vast canvas of the Spanish victory at Tetuán, Spanish Morocco, in which 500 Catalan volunteers had taken part. It is now in the MNAC *(see p91)*.

In 1892, 18 years after the first Impressionist exhibition in Paris, Mas i Fontdevila staged an exhibition in Sitges bringing together the Olot School and the Luminists. It was seen as the first Modernista event and featured two other artists: Santiago Rusiñol (1861–1931) and Ramon Casas (1866–1932), the towering figures of Modernista painting. Rusiñol, the son of a textile magnate, bought a house in Sitges, Cau Ferrat *(see p130)*, which became a Modernista haunt. Casas, the first man in Barcelona to own a car, drew all the famous people of the day and also painted large, powerful canvases such as *The Charge* and *Garrotte*. Both Rusiñol and Casas were founding members of Els Quatre Gats café, which was modelled on Le Chat Noir in Paris.

Waiting for Soup (1899) by Isidre Nonell

in the Museu Picasso *(see p66)*, as well as by the leading Catalan artists – landscape painter Isidre Nonell (1873–1911), Joaquim Mir (1873–1940), Rusiñol and Casas. He shared their view that Paris was vital to an artistic life and joined its Catalan fraternity. Despite a self-imposed exile during the Franco years, he kept in touch with Catalonia all his life.

Joan Miró (1893–1983) also attended the La Llotja art school. Thrown out for poor draughtsmanship, he went on to become one of the 20th-century's most original talents, remarkable for his playful abstracts.

A sense of play was also never far from Salvador Dalí *(see p119)*, whom Miró encouraged in the way that he himself had been inspired by Picasso. Dalí joined both of them in Paris, where Miró introduced him to the Surrealists. Unlike his mentors, Dalí stayed in Catalonia after the Civil War. His house in Port Lligat *(see p122)* is his finest creation.

Also to remain was Josep-Maria Sert (1876–1945). A more traditional painter, he is best remembered for his vast murals in Barcelona's Casa de la Ciutat *(see p59)*, and in the Rockefeller Center and the dining room of the Waldorf Astoria in New York. His startling work in Vic cathedral *(see p126)* was burnt out in the Civil War, but he was able to repaint it before he died.

Today, Catalonia's best-known painter is Antoni Tàpies (1923–2012). A modest, uncompromising man, he was rooted in his own culture. Though an abstract painter, he often used the colours of the Catalan flag and admitted to being influenced by Romanesque art. Like Picasso and Miró, he has his own museum *(see p80)*. A wide variety of work by other contemporary Catalan artists, such as Antoni Abad, can be seen at Barcelona's Museu d'Art Contemporani *(see p64)*.

The 20th and 21st Centuries

Although Pablo Ruiz Picasso (1881–1973) lived in Barcelona for only eight years *(see p66)*, they were very formative. His early work was much influenced by the city and its environs, as can be seen

The Cathedral of the Poor (1897) by Joaquim Mir

Lithograph (1948) in Catalan flag colours by Antoni Tàpies

The Flavours of Catalonia

Food is central to the Catalan soul, and it's no accident that Barcelona's most famous literary creation, detective Pepe Carvalho, is a discerning gourmet. Reflecting Barcelona's status as the undisputed style capital of the Mediterranean, the culinary scene in Catalonia is now one of the most exciting in Europe, with innovative chefs like Ferran Adrià, of the legendary El Bullí restaurant (now closed) and Tickets tapas bar, taking Catalonia's venerable gastronomic traditions and transforming them with spectacular flair. But the old ways survive in small, family-run restaurants, authentic, sawdust-strewn tapas bars, and particularly in the superb local markets.

Ceps *(bolets)*

Barcelona café serving traditional pastries and desserts

Visit any one of Barcelona's excellent markets to see the spectacular variety of fresh produce that is available in Catalonia: stalls are heaped high with glistening fish from the Mediterranean; superb-quality meat and game from the mountains; and a quite dazzling array of fruit and vegetables from the plains. Catalan cuisine, even at its most experimental, is essentially simple, and relies on the superb quality and range of the local produce. It is also very much a seasonal cuisine, and each time of the year has its specialities, from the onion-like *calçots* that appear in the spring, and the luscious plethora of summer fruit, to the wild mushrooms, roasted meats and hearty, warming stews of the autumn and winter.

Meat and Game

Catalan cured meats are justly famous throughout Spain, particularly the pungent cured sausage *fuet*. Pork finds its way onto almost every menu, with *peus de porc* (pigs' trotters) an old-fashioned favourite. Its mountain cousin, wild boar *(porc sanglar)* is popular in late autumn, along with game, especially partridge *(perdiu)*.

Xoriço picant

Fuet

Llonganissa

Xoriço

Pernil salat

Xoriço curat

Selection of Catalan cured meats, known as *embutits*

Local Dishes and Specialities

Some things are hallowed in Catalan cuisine, and none more so than the quartet of classic sauces that underpin almost everything. King of them all is *sofregit* (mentioned in the first Catalan cookbook of 1324), a reduction of caramelized onions, fresh tomatoes and herbs. *Samfaina* is made like *sofregit*, but with the addition of roast aubergines (eggplant), courgettes (zucchini) and peppers. *Picada* is spicier, and ingredients vary, but normally include breadcrumbs, garlic, almonds, saffron and pine nuts. *All i oli* is a garlicky, mayonnaise-like (but eggless) sauce, usually served with grilled meat and vegetables. But the classic Catalan dish is *pa amb tomàquet* – crusty bread rubbed with fresh tomatoes and garlic, then drizzled with olive oil. Simple, but utterly delicious.

Pa amb tomàquet

Escalivada is a salad made of marinated onions, peppers and aubergines (eggplant) that have been roasted until sweet.

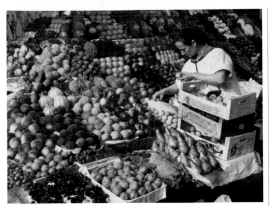

Summer fruits and vegetables lovingly displayed at La Boquería market

Fruit and Vegetables

Spring is heralded by *calçots*, a cross between leeks and onions, tiny broad (fava) beans and delicate asparagus spears. In summer, market stalls blaze with the colours of cherries, strawberries, figs, peaches and melons, aubergines (eggplants), courgettes (zucchini), tomatoes and artichokes. In autumn, Catalans head for the hills to seek out wild mushrooms (*bolets*), and classic Catalan bean dishes appear on menus as winter approaches.

Rabbit (*conill*) and snails (*cargols*) come into their own in hearty winter dishes. Meat and fish are sometimes combined in dishes known as *mar i muntanya* (sea and mountain).

Fish

Barcelona excels at seafood. Tapas bars commonly serve mouthwatering sardines, and rosy prawns grilled or tossed in garlic. Restaurants and markets offer a dizzying array of fresh fish, including monkfish, bass, hake, sole, squid, octopus and every possible variety of shellfish. Fish is often served simply grilled (*a la brasa*), or perhaps with a simple sauce. It's especially good cooked

paella-style in *fideuà*, or in a stew such as *suquet de peix*. But humble dried, salted cod (*bacallà*) still reigns supreme in Catalan cuisine, and is at its most delicious when baked with tomatoes, garlic and wine (*a la llauna*).

Locally caught sardines being grilled over charcoal

Best Food Shopping

La Boqueria (*see p155*).

Bombones Blasi Alfons XII 26 and Còrsega 218 (93 414 26 38). Exquisite chocolates.

Olis Oliva Mercat de Santa Caterina (93 268 14 72). A huge range of olive oils, plus salt.

La Pineda Carrer del Pi 16 (93 302 43 93). Delightful old grocer's, specializing in hams.

Tot Formatge Passeig del Born 13 (93 319 53 75). Superb cheeses from Catalonia, Spain and elsewhere.

La Botifarrería de Santa María Carrer Santa María 4 (93 319 91 23). Cured meats of all kinds.

La Llavor dels Orígens Carrer Vidreria 6–8 (93 310 75 31). Catalan fare, organic where possible, including cheeses, hams, oils and conserves.

Conill amb cargols is a hearty country stew of rabbit and snails with tomatoes, spices and a splash of wine.

Suquet de peix is a rich stew of firm-fleshed fish (often hake), with tomatoes, garlic and toasted almonds.

Crema Catalana, the Catalan version of crème brûlée, is a rich, eggy custard with a caramelized sugar topping.

Cava Country

Cava is one of Catalonia's most appreciated exports. This relatively inexpensive sparkling wine is made in the same way as French champagne, undergoing a second fermentation in the bottle in which it is sold. It was made commercially from the mid-19th century and, in 1872, full-scale production was begun by Josep Raventós, head of Codorníu. This famous winery is still run by his descendants in Sant Sadurní d'Anoia, *cava* capital of the Penedès wine-producing region. Today, *cava* continues to be made using local grape varieties – Macabeo, Xarel·lo and Parellada – and some pleasant pink *cava* is also produced. The literal meaning of *cava* is simply "cellar".

Codorníu, the first wine to be made using the *méthode champenoise*, brought *cava* international renown as one of the great sparkling wines.

Freixenet was established by the Sala family in 1914 and is now one of the leading *cava* brands. Their estate is in Sant Sadurní d'Anoia, heart of *cava* country, and Freixenet's distinctive black bottle is recognized throughout the world.

Raïmat, developed by the Raventós family using the Chardonnay grape, is considered by many to be the ultimate *cava*. Wrested from wasteland, the 3,000 hectare (7,410 acre) Raïmat estate, 14 km (9 miles) west of Lleida, has its own railway station and workers' village and has been declared a "model agricultural estate" by the Spanish government.

Bell-lloc d'Urgell
Lleida
Alcarràs
Bellpuig
N240
AP2
Juneda
A2
Seròs
Coster del Seg
Maials
La Granadella
La Bisbal de Falset
Flix
Priorat
Falset
N420
Cambrils
L'Hospitalet de l'Infant
L'Ametlla de Mar

The Other Wines of Catalonia

Wine (*vi*) in Catalonia is *negre* (red), *rosat* (pink) or *blanc* (white). *Garnatxa* is a dessert wine named after the grape it comes from; *ranci* is a matured white wine. A tradition, now only practised at local *festes* or old-style bars, is to pour wine into the mouth from a *porró* (long-spouted wine jug). There are 11 official DO (*Denominació de Origen*) regions, which include: **Empordà-Costa Brava:** light wines from the northeast. They include *vi de l'any*, drunk in the year it is produced. *Cava* is made in Peralada. **Alella:** a tiny region, just north of Barcelona, with good light whites. **Penedès:** great reds as well as some whites, with names such as Torres and Codorníu. Visit the wine museum in Vilafranca del Penedès (*see p127*). **Conca de Barberà:** small quantities of both reds and whites. **Costers del Segre:** includes the delicious reds from the Raïmat estate. **Priorat:** characterful reds and good whites (Falset) from a pretty region of small villages west of Tarragona. **Tarragona and Terra Alta:** traditionally hefty wines, but getting lighter.

A *porró*, for drinking wine

The Art Nouveau winery in Sant Sadurní d'Anoia is Codorníu's Modernista showpiece, designed by Josep Puig i Cadafalch in 1906. There are 26 km (16 miles) of cellars on five floors and visitors are taken round on a small train.

Key

Main *cava* districts

0 kilometres   20

0 miles   20

Gold medals were awarded to Codorníu for its *cava* as early as 1888. By 1897, it was being served at state functions instead of Champagne.

Calaf   C25   Manresa

Tàrrega

Igualada   Castellolí   Terrassa   Granollers

Santa Coloma de Queralt   Masquefa ⑥   Sabadell

Sabadell   *Alella*   Mataró

Rubí   Premià de Mar

Conca de Barberà   *Penedès*   ②①   Santa Coloma de Gramanet

Montblanc   ③ Sant Sadurní d'Anoia

Barcelona

④   L'Hospitalet de Llobregat

Vilafranca del Penedès   El Prat de Llobregat

Valls   AP2

Tarragona   Sitges

El Vendrell   Vilanova i la Geltrú

Reus   A7   Castelldefels

Torredembarra

Tarragona   *Mediterranean Sea*

Salou

Cap de Salou

Best Producers

① Codorníu
  Sant Sadurní d'Anoia

② Freixenet
  Sant Sadurní d'Anoia

③ Gramona
  Sant Sadurní d'Anoia

④ Mascaró
  Vilafranca del Penedès

⑤ Raïmat
  Costers del Segre

⑥ Raventós Rosell
  Masquefa

Cava Tips

What to buy

The driest *cavas* are *brut nature* and *extra brut. Brut, extra seco* and *seco* are slightly less dry. Sweet *semiseco* and *dulce* (in Catalan, *dolç*) are best with desserts. Although inexpensive compared with the French equivalent, costs do vary, with small, specialist producers commanding high prices.

Visiting a winery

The main *cava* producers are open to the public during office hours (but many close in August). Sant Sadurní d'Anoia is 45 minutes by train from Barcelona's Sants station and the most impressive cellars to visit here are Freixenet's and Codorníu's. Vilafranca del Penedès tourist office (see p127) has details of all *cava* winery visits.

A rewarding tour can be had by visiting the Freixenet cellars. The company sells more bottles of *cava* each year than the French sell champagne.

CATALONIA THROUGH THE YEAR

Each *barri* (district) in Barcelona and every town and village in Catalonia has a saint's day to be celebrated in an annual *festa major*. The *sardana* (see p131) is danced and, on the Costa Brava, *havaneres* (habaneras) are sung. Food is central to any event, and open-air feasts and special pastries and cakes feature strongly. Many towns, including Barcelona, have parades of giants *(gegants)*, bigheads *(capgrosses)* and dwarfs *(nans)* – papier-mâché caricatures of people once linked with local trade guilds. Demons and dragons provide drama. Catalans love pyrotechnics, and the fires at the midsummer *Revetlla de Sant Joan* are a lavish incendiary event. Many celebrations often start on the eve of the feast day proper.

Book stalls set up in Barcelona on Sant Jordi's Day, *el dia del llibre*

Spring

Almond blossom gives way to cherry and apple as the earth warms and the melting snows swell the rivers. The fishing season for trout and other freshwater fish starts in late March. At Easter, families get together, often going out of town to visit relatives, or to picnic and search for wild asparagus. May is the best month in which to see wild flowers, which are particularly spectacular in the Pyrenees.

March

Terrassa Jazz Festival *(two weeks in Mar)*. Concerts by musicians from all over the world.
Sant Medir *(3 Mar)*. Processions distribute sweets in the Gràcia district, and in Sants a week later.
Sant Josep *(19 Mar)*. Although not a holiday as it is elsewhere in Spain, in Catalonia there are plenty of "Pep"s (short for Josep) celebrating their name day (more important in Spain than birthdays). It's also Father's Day, as Josep was Jesus's foster-father.

Setmana Santa (Holy Week), Easter and the week that leads up to it, is filled with events.

April

Diumenge de Rams *(Palm Sunday)*. Palm leaves are blessed in church, notably at the Sagrada Família in Barcelona. Processions of Roman soldiers turn out in Girona, and *via crucis* (passion plays) are put on in several places, notably the spa town of Sant Hilari Sacalm, Girona province.
Dijous Sant *(Maundy Thu)*. Verges, Girona province. Men dressed as skeletons perform a death dance *(dansa de la mort)* thought to date back to times of plague in the 1300s.
Pasqua *(Easter)*. On Good Friday *(Divendres Sant)*, crucifixes are carried through the streets following the Stations of the Cross. On Easter Monday *(Dilluns de Pasqua)*, godparents buy godchildren *mona* (egg cake) and bakers compete to make the most elaborate confections.

Sant Jordi *(23 Apr)*. Feast of St George, patron saint of Catalonia, and a day devoted to the memory of Cervantes *(see p45)*, who died on this day in 1616. Men and boys give single red roses to wives, mothers and girlfriends, who give them books in return. The *festa* is also known as *el dia del llibre* (book day).
Feria de Abril *(end Apr)*. This popular spring festival is held at the Forum Park, and features flamenco dancing, concerts, tapas stalls, attractions for kids and plenty more.

May

Fira de Sant Ponç *(11 May)*. Ancient celebration around the Carrer de l'Hospital in Barcelona, once the site of the city hospital. Aromatic and medicinal herbs and honey are sold.
Corpus Christi *(May/Jun)*. Flowers are laid in the streets of Sitges, and in the town of Berga, Barcelona province, a monster dragon *(la Patum)* dances through the streets.

The feast of Corpus Christi, when carpets of flowers cover the streets

Average daily hours of sunshine

Hours

| 10 | 8 | 6 | 4 | 2 | 0 |

Jan Feb Mar Apr May Jun Jul Aug Sep Oct Nov Dec

Hours

| 10 | 8 | 6 | 4 | 2 | 0 |

Sunshine Chart
Barcelona is a sunny city, enjoying clear blue skies for a large part of the year and often up to ten hours' sunshine a day in summer. In winter, even though it can be cold in the shade, the sun is high enough to give it warming power and it can be pleasant to sit outdoors on a sheltered, sunny terrace or patio.

Summer

The majority of Barcelona's inhabitants live in apartments, so they like to head out of town at weekends, either to the coast or the mountains. Motorways (highways) on Friday afternoons and Sunday evenings are best avoided. School holidays are long, starting at the end of June when the sea is warm enough for swimming. Crowds throng the marinas, the aroma of barbecued sardines fills the air, and a plethora of summer entertainment provides limitless options. Some shops and restaurants close in August.

June
Revetlla de Sant Joan
(23 & 24 Jun). St John's (Midsummer's) Eve is celebrated with fireworks, especially on the beaches of Barcelona. Bonfires are lit throughout Catalonia and lighted torches are brought down from the top of Mont Canigó, just over the border in France. *Cava* – a sparkling white wine *(see pp34–5)* – is drunk with a special *coca* (cake) sprinkled with pine nuts and crystallized fruit.
Castellers *(24 Jun)*. In Valls, Tarragona, a province famous for its *casteller* festivals, teams of men stand on each other's shoulders hoping to take the prize for building the highest human tower *(see p127)*.
Concert season *(Jun/Jul)*. Classical music concerts, held at different parks in Barcelona, are organized by the Institut Municipal de Parcs i Jardins.

Holiday-makers at Platja d'Aro, a popular Costa Brava resort

Grec Festival de Barcelona *(Jun/ Jul)*. National and international performances throughout Barcelona; the main venues are the Teatre Grec, Mercat de les Flors and Poble Espanyol.

July
Cantada d'havaneres *(first Sun in Jul)*. Drinking *cremat* (coffee and rum), musicians and singers belt out *havaneres* in towns along the coast, most famously at Calella de Palafrugell.

A team of *castellers* in action

Verge del Carme *(16 Jul)*. A maritime festival that takes place around Barcelona's port. As well as processions, there are bands playing *havaneres*.
Santa Cristina *(24 Jul)*. The biggest festival of Lloret de Mar, Costa Brava, when a statue of the Virgin is brought ashore by a decorated flotilla.

August
Festa major de Gràcia *(one week beginning around 15 Aug)*. Each district of Barcelona hosts its own *festa*, in which streets try to outdo each other in the inventiveness of their decorations. The *festa* in the old district of Gràcia is the biggest and most spectacular and incorporates concerts, balls, music, competitions and street games.
Festa major de Vilafranca del Penedès *(mid-Aug)*. This town's annual festival is one of the best places to see *casteller* (human tower) competitions *(see p127)*.
Festa major de Sants *(around 24 Aug)*. The big annual *festa* takes place in the Sants district of Barcelona.

Average monthly rainfall (Barcelona)

Rainfall Chart
Barcelona experiences modest rainfall year-round – just sufficient to maintain the city's green spaces. However, rain tends to fall in sudden, but short-lived, torrential downpours and heavy thunderstorms are a feature of the summer months. Grey, drizzly weather lasting for days on end is very rare.

Autumn

The grape harvest *(verema)* is a highlight of the autumn, just before the vines turn red and gold. It is the season for seeking out mushrooms, which swell the market stalls. From October, hunters set off to bag red-legged partridge, migrating ducks and wild boar. Hardier people can be seen swimming in the sea right up until November.

Cattle descending from the Pyrenees at the end of the summer

September

Diada de Catalunya *(11 Sep)*. Catalonia's national day marks Barcelona's fall to Felipe V in 1714 *(see p47)*, when the region lost its autonomy. Political demonstrations convey strong separatist sentiment. *Sardana (see p131)* bands and people singing *Els segadors (see p46)* can be heard and Catalan flags are everywhere.

La Mercè *(24 Sep)*. This annual festival in Barcelona honours *Nostra Senyora de la Mercè* (Our Lady of Mercy) in a week of concerts, masses and dances. Look out for the *correfoc* – a

Harvesting grapes in autumn, with high hopes for a successful crop

lively parade of fire-breathing dragons, giants and monsters; and the *piro musical* – fireworks set to music.

Sant Miquel *(29 Sep)*. Celebrations for Barceloneta's patron saint recall Napoleon's occupation of Spain *(see p47)*. Bum Bum, a Napoleonic general, parades through the streets to salvoes of gunfire. There is dancing on the beach.

October

Festes de Sarrià i de Les Corts *(first Sun in Oct)*. Each of these Barcelona districts has a festival for its patron saint.

Día de la Hispanitat *(12 Oct)* National holiday to mark the discovery of America in 1492 *(see p46)*, but most Catalans do not celebrate this anniversary.

November

Tots Sants (All Saints' Day) *(1 Nov)*. Roast chestnuts and sweet potatoes are eaten and on the next day – *Dia dels difunts* (All Souls' Day) – people visit the graves of their relatives.

Public Holidays

Any Nou *(New Year's Day)* 1 Jan

Reis Mags *(Epiphany)* 6 Jan

Divendres Sant *(Good Friday)* Mar/Apr

Dilluns de Pasqua *(Easter Monday)* Mar/Apr

Festa del Treball *(Labour Day)* 1 May

Sant Joan *(Saint John's Day)* 24 Jun

Assumpció *(Assumption Day)* 15 Aug

Diada de Catalunya *(National Day)* 11 Sep

La Mercè 24 Sep

Dia de la Hispanitat *(Day of the Spanish-speaking nations)* 12 Oct

Tots Sants *(All Saints' Day)* 1 Nov

Dia de la Constitució *(Constitution Day)* 6 Dec

Immaculada Concepció *(Immaculate Conception)* 8 Dec

Nadal *(Christmas)* 25 Dec
Sant Esteve 26 Dec

Average daily temperature (Barcelona)

Temperature Chart
This chart shows the average minimum and maximum daily temperatures recorded in Barcelona. The sunshine in winter can be deceptive, as daytime temperatures can occasionally dip to near-freezing. Summer days are consistently hot. Hats and a high-factor sun screen are essential.

Winter

Ski resorts in the Pyrenees are a popular destination at weekends. Though days can be sunny and lunches still taken alfresco, the weather is unpredictable and the nights can be chilly. Christmas is a particularly delightful time to be in Barcelona, when the city vibrates with the spirit of celebration and sharing. Crafts and decorations are on sale in the Feria de Santa Llúcia in front of the Cathedral.

A ski resort in the Pyrenees, a popular destination for weekenders

December

Nadal and **Sant Esteve** *(25 & 26 Dec)*. Christmas is a time for people to come together. Traditional Christmas lunch consists of an *escudella* (meat stew) followed by turkey stuffed with apples, apricots, prunes, pine nuts and raisins.

Revellón *(31 Dec)*. All over Spain on New Year's Eve it has become a custom for people

to eat a grape between each chime of the midnight bell. To manage the feat brings good luck all year.

January

Reis Mags *(6 Jan)*. On the eve of the Epiphany, the three kings arrive in various guises throughout Catalonia giving sweets to children. The main cavalcade in Barcelona is down by the port.

Els Tres Tombs *(17 Jan)*. Horsemen in top hats and tails ride three times through the

city to honour St Anthony, patron saint of animals.

Pelegrí de Tossa *(20 & 21 Jan)*, Tossa de Mar. A 40 km (25 mile) pilgrimage marking the end of the plague is this town's biggest annual event.

February

De Cajón! Flamenco Festival *(early Feb–Mar)*. Concerts and classes are held in venues across Barcelona.

Santa Eulàlia *(mid-Feb)*. The feast of the ancient patron saint of Barcelona is celebrated in the old town with dancing, *gegant* parades and other festivities.

Carnestoltes (Carnival) *(Feb/Mar)*. King Carnival presides over the pre-Lent celebrations, children dress up and every *barri* (district) in Barcelona puts on a party. Sausage omelettes are eaten on Shrove Tuesday *(Dijous gras)*, and on Ash Wednesday *(Dimecres de cendra)* a sardine is ceremoniously buried *(Enterrament de la sardina)*. There are major celebrations in Platja d'Aro on the Costa Brava and Vilanova on the Costa Daurada. Sitges is the place to go to see the full transvestite indulgence of the feast.

The winter festival of Els Tres Tombs in Vilanova i la Geltrú

Castellers build themselves into human towers during the September festival of La Mercè in Barcelona ▶

The Moors and Charlemagne

The Visigoths established their capital at Toledo, just south of modern Madrid. When King Witiza died in 710, his son, Agila, is said to have called on the Saracens from north Africa for help in claiming the throne. In 711, with astonishing speed, Muslim and Berber tribes began to drive up through the Iberian peninsula, reaching Barcelona in 717, then Poitiers in France in 732, where they were finally stopped by the Frankish leader, Charles Martel.

Page from a 15th-century manuscript of the *Llibre del Consolat de Mar*

The Muslims made their capital the city of Córdoba in southern Spain, while the Visigothic nobles found hiding places in the Pyrenees, from which they conducted sorties against the invaders. They were aided by Charles Martel's

Ramon Berenguer I of Barcelona (1035–76)

grandson, Charles the Great (Charlemagne). In 801, Barcelona was retaken by the Franks, only to be lost and taken again. The shortness of the Muslim occupation left Catalonia, unlike the rest of Spain, unmarked by the culture and language of Islam.

The Counts of Barcelona

Charlemagne created the *Marca Hispanica*, a buffer state along the Pyrenees, which he entrusted to local lords. The most powerful figure in the east was Guifré el Pelós (Wilfred the Hairy), who consolidated the counties of Barcelona, Cerdanya, Conflent, Osona, Urgell and Girona and founded the monastery of Ripoll *(see p116)* – *el bressol de Catalunya* (the cradle of Catalonia). Guifré died in battle against the Moors in 897, but he had started a dynasty of Counts of Barcelona that was to last, unbroken, for 500 years.

Before the end of the 11th century, under Ramon Berenguer I, Catalonia had established the first constitutional government in Europe with a bill of rights, the *Usatges*. By the early 12th century, under Ramon Berenguer III, Catalonia's boundaries had pushed south past Tarragona. Catalan influence also spread north and east when he married Dolça of Provence, linking the two regions and, more lastingly, the principality of Barcelona was united with its neighbour Aragon in 1137 by the marriage of Ramon Berenguer IV and Petronila of Aragon. In 1196, the great monastery of Poblet *(see pp128–9)* in Tarragona province took the place of Ripoll as the pantheon of Catalan royalty.

717 Catalonia occupied by Muslims

801 Moors ejected. Charlemagne sets up buffer state

Charlemagne (742–814)

1060 Constitution, *Usatges*, is drawn up around the time that the word Catalan is first recorded

700   **800**   **900**   **1000**

711 North African Muslims invade Spanish mainland

Moorish sword

778 Charlemagne, leader of the Franks, begins campaign to drive Moors from Spain

878 Guifré el Pelós (Wilfred the Hairy), Count of Cerdanya-Urgell, consolidates eastern Pyrenees and gains virtual autonomy. He starts 500-year dynasty of Counts of Barcelona

1008–46 Abbot Oliv builds church at Rip and oversees Benedictine buildin including Vic and Monserrat

Maritime Expansion

Under Jaume I the Conqueror (1213–76), Catalonia began a period of prosperity and expansion. By the end of the 13th century, the Balearic islands and Sicily had been conquered; many of the ships used in the enterprise were built at the vast Drassanes shipyards in Barcelona (see p71). Catalonia now ruled the seas and the *Llibre del Consolat de Mar* was a code of trading practice that held sway throughout the Mediterranean. Swashbuckling admirals included Roger de Llúria, who won a definitive victory over the French fleet in the Bay of Roses in 1285, and Roger de Flor, leader of a bunch of fierce Catalan and Aragonese mercenaries, the Almogàvers. These won battles for both the King of Sicily and the Byzantine emperor before Roger de Flor was murdered in 1305.

During Jaume I's long reign, the *Corts* (parliament) was established, the city walls were rebuilt to enclose an area ten times larger than that enclosed by the old Roman walls, and noble houses arose down the new Carrer Montcada (see p66).

La Llotja (the stock exchange) was sited by what was then the main port, and the church of Santa Maria del Mar (see p66) was built by grateful merchants. Under Pere IV (1336–87), two great halls were built: the Royal Palace's Saló del Tinell and the Casa de la Ciutat's Saló de Cent (see pp56–7).

Model of a 15th-century ship

Prosperity brought a flowering of Catalan literature. Jaume I wrote his own *Llibre dels Feits (Book of Deeds)*, and Pere el Gran's conquest of Sicily in 1282 was described in glowing terms in a chronicle of Catalan history written by Bernat Desclot around 1285. The great Catalan poet Ramon Llull (1232–1315), born in Mallorca, was the first to use a vernacular language in religious writing. From 1395, an annual poetry competition, the Jocs Florals, was held in the city, attracting the region's troubadours. In 1450, Joanot Martorell began writing his Catalan chivalric epic narrative *Tirant lo Blanc*, though he died in 1468, 22 years before it was published. Miguel de Cervantes, author of *Don Quijote*, described it as simply "the best book in the world".

Wall painting showing Jaume I during his campaign to conquer Mallorca

1100	1200	1300	1400
1148 Frontier with Moors pushed back to Riu Ebre	**1258–72** *Consolat de Mar*, a code of trading practice, holds sway throughout the Mediterranean	**1282** Pere el Gran takes Sicily. His exploits are recorded in Desclot's *Chronicles*	**1347–8** Black Death kills a quarter of the population
			1359 Generalitat founded
			1423 Conquest of Naples
1137 Barcelona united to neighbouring Aragon by royal marriage	**1213–35** Jaume I (The Conqueror) takes Mallorca, Ibiza and Formentera	**1302–5** Catalan mercenaries under Admiral Roger de Flor aid Byzantium against the Turks	
	Jaume I (1213–76)	**1287** Conquest of Mallorca under Alfonso III	

Fernando and Isabel of Castile

Catholic Spain was united in 1479 when Fernando II of Catalonia-Aragon married Isabel of Castile, a region which by then had absorbed the rest of northern Spain. In 1492, they drove the last of the Moors from the peninsula, then, in a fever

Baptizing Jews during the era of the Catholic Monarchs

of righteousness, also drove out the Jews, who had large and commercially important populations in Barcelona (see p58) and Girona. This was the same year in which Columbus had set foot in America, returning in triumph to Barcelona with six Carib Indians (see p60). However, the city lost out when the monopoly on New World trade was given to Seville and Cádiz. Though it still had great moments, such as its involvement in the victory over the Turks at Lepanto in 1571 (see p71), Barcelona went into a period of decline.

Revolts and Sieges

During the Thirty Years' War with France (1618–48), Felipe IV forced Barcelona's *Corts* to raise an army to fight the French, towards whom the Catalans bore no grudge. A viceroy was imposed on the city and unruly Spanish troops were billeted throughout the region. In June 1640, the population arose, and harvesters (*segadors*) murdered the viceroy. The *Song of the Harvesters* is still sung at Catalan gatherings. Barcelona then allied itself with France, but was besieged and defeated by Felipe. The peace of 1659 ceded Catalan lands north of the Pyrenees to France.

Wall tile for a Catalan trade guild

A second confrontation with Madrid arose during the War of the Spanish Succession, when Europe's two dominant royal houses, the Habsburgs and Bourbons, both laid claim to the throne. Barcelona, with England as an ally, found itself on the losing side, supporting the Habsburgs. As a result, it was heavily besieged by troops of

The great siege of Barcelona in 1714, during the War of the Spanish Succession

1450	1500	1550	1600	1650
1492 Columbus discovers Americas. Barcelona barred from trade with the New World. Jews expelled	**1494** Supreme Council of Aragon brings Catalonia under Castilian control	*The Spanish Inquisition, active from 1478*	**1619** Spanish capital established in Madrid	**1659** Treaty of the Pyrenees at end of Thirty Years' War draws new border with France; Roussillon ceded to France
1479 Fernando II of Catalonia-Aragon marries Isabel of Castile, uniting all the houses of Spain	**1490** *Tirant lo Blanc*, epic tale of chivalry by Martorell (see p45), published in Catalan	**1571** Vast fleet sets sail from Barcelona to defeat the Ottomans at sea at Lepanto	**1640** Revolt of the harvesters (*segadors*) against Spanish exploitation of Catalan resources during Thirty Years War with France	

Women joining in the defence of Girona against the Napoleonic French in 1809

the incoming Bourbon king, Felipe V. The city fell on 11 September 1714, today commemorated as National Day *(see p38)*. Felipe then proceeded to annul all of Catalonia's privileges. Its language was banned, its universities closed and Lleida's Gothic cathedral became a barracks. Felipe tore down the Ribera district of Barcelona and, in what is now Ciutadella Park *(see p67)*, built a citadel to keep an eye on the population.

With the lifting of trade restrictions with the Americas, Catalonia began to recover economically. Progress, however, was interrupted by the 1793–95 war with France and then by the 1808–14 Peninsular War (known in Spain as the War of Independence), when Napoleon put his brother Joseph on the Spanish throne. Barcelona fell in early 1808, but Girona withstood a seven-month siege. Monasteries, including Montserrat *(see pp124–5)* were sacked and pillaged. They suffered further in 1835 under a republican government, when many were seen as too rich and powerful and were dissolved. This was a politically vigorous time, when a minority of largely rural reactionaries fought a rearguard action against the liberal spirit of the century in the Carlist Wars.

The Catalan Renaixença

Barcelona was the first city in Spain to industrialize, mainly around cotton manufacture from raw material imported from the Americas. It brought immigrant workers and a burgeoning population, and, in 1854, the city burst out of its medieval walls *(see p73)*. Inland, industrial centres such as Terrassa and Sabadell flourished and *colònies industrials* (company-built workers' villages) grew up along the rivers where mills were powered by water.

Just as the wealth of the 14th century inspired Catalonia's first flowering, so the wealth from industry inspired the *Renaixença*, a renaissance of Catalan culture. Its literary rallying points were Bonaventura Aribau's *Oda a la patria* and the poems of a young monk, Jacint Verdaguer, who won poetry prizes in the revived Jocs Florals *(see p45)*.

Well-to-do *barcelonins* selecting from a wide range of locally produced calico in the early 19th century

Felipe V
(1700–24)

1808–14 Peninsular War (War of Independence): Girona besieged, Barcelona occupied, Monastery of Montserrat sacked

1823–6 French occupy Catalonia

1835 Monasteries dissolved

1833–9 First Carlist War

1859 Revival of Jocs Florals poetry competition feeds renaissance of Catalan culture

1700	1750	1800	1850

1714 Barcelona sacked by Felipe V, first Bourbon king. Catalan universities closed. Catalan language banned

1778 Catalonia allowed to trade with the Americas, bringing new wealth

1833 Aribau's *Oda a la patria* published

1849 Spain's first railway built to link Barcelona and Mataró

Poet Bonaventura Carles Aribau i Farriols

A hall of Spanish goods at the 1888 Universal Exhibition

Catalanism and Modernisme

The *Renaixença* produced a new pride in Catalonia, and "Catalanism" was at the heart of the region's accelerating move towards autonomy, a move echoed in Galicia and the Basque Country. Interruptions by the Carlist Wars came to an end in 1876 and resulted in the restoration of the Bourbon monarchy.

The first home-rule party, the *Lliga de Catalunya*, was founded in 1887, and disputes with the central government continued. It was blamed for the loss of the American colonies, and therefore lucrative transatlantic trade, and for involving Spain in unnecessary conflict in Morocco. *La setmana tràgica* (tragic week) of 1909 saw the worst of the violent protests: 116 people died and 300 were injured.

Meanwhile, on a more cultural and artistic level and in order to show off its increasing wealth, Barcelona held in 1888 a Universal Exhibition in the Parc de la Ciutadella where Felipe V's citadel had recently been torn down. The urban

Poster for 1929 Exhibition

expansion *(eixample)* inland was carefully ordered under a plan by Ildefons Cerdà *(see p73)* and industrial barons employed imaginative architects to show off their wealth, most successfully Eusebi Güell and Antoni Gaudí *(see pp26–7)*. The destruction of the monasteries had left spaces for sumptuous buildings, such as the Palau de la Música Catalana *(see p65)*, the Liceu opera house and La Boqueria market *(see p155)*.

Spain's noninvolvement in World War I meant that Catalonia's Modernista architecture remained unscathed. Barcelona's place as a showcase city was confirmed with the 1929 International Exhibition on Montjuïc, many of whose buildings still remain.

Antoni Gaudí, Modernisme's most creative architect

Civil War

The *Mancomunitat*, a local council established in 1914, disappeared on the arrival in 1923 of the dictator Primo de Rivera, Barcelona's military governor. In 1931, Francesc Macià declared himself President of the Catalan Republic, which lasted three days. Three years later, Lluís Companys was arrested and sentenced to 30 years' imprisonment for attempting to do the same. Finally, on 16 July 1936, General Francisco Franco led an army revolt against the Republican government and the fledgling autonomous states. The government fled Madrid to

1888 Universal Exhibition held in Parc de la Ciutadella, showing off the new Modernista style

1872–6 Third and last Carlist War

1909 *Setmana tràgica*: violent protest against Moroccan Wars

Primo de Rivera (1870–1930)

1947 Spain declared a monarchy with Franco as regent

1931 Francesc Macià declares independence for Catalonia

1875

1900

1925

1893 Anarchist bombs in Liceu opera house kill 14

1901 *Lliga Regionalista*, new Catalan party, wins elections

1929 International Exhibition on Montjuïc

1939 50,000 go into exile in France. Catalan President Companys executed

1936–9 Spanish Civil War. Republican government retreats from Madrid to Valencia, then Barcelona

Carlist soldiers

Refugees on the march in 1939, fleeing towards the Pyrenees to seek asylum in France

Valencia, then Barcelona. City and coast were bombed by German aircraft, and shelled by Italian warships. When Barcelona fell three years later, thousands, including Companys, were executed in Franco's reprisals. Catalonia lost all it had gained, and its language was outlawed once more. The *negre nit*, the dark night that followed Franco's victory, left Barcelona short of resources and largely neglected by Madrid. The 1960s, however, brought new economic opportunities, and between 1960 and 1975, two million Spaniards came to work in the city. The arrival of the first tourists to the coast during that time, to the Costa Brava and Costa Daurada, changed the face of Spain for ever.

Life after Franco

Champagne flowed freely in Barcelona's streets on the news of Franco's death in 1975. Democracy and the monarchy, under the Bourbon Juan Carlos, was restored. Catalonia has since won a large degree of autonomy and, in June 2006, a Statute of Autonomy of Catalonia was approved, providing a new legal framework for greater political independence. Pasqual Maragall, Barcelona's mayor until 1997 and president of Catalonia from 2003 to 2006, steered the radical shake-up of the city for the 1992 Olympic Games. Barcelona changed dramatically, with a bold new waterfront, inspired urban spaces, and state-of-the-art museums and galleries. In 2011, after 32 years of socialist government, the centre-right Catalan nationalist party (CiU) rose to power in Barcelona. Parties supporting Catalonian independence continue to gain ground. A planned referendum at the end of 2014 was decreed illegal by the Spanish government, but an estimated 80 percent of Catalans voted "yes" in a symbolic referendum held in November.

Opening ceremony, 1992 Barcelona Olympic Games

1953 US bases welcomed

1975 Franco dies. King Juan Carlos restores Bourbon line

1979 Partial autonomy granted to Catalonia

1992 Olympic Games held in Barcelona

2008 High Speed AVE train line between Barcelona and Madrid inaugurated

2014 1.8 million pro-independence Catalans form a gigantic "V" for victory in Barcelona

950   1975   2000   2025

1960s Costa Brava leads package-holiday boom

1985 Medes Islands become Spain's first marine nature reserve

1986 Spain enters European Union

2004 Universal Forum of Cultures held in Barcelona

2012 Large demonstrations are held in favour of Catalan independence.

Cobi, the Olympic mascot

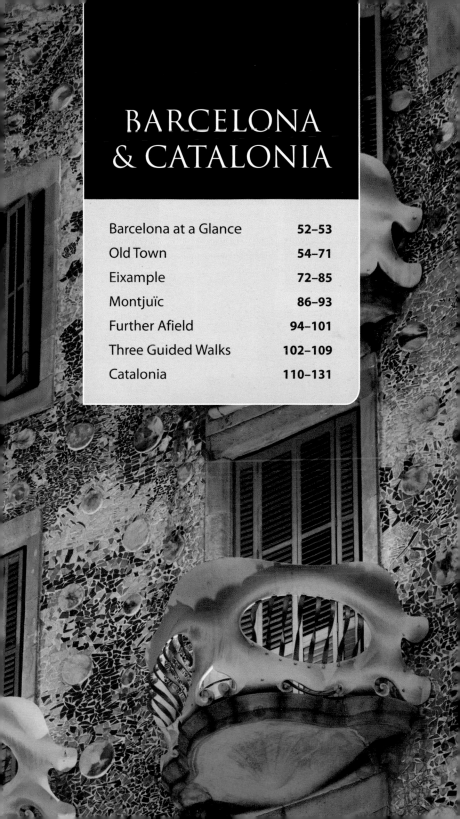

BARCELONA & CATALONIA

Barcelona at a Glance	52–53
Old Town	54–71
Eixample	72–85
Montjuïc	86–93
Further Afield	94–101
Three Guided Walks	102–109
Catalonia	110–131

OLD TOWN

The old town, traversed by Barcelona's most famous avenue, La Rambla, is one of the most extensive medieval city centres in Europe. The Barri Gòtic contains the cathedral and a maze of streets and squares. Across from the Via Laietana, the El Born neighbourhood is dominated by the Santa Maria del Mar church and is replete with 14th-century mansions. This area is bounded by the leafy Parc de la Ciutadella, home to the city's zoo. The revitalized seafront is a stimulating mix of old and new. Trendy shops and restaurants make up the fashionable marina, contrasted with the old maritime neighbourhood of Barceloneta and the new Olympic port.

Sights at a Glance

Museums and Galleries
- ❷ Museu Frederic Marès
- ❿ Museu d'Art Contemporani
- ⓭ Museu Picasso
- ⓯ Museu de la Xocolata
- ⓲ Castell dels Tres Dragons
- ⓳ Museu d'Idees i Invents (MIBA)
- ⓴ Museu Martorell
- ㉕ Aquàrium
- ㉖ Museu d'Història de Catalunya
- ㉙ Museu Marítim and Drassanes

Parks and Gardens
- ⓱ Parc de la Ciutadella
- ㉑ Zoo de Barcelona

Harbour Sights
- ㉒ Port Olímpic
- ㉔ Port Vell
- ㉘ Golondrinas

Monuments
- ⓰ Arc del Triomf
- ㉗ Monument a Colom

Churches
- ❻ Cathedral pp60 61
- ⓮ Basílica de Santa Maria del Mar

Historic Building
- ❶ Casa de l'Ardiaca
- ❸ Museu d'Història de Barcelona – Plaça del Rei
- ❹ Casa de la Ciutat
- ❺ Palau de la Generalitat
- ❽ Palau Güell
- ⓫ Palau de la Música Catalana
- ⓬ La Llotja

Streets and Districts
- ❼ La Rambla
- ❾ El Raval
- ㉓ Barceloneta

See also Street Finder maps 2, 5 and 6

Street-by-Street: Barri Gòtic

The Barri Gòtic (Gothic Quarter) is the true heart of Barcelona. The oldest part of the city, it was the site chosen by the Romans in the reign of Augustus (27 BC–AD 14) on which to found a new *colonia* (town), and has been the location of the city's administrative buildings ever since. The Roman forum was on the Plaça de Sant Jaume, where now stand the medieval Palau de la Generalitat, the seat of Catalonia's government, and the Casa de la Ciutat, the city's town hall. Close by are the Gothic cathedral and royal palace, where Columbus was received by Fernando and Isabel on his return from the New World in 1492 *(see p46)*.

❶ Casa de l'Ardiaca
Built on the Roman city wall, the Gothic-Renaissance archdeacon's residence now houses Barcelona's historical archives.

To Plaça de Catalunya

SANT SEVER

CARRER DEL BISBE

PIETA

❻ ★ Cathedral
The façade and spire are 19th-century additions to the original Gothic building. Among the artistic treasures inside are medieval Catalan paintings.

SANT DOMÈNEC DEL CALL

SANT HONORAT

❺ Palau de la Generalitat
Catalonia's seat of government has superb Gothic features, such as the chapel and a staircase to an open-air, arcaded gallery.

CARRER DE FERRAN

PLAÇA DE SANT JAUME

CARRER DE LA CIUTAT

To La Rambla

❹ Casa de la Ciutat (Ajuntament)
Barcelona's town hall was built in the 14th and 15th centuries. The façade is a Neo-Classical addition. In the entrance hall stands *Three Gypsy Boys* by Joan Rebull (1899–1981), a 1976 copy of a sculpture he originally created in 1946.

Key

— Suggested route

❷ Museu Frederic Marès
This medieval doorway is from an extensive display of Spanish sculpture – the mainstay of this museum's extraordinarily eclectic and high-quality collections.

Locator Map
See Barcelona City Centre map pp16–17

EIXAMPLE

OLD TOWN

MONTJUÏC

Roman city wall

Saló del Tinell

❸ ★ Palau Reial
The 14th-century Capella Reial de Santa Àgata, with a 1466 altarpiece, is one of the best surviving sections of the palace.

Capella Reial de Santa Àgata

Plaça del Rei

Palau del Lloctinent

Cereria Subirà candle shop

CARRER DELS COMTES DE BARCELONA

TAPINERIA

VIA LAIETANA

CARRER DE JAUME I

Jaume I Metro

CARRER DEGUERIA

SOTS-TINENT NAVARRO

0 metres   100
0 yards   100

The Museu d'Història de Barcelona features the most extensive subterranean Roman ruins in the world. Accessed through this 14th-century mansion, visitors can view the streets and squares of Roman Barcelona. The ruins extend underground, through to the exit at the Palau Reial.

Pillars from the Temple of Augustus can be seen just off the courtyard of the Centre Excursionista de Catalunya, which is housed in a medieval mansion. The temple site is marked by a millstone in the street.

For keys to symbols *see back flap*

Decorated marble postbox, Casa de l'Ardiaca

❶ Casa de l'Ardiaca

Carrer de Santa Llúcia 1. **Map** 5 B2.
Tel 93 256 22 55. 🚇 Jaume I. **Open**
for research only. Courtyard open
9am–8:45pm Mon–Fri (to 7:30pm Jul
& Aug), 9am–1pm Sat (not Jul & Aug).
W bcn.cat/arxiu/arxiuhistoric

Standing beside what was
originally the Bishop's Gate in
the Roman wall is the Archdeacon's House. It was first built
in the 12th century, but in its
present form it dates from
around 1500, when it was
remodelled, including the
addition of a colonnade. In 1870,
this was extended to form the
Flamboyant Gothic patio around
a fountain. The Modernista
architect Domènech i Montaner
(1850–1923) added the fanciful
marble mailbox, carved with
three swallows and a tortoise,
beside the Renaissance portal.
Upstairs is the Arxiu Històric de
la Ciutat (City Archives).

❷ Museu Frederic Marès

Plaça de Sant Iu 5. **Map** 5 B2. **Tel** 93
256 35 00. 🚇 Jaume I. **Open** 10am–
7pm Tue–Sat, 11am–8pm Sun &
public hols. **Closed** 1 Jan, 1 May, 24
Jun, 25 Dec. 🎟 free for under 16s,
also Sun after 3pm & 1st Sun of every
month. 📷 ♿
W museumares.bcn.cat

The sculptor Frederic Marès i
Deulovol (1893–1991) was also
a traveller and collector, and this
museum is a monument to his
eclectic taste. As part of the
Royal Palace, it was occupied by

13th-century bishops, 14th-
century counts of Barcelona,
15th-century judges and
18th-century nuns, who lived
here until they were expelled in
1936. Marès, who had a small
apartment in the building,
opened this museum in 1948.
It contains a fascinating
collection of works, including
some outstanding examples
of Romanesque and Gothic
religious art. In the crypt and
on the ground floor are stone
sculptures and two complete
Romanesque portals. The first
floor has Renaissance and
Baroque sculpture. Exhibits on
the second and third floors
range from children's toys,
clocks, crucifixes and costumes
to antique cameras, pipes
and postcards.

❸ Museu d'Història de Barcelona – Plaça del Rei

Plaça del Rei. **Map** 5 B2. **Tel** 93 256
21 22. 🚇 Jaume I. **Open** 10am–7pm
Tue–Sat, 10am–8pm Sun, 10am–2pm
public hols. **Closed** 1 Jan, 1 May, 24
Jun, 25 Dec. 🎟 free for under 16s,
also Sun after 3pm & 1st Sun of month.
📷 **W** museuhistoria.bcn.cat

The Royal Palace was the
residence of the count-kings of
Barcelona from its foundation in
the 13th century. The complex
includes the 14th-century
Gothic Saló del Tinell, a vast
room with arches spanning
17 m (56 ft). This is where Isabel
and Fernando (see p46) received
Columbus after his triumphal
return from America. It is also
where the Holy Inquisition sat,

Gothic nave of the Capella de Santa Àgata,
Palau Reial

Barcelona's Early Jewish Community

Hebrew tablet

From the 11th to the 13th centuries Jews,
dominated Barcelona's commerce and culture,
providing doctors and founding the first seat of
learning. But in 1243, 354 years after they were
first documented in the city, violent anti-
Semitism led to the Jews being consigned to a
ghetto, El Call. Ostensibly to provide protection,
the ghetto had only one entrance, which led
into the Plaça de Sant Jaume. Jews were heavily
taxed by the monarch, who viewed them as "royal
serfs"; but in return they also received privileges,
as they handled most of Catalonia's lucrative trade with North
Africa. However, official and popular persecution finally led to the
disappearance of the ghetto in 1401, 91 years before Judaism was
fully outlawed in Spain (see p46).

Originally, there were three synagogues, the main one being in
Carrer Sant Domènec del Call, but only the foundations are left. A
14th-century Hebrew tablet is embedded in the wall at No. 5 Carrer
de Marlet, which reads: "Holy Foundation of Rabbi Samuel Hassardi.
His soul will rest in Heaven".

believing the walls would move if lies were told. On the right, built into the Roman city wall, is the royal chapel, the Capella de Santa Àgata, with a painted wood ceiling and an altarpiece (1466) by Jaume Huguet *(see p30)*. Its bell tower is formed by part of a watchtower on the Roman wall. Stairs on the right of the altar lead to the 16th-century tower of Martí the Humanist (who reigned from 1396 to 1410), the last ruler of the 500-year dynasty of the count-kings of Barcelona. Sadly, the tower can no longer be climbed by visitors.

The main attraction of the Museu d'Història lies below the ground. Entire streets and squares of old Barcino are accessible via a lift and walkways suspended over the ruins of Roman Barcelona. The site was discovered when the Casa Clariana-Padellàs, the Gothic building from which you enter, was moved here, stone by stone, in 1931, as demonstrated by an extraordinary photo of the original dig towards the end of the exhibit. The water and drainage systems, baths, homes with mosaic floors, dye works, laundries and even the old forum now make up the most extensive and complete subterranean Roman ruins in the world.

❹ Casa de la Ciutat

Plaça de Sant Jaume 1. **Map** 5 A2. **Tel** 93 402 70 00. 🚇 Jaume I or Liceu. **Open** 10am–1:30pm Sun (also 12 Feb, 23 Apr and May 30: 10am–8pm), or by appointment. 🗓 11am in English. ♿

The magnificent 14th-century city hall *(ajuntament)* faces the Palau de la Generalitat. Flanking the entrance are statues of Jaume I *(see p45)*, who granted the city rights to elect councillors in 1249, and Joan Fiveller, who levied taxes on court members in the 1500s. Inside is the huge council chamber, the 14th-century Saló de Cent, built for the city's 100 councillors. The Saló de les Cròniques was commissioned for the 1929 International Exhibition and decorated by Josep-Maria Sert *(see p31)* with murals of events in Catalan history.

❺ Palau de la Generalitat

Plaça de Sant Jaume 4. **Map** 5 A2. 🚇 Jaume I. **Open** 23 Apr, 11 & 24 Sep, 2nd & 4th Sat & Sun of month: 10:30am–1:30pm by appointment only via website. Passport needed for entry. ♿ 🗓 🌐 **gencat.cat**

Since 1403, the Generalitat has been the seat of the Catalonian Government. Above the

The Italianate façade of the Palau de la Generalitat

entrance, in its Renaissance façade, is a statue of Sant Jordi (St George) – the patron saint of Catalonia – and the Dragon. The late Catalan Gothic courtyard is by Marc Safont (1416).

Among the fine interiors are the Gothic chapel of Sant Jordi, also by Safont, and Pere Blai's Italianate Saló de Sant Jordi. The building is open to the public only on the saint's feast day. At the back, one floor above street level, lies the *Pati dels Tarongers*, the Orange Tree Patio, by Pau Mateu, which has a bell tower built by Pere Ferrer in 1568.

The Catalan president has offices here as well as in the Casa dels Canonges. The two buildings are connected across Carrer del Bisbe by a bridge built in 1928 and modelled on the Bridge of Sighs in Venice.

The magnificent council chamber, the Saló de Cent, in the Casa de la Ciutat

⊙ Barcelona Cathedral

This compact Gothic cathedral, with a Romanesque chapel (the Capella de Santa Llúcia) and beautiful cloister, was begun in 1298 under Jaume II, on the foundations of a Roman temple and Moorish mosque. It was not finished until the early 20th century, when the central spire was completed. A white marble choir screen, sculpted in the 16th century, depicts the martyrdom of St Eulàlia, the city's patron. Next to the font, a plaque records the baptism of six native Caribbeans, brought back from the Americas by Columbus in 1493.

Nave Interior
The Catalan-style Gothic interior has a single wide nave with 28 side chapels. These are set between the columns supporting the vaulted ceiling, which rises to 26 m (85 ft).

KEY

① **The main façade** was not completed until 1889, and the central spire until 1913. It was based on the original 1408 plans of the French architect Charles Galters.

② **The twin octagonal bell towers** date from 1386–93. The bells were installed in this tower in 1545.

③ **Porta de Santa Eulàlia,** entrance to cloisters

④ **The Sacristy Museum** has a small treasury. Pieces include an 11th-century font, tapestries and liturgical artifacts.

⑤ **Capella de Santa Llúcia**

★ **Choir Stalls**
The top tier of the beautifully carved 15th-century stalls contains painted coats of arms (1518) of several European kings.

Capella del Santíssim Sagrament
This small chapel houses the 16th-century Christ of Lepanto crucifix.

Capella de Sant Benet
This chapel, dedicated to the founder of the Benedictine Order and patron saint of Europe, houses a magnificent altarpiece showing *The Transfiguration* by Bernat Martorell (1452).

★ Crypt
In the crypt, beneath the main altar, is the alabaster sarcophagus (1339) of St Eulàlia, martyred for her beliefs by the Romans during the 4th century AD.

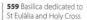

★ Cloisters
The fountain, set in a corner of the Gothic cloisters and decorated with a statue of St George, provided fresh water.

400	700	1000	1300	1600	1900
559 Basilica dedicated to St Eulàlia and Holy Cross	**877** St Eulàlia's remains brought here from Santa Maria del Mar	**1339** St Eulàlia's relics transferred to alabaster sarcophagus		**1913** Central spire completed	
		1046–58 Romanesque cathedral built under Ramon Berenguer I		**1889** Main façade completed, based on plans dating from 1408 by architect Charles Galters	
4th century Original Roman (paleo-Christian) basilica built	**985** Building destroyed by the Moors	**1257–68** Romanesque Capella de Santa Llúcia built	**1493** Indians brought back from the Americas are baptized		
		1298 Gothic cathedral begun under Jaume II		*Plaque of the Caribbeans' baptism*	

❼ La Rambla

The historic avenue of La Rambla, leading to the sea, is busy around the clock, especially in the evenings and at weekends. Newsstands, flower stalls, tarot readers, musicians and mime artists throng the wide, tree-shaded central walkway. Among its famous buildings are the Liceu Opera House, the huge Boqueria food market and some grand mansions.

Exploring La Rambla

The name of this long avenue, also known as Las Ramblas, comes from the Arabic *ramla*, meaning the dried-up bed of a seasonal river. The 13th-century city wall followed the left bank of such a river which flowed from the Collserola hills to the sea. Convents, monasteries and the university were built on the other bank in the 16th century. As time passed, the riverbed was filled in and those buildings demolished, but they are remembered in the names of the five consecutive Ramblas that make up the great avenue between the Port Vell and Plaça de Catalunya.

Mercat de Sant Josep Plaza de la Boqueria. **Map** 2 F3. **Tel** 93 318 20 17. 🅜 Liceu. **Open** 8am–8:30pm Mon–Sat.

Palau de la Virreina La Rambla 99. **Map** 5 A2. **Tel** 93 316 10 00. 🅜 Liceu. **Open** noon–8pm Tue–Sun. **Closed** 1 Jan, 1 May, 25 & 26 Dec.

Museu de Cera Pg de la Banca 7. **Map** 2 F4. **Tel** 93 317 26 49. 🅜 Drassanes. **Open** 10am–1:30pm, 4–7:30pm Mon–Fri, 11am–2pm, 4:30–8:30pm Sat, Sun & public hols (Jul–Aug: 10am–10pm daily). 🖼 ♿

The busy, tree-lined avenue of La Rambla

⑤ Mercat de Sant Josep
Popularly known as "La Boqueria", the Mercat de Sant Josep is Barcelona's most colourful food market.

⑦ Gran Teatre del Liceu
Barcelona's opera house has had to be restored twice following damage caused by fires in 1861 and 1994.

The monument to Columbus at the bottom of the tree-lined Rambla

⑨ Palau Güell
This Neo-Gothic palace, completed in 1889, is considered to be one of Gaudí's most important works (*see p64*).

CARF

C. NOU
LA RAM

CARRER LANCASTER

C. DE L
DEL TE

Drassanes 🅜

RAMBLA DE

① Font de Canaletes

This 19th-century fountain has four taps from which to drink. Saying that someone "drinks the waters of Canaletes" indicates that he or she is from Barcelona

② Reial Acadèmia de Ciències i Arts

Converted to a theatre in 1910, this building is the home of Barcelona's first official public clock.

③ Palau Moja

This Classical building dates back to 1790. The Baroque first-floor salon of Palau Moja is used for exhibitions.

④ Palau de la Virreina

The first person to live in this great palace, in 1777, was the widowed *virreina* (viceroy's wife) of Spain in Peru.

⑥ Plaça de la Boqueria

This square features a colourful mosaic pavement by Joan Miró (1976) and a Modernista dragon designed for a former umbrella shop.

⑧ Plaça Reial

Barcelona's liveliest square was built in the 1850s and is adorned with palms. Its Neo-Classical carriage lamps were designed by Gaudí.

⑩ Museu de Cera

This waxwork museum is housed in an atmospheric, 19th-century stately home. The museum was established in 1973 and contains over 300 exhibits.

0 metres		100
0 yards		100

For keys to symbols *see back flap*

❽ Palau Güell

Nou de la Rambla 3–5. **Map** 2 F3. **Tel** 93 472 57 75. 🚇 Liceu. **Open** 10am–8pm Tue–Sun (to 5:30pm Nov–Mar). **Closed** 1, 6 & 19–25 Jan, 25 & 26 Dec. 🎫 free for under 10s, also Sun 5–8pm (Apr–Oct), 2:30–5:30pm (Nov–Mar), and all day 1st Sun of month. 📷 ♿ except roof terrace. 🌐 **palauguell.cat**

Gaudí's first major work in Barcelona's city centre was commissioned by his wealthy patron Eusebi Güell. Güell made it known that, even if he was investing in an inexperienced architect, there would be no limit to the budget at Gaudí's disposal. Gaudí took his patron at his word, as can be seen in the quality of the materials used for what was a disproportionately grand building raised on a small plot in a narrow street. The stonework is clad with marble and inside, high quality woods are employed throughout.

As in his other buildings, Gaudí designed furniture, lights, stained glass, and many other fittings, working closely with craftsmen to realise his ideas. The house was finished in 1889 and was used not only as a luxurious family home for a wealthy man, but also as a place to hold political meetings, chamber concerts and to put up important guests.

From the street, there is little hint of the colour and playfulness to come in Gaudí's mature work, except in the spire-like chimneys behind the parapet on the roof. The austere façade of Palau Güell is symmetrical and characterised mostly by straight lines, both horizontal and vertical. The only indication of Gaudí's later preference for curves is in the two doorways, each formed by a parabolic arch – a geometric shape he would subsequently employ to great effect.

Inside, the most notable feature of the house is its very high central room on the main floor. Something between a sitting room and a covered courtyard, this central room rises fully three floors (of a six floor building) and is spanned by a cupola. The other rooms are grouped around it.

Palau Güell's spire-like roof chimneys

❾ El Raval

Map 2 F3. 🚇 Catalunya, Liceu.

The district of El Raval lies west of La Rambla and includes the old red-light area near the port, once known as Barri Xinès (Chinese quarter).

From the 14th century, the city hospital was located in Carrer de l'Hospital, which still has several herbal and medicinal shops today. Gaudí (*see p80*) was brought here after being fatally hit by a tram in 1926. The buildings now house the Biblioteca de Catalunya (Catalonian Library), but the elegant former dissecting room has been fully restored.

Towards the port in Carrer Nou de la Rambla is Gaudí's Palau Güell. At the end of Carrer

Sant Pau is the city's most complete Romanesque church, the 12th-century Sant Pau del Camp, with a charming cloister featuring exquisitely carved capitals.

❿ Museu d'Art Contemporani

Plaça dels Angels 1. **Map** 2 F2. **Tel** 93 412 08 10. 🚇 Universitat, Catalunya. **Open** 25 Jun–24 Sep: 11am–8pm Mon, Wed, & Thu, 11am–10pm Fri, 10am–10pm Sat, 10am–3pm Sun; 25 Sep–24 Jun: 11am–7:30pm Mon & Wed–Fri, 10am–9pm Sat, 10am–3pm Sun. **Closed** 1 Jan, 25 Dec. 🎫 free for under 14s. ♿ 📷 tours in English 4pm & 6pm Mon, 4pm Wed–Sat. 🌐 **macba.cat** Centre de Cultura Contemporània: Montalegre 5. **Tel** 93 306 41 00. 🌐 **cccb.org**

This dramatic, glass-fronted building was designed by the American architect Richard Meier. Its light, airy galleries act as the city's contemporary art mecca. The permanent collection of mainly Spanish painting, sculpture and installations from the 1950s onwards is complemented by temporary exhibitions by foreign artists like South African photo-journalist David Goldblatt and US painter Susana Solano.

Next to the MACBA is the **Centre de Cultura Contemporània de Barcelona** (CCCB), a lively arts centre.

Façade of the Museu d'Art Contemporani

Glorious stained-glass dome, Palau de la Música Catalana

⑪ Palau de la Música Catalana

Carrer de Sant Pere Més Alt, s/n. **Map** 5 B1. **Tel** 93 295 72 00. 🚇 Urquinaona. **Open** 10am–3:30pm daily (to 6pm Easter, 9am–8pm Aug); and for concerts. Buying tickets in advance online is recommended. 🎧♿📷 on the hour in English. **W** palaumusica.org

This is a real palace of music, a Modernista celebration of tilework, sculpture and glorious stained glass. It is the only concert hall in Europe lit by natural light. Designed by Lluís Domènech i Montaner, it was completed in 1908. Although a few extensions have been added, the building still retains its original appearance. The elaborate red-brick façade is hard to appreciate fully in the confines of the narrow street. It is lined with mosaic-covered pillars topped by busts of the great composers Palestrina, Bach and Beethoven. The large

stone sculpture of St George and other figures at the corner of the building portray an allegory from Catalan folksong by Miquel Blay.

But it is the interior of the building that is truly inspiring. The auditorium is lit by a huge inverted dome of stained glass depicting angelic choristers. The sculptures of composers Wagner and Clavé on the proscenium arch that frames the stage area were designed by Domènech, but finished by Pau Gargallo. The stunning "Muses of the Palau", the group of 18 highly stylized, instrument-playing maidens are the stage's backdrop. Made of terracotta and *trencadís* (broken pieces of ceramic), they have become the building's most admired feature.

The work of Josep Anselm Clavé (1824–74) in promoting Catalan song led to the creation of the Orfeó Català choral society in 1891, a focus of Catalan nationalism and the

inspiration behind the Palau. Although the Orfeó is now based at the more state-of-the-art L'Auditori in Plaça de les Glòries (see p166), there is a concert at the Palau nearly every night; it is the main venue for the city's jazz and guitar festivals, and national and international symphony orchestras regularly grace its flamboyant stage.

The Palau's new era began with the completion of the work carried out by the top local architect Oscar Tusquets. An underground concert hall and an outdoor square for summer concerts were added, consolidating the Palau's reputation as Barcelona's most loved music venue.

⑫ La Llotja

Carrer del Consolat de Mar 2. **Map** 5 B3. **Tel** 93 547 88 49. 🚇 Barceloneta. **Closed** to public (except twice a year, days vary). **W** casallotja.com

La Llotja (meaning commodity exchange) was built in the 1380s as the headquarters of the Consolat de Mar (see p45). It was remodelled in Neo-Classical style in 1771 and housed the city's stock exchange until 1994, the original Gothic hall acting as the main trading room. It can still be seen through the windows.

The upper floors housed the Barcelona School of Fine Arts from 1849 to 1970, attended by the young Picasso and Joan Miró (see p31). They are now occupied by local government offices.

Statue of Poseidon in the courtyard of La Llotja

A wedding service in the Gothic interior of Santa Maria del Mar

⑬ Museu Picasso

Carrer de Montcada 15–23. **Map** 5 B2.
Tel 93 256 30 00. 🚇 Jaume I. **Open**
9am–7pm Tue–Sun (to 9:30pm Thu).
Closed 1 Jan, 1 May, 24 Jun, 25 & 26
Dec. 🎫 free for under 18s, also 1st
Sun of month, every Sun from 3pm.
♿ 🅿 email: museupicasso_
reserves@bcn.cat. Free tours in
English 11am Sun (not August).
📷 🌐 **museupicasso.bcn.cat**

The popular Picasso Museum is
housed in five adjoining medieval
palaces on Carrer Montcada:
Berenguer d'Aguilar, Baró de
Castellet, Meca, Mauri and
Finestres. The museum opened

in 1963, showing works donated
by Jaime Sabartes, a friend of
Picasso. After Sabartes' death in
1968, Picasso himself donated
paintings. Works were also left
in his will and donated by his
widow, Jacqueline.

The strength of the 4,200-
piece collection is Picasso's early
works. Even at the age of 15, he
was painting major works such
as *The First Communion* (1896)
and *Science and Charity* (1897).
There are a few works from his
Blue and Rose periods. Most
famous is his series of 44 paintings, *Las Meninas*, inspired by
Velázquez's masterpiece.

⑭ Basílica de Santa Maria del Mar

Pl Sta Maria 1. **Map** 5 B3. **Tel** 93 310 23
90. 🚇 Jaume I. **Open** 9am–1pm,
5–8:30pm Mon–Sat, 10am–2pm,
5–8pm Sun. ♿ 🅿 hourly
throughout the day (in English pm).

This beautiful building, the city's
favourite church with superb
acoustics for concerts, is the
only example of a church
entirely in the Catalan Gothic
style. It took just 55 years to
build, with money donated by
merchants and shipbuilders. The
speed – unrivalled in the Middle

Pablo Picasso in Barcelona

Picasso (1881–1973) was 13 when he arrived in Barcelona, where
his father, José Ruiz y Blasco, had found work teaching in the
city art school situated above the Llotja. The city was rich, but it
also possessed a large, poor working class that was becoming
organized and starting to rebel. Shortly after the family's arrival,
a bomb was thrown into a Corpus Christi procession.

The family settled at No. 3 Carrer de la Mercè, a gloomy, five-
storeyed house not far from the Llotja. Picasso's precocious talent
gave him admittance to the upper school, where all the other
pupils were aged at least 20. Here, he immediately made friends
with another artist, Manuel Pallarès Grau, and the two lost their
virginity to the whores of Carrer d'Avinyó, who were to inspire
Les Demoiselles d'Avignon (1906–7), considered by many art critics
to be the wellspring of modern art. Picasso travelled with Pallarès
to the Catalan's home town of Horta, where he painted some early
landscapes, now in the Museu Picasso. The two remained friends
for the rest of their lives.

Pablo Picasso, *Self-Portrait* in charcoal
(1899–1900)

Ages – gave it a unity of style both inside and out. The west front has a 15th-century rose window of the Coronation of the Virgin. More stained glass from the 15th–18th centuries lights the wide nave and high aisles. When the choir and furnishings were burned in the Civil War *(see p48)*, it added to the sense of space and simplicity.

⓯ Museu de la Xocolata

Comerç 36. **Map** 5 C2. **Tel** 93 268 78 78. ⓜ Jaume I, Arc de Triomf. **Open** 10am–7pm Mon–Sat, 10am–3pm Sun & pub hols. **Closed** 1 Jan,1 May, 25 & 26 Dec. 🅿 free 1st Mon of month ⓰ ⓰ by appointment. ⬜ ⓦ **museuxocolata.cat**

Founded by Barcelona's pastry- and chocolate-makers' union, this museum takes you through the history of one of the most universally loved foodstuffs: from the discovery of cocoa in South America to the invention of the first chocolate machine in Barcelona. This is done using old posters, photographs and footage. The real thing is displayed in a homage to the art of the *mona*. A Catalan invention, this was a traditional Easter cake that over centuries evolved into an edible sculpture. Every year, *pastissiers* compete to create the finest piece, decorating their chocolate versions of well-known buildings or folk figures with jewels, feathers and other materials.

⓰ Arc del Triomf

Passeig Lluís Companys. **Map** 5 C1. ⓜ Arc de Triomf.

The main gateway to the 1888 Universal Exhibition, which filled the Parc de la Ciutadella, was designed by Josep Vilaseca i Casanovas. It is built of brick in Mudéjar (Spanish Moorish) style, with sculpted allegories of crafts, industry and business. The frieze by Josep Reynés on the main façade represents the city welcoming foreign visitors.

The pink brick façade of the late 19th-century Arc del Triomf

⓱ Parc de la Ciutadella

Passeig Picasso 1. **Map** 5 C3. ⓜ Barceloneta, Ciutadella-Vila Olímpica. **Open** 8am–sunset daily. ⓰

This popular park has a boating lake, orange groves and parrots living in the palm trees. It was once the site of a massive star-shaped citadel, built for Felipe V between 1715 and 1720 following a 13-month siege of

the city *(see p47)*. The fortress was intended to house soldiers to keep law and order, but was never used for this purpose. Converted into a prison, the citadel became notorious during the Napoleonic occupation *(see p47)*, and, during the 19th-century liberal repressions, it was hated as a symbol of centralized power.

In 1878, under General Prim, whose statue stands in the middle of the park, the citadel was pulled down and the park given to the city, to become, in 1888, the venue of the Universal Exhibition *(see p48)*. Three buildings survived: the Governor's Palace, now a school; the chapel; and the arsenal, which continues to be occupied by the Catalan parliament.

The park offers more cultural and leisure activities than any other in the city and is particularly popular on Sunday afternoons when people gather to play instruments, dance and relax, or visit the museum and zoo. A variety of works by Catalan sculptors, such as Marès, Arnau, Carbonell, Clarà, Llimona, Gargallo, Dunyach and Fuxà, can be seen in the park, alongside work by modern artists such as Tàpies and Botero.

The northeastern corner of the park boasts a magnificent fountain designed by architect Josep Fontseré, with the help of Antoni Gaudí, who was a young student at the time.

Ornamental cascade in the Parc de la Ciutadella, designed by Josep Fontseré and Antoni Gaudí

⑱ Castell dels Tres Dragons

Passeig de Picasso. **Map** 5 C2.
Tel 93 256 22 00. 🚇 Arc de Triomf,
Jaume I. **Closed** to the general public.

At the entrance to the Parc de
la Ciutadella is the fortress-like
Castell dels Tres Dragons
(Castle of the Three Dragons),
named after a play by Frederic
Soler. A fine example of
Modernista architecture, this
crenellated brick edifice was
built by Lluís Domènech i
Montaner for the 1888
Universal Exhibition. He later
used the building as a
workshop for Modernista
design, and it became a focus
of the movement. Shortly
afterwards it housed the
History Museum and later on
the Biology Museum. It is now
a laboratory of the Science
Museum and is open only
to researchers.

Castell dels Tres Dragons, a prime example
of Modernista architecture

⑲ Museu d'Idees i Invents (MIBA)

Carrer de la Ciutat 7. **Map** 5 A2. **Tel** 93
332 79 30. 🚇 Jaume I. **Open** 10am–
2pm, 4–7pm Tue–Fri, 10am–8pm Sat,
10am–2pm Sun. **Closed** 1 & 6 Jan, 25
& 26 Dec. 🎫 free for under 4s. ♿
🌐 mibamuseum.com

Inventor, writer and local
TV personality Pep Torres
founded the Museum of Ideas
and Inventions in 2011 to
celebrate entrepreneurship,
innovation and creativity. The
museum has three sections:
Limitless Society, a space for
inventors to showcase their
ideas; Corner of the Absurd,

Visitors peering into an animal enclosure at the Zoo de Barcelona

displaying humorous ideas
intended to prompt a smile or
a laugh; and Reflectionarium,
which has inventions that
provoke thought.

⑳ Museu Martorell

Parc de la Ciutadella. **Map** 5 C3.
Tel 93 256 60 02. 🚇 Arc de Triomf,
Jaume I. **Closed** for renovation.

This landmark, Barcelona's
oldest museum, opened in
1882, the same year the Parc
de la Ciutadella became a
public space. It was founded
to house the natural science
and archaeological collection
bequeathed by Francesc
Martorell i Peña to the city of
Barcelona. This Neo-Classical
building, designed by architect
Antoni Rovira i Trias, was the
city's first public museum.
It is currently being renovated

as a branch of the Science
Museum in the Fòrum area.
It will house a permanent
exhibition on the history
of the natural sciences in
Barcelona. Beside it is the
Hivernacle, a glasshouse by
Josep Amargós, and the
Umbracle, a brick and wood
conservatory by the park's
architect, Josep Fontseré.
Both date from 1884.

㉑ Zoo de Barcelona

Parc de la Ciutadella. **Map** 6 D3.
Tel 90 245 75 45. 🚇 Ciutadella–Vila
Olímpica. **Open** Apr–Oct: 10am–7pm
daily (to 8pm mid-May–mid-Sep);
Nov–Mar: 10am–5:30pm daily. 🎫 ♿
🌐 zoobarcelona.com

This zoo was laid out in the
1940s to what was, for the
time, a relatively enlightened
design – although the

Hivernacle glasshouse, next to Museu Martorell in Parc de la Ciutadella enclosures are not large, the animals are separated by moats instead of bars. Roig i Soler's 1885 sculpture by the entrance, *The Lady with the Umbrella*, has become a symbol of Barcelona. The zoo has pony rides, electric cars and a train for children. There are also dolphin and sea-lion shows, a face-painting area, and a petting zoo that is ideal for smaller children.

Yachts at the Port Olímpic, overlooked by Barcelona's tallest skyscrapers

⓳ Port Olímpic

Map 6 F4. Ⓜ Ciutadella-Vila Olímpica.

The most dramatic rebuilding for the 1992 Olympics was the demolition of the old industrial waterfront and the laying out of 4 km (2 miles) of promenade and pristine sandy beaches. At the heart of the project was a 65 ha (160 acre) new estate of 2,000 apartments and parks called Nova Icària. The area is still popularly known as the Vila Olímpica, because the buildings originally housed the Olympic athletes.

On the sea front there are twin 44-floor buildings, Spain's second- and third- tallest skyscrapers, one occupied by offices, the other by the Hotel Arts *(see p137)*. They stand beside the central building complex of the Port Olímpic marina, which was also built for 1992. This has shops, bars and nightclubs, as well as two levels

Sandy, palm-fringed beach at Barcelona's Port Olímpic

of restaurants around the waterside that have made it a popular place to eat out. There is a wide variety of international cuisines on offer, catering to the tastes of the visitors who make use of the berthing facilities here. The breezy outdoor setting attracts business people at lunchtime and pleasure-seekers in the evenings and at weekends.

Lunch can be walked off along the string of beaches, edged by a palm-fringed promenade with cafés. Behind the promenade, the coastal road heads around a park that is full of palm trees and lies beside the last three beaches, divided by rocky breakwaters. Swimming is safe on the gently sloping, sandy strands. For a more energetic experience, several of the marina's charter firms offer excursions by boat, "taster" sailing trips, kayaking and paddle-surfing.

㉓ Barceloneta

Map 5 B5. Ⓜ Barceloneta.

Barcelona's fishing "village", which lies on a triangular tongue of land jutting into the sea just below the city centre, is renowned for its little restaurants and cafés. Its beach is also the closest to the city centre and is well equipped with lifeguards, disabled access, showers and play areas for children.

The area was designed in 1753 by the architect and military engineer Juan Martín de Cermeño to rehouse people made homeless by the construction, just inland, of the Ciutadella fortress *(see p67)*. Since then it has housed largely workers and fishermen. Laid out in a grid system with narrow two- and three-storey houses, in which each room has a window on the street, the area has a friendly, intimate air.

In the small Plaça de la Barceloneta is the Baroque church of Sant Miguel del Port, also by Cermeño. The square itself is dominated by a popular covered market.

Today, Barceloneta's fishing fleet is still based in the nearby Moll del Rellotge (the clock dock), by a small clock tower. On the opposite side of this harbour is the Torre de Sant Sebastià, terminus of the cable car that runs right across the port, via the World Trade Centre, to Montjuïc.

Fishing boat moored in Barceloneta harbour

Maremagnum shopping complex on the Moll d'Espanya, Port Vell

ⓩ Port Vell

Map 5 A4. 🚇 Barceloneta, Drassanes.

Barcelona's marina is located at the foot of La Rambla, just beyond the old customs house. This was built in 1902 at the Portal de la Pau, the city's former maritime entrance. To the south, the Moll de Barcelona, with a new World Trade Centre, serves as the passenger pier for visiting liners. In front of the customs house, La Rambla is connected to the yacht clubs on the Moll d'Espanya by a swing bridge and a pedestrian jetty, known as La Rambla de Mar. The Moll d'Espanya boasts Barcelona's impressive Aquàrium (see below) and a vast shopping and restaurant complex, the Maremagnum.

On the shore, the Moll de Fusta (Timber Wharf), with terrace cafés, has red structures inspired by the bridge at Arles painted by Van Gogh. At the end of the wharf is *El Cap de Barcelona (Barcelona Head)*, a 20 m (66 ft) tall sculpture by Pop artist Roy Lichtenstein.

The attractive Sports Marina on the other side of the Moll d'Espanya was once lined with warehouses. The only one left – and the sole building still standing from Barcelona's Old Port – is the former General Stores building. The Stores were designed in 1881 by the

engineer Maurici Garrán and were intended for use as trading depots. They were refurbished in 1992 and today house the Museu d'Història de Catalunya (see below).

Spectacular glass viewing tunnel at the aquarium, Port Vell

ⓤ Aquàrium

Moll d'Espanya. **Map** 5 B4.
🚇 Barceloneta, Drassanes. **Tel** 93 221 74 74. **Open** 9:30am–9pm daily (to 9:30pm Sat, Sun & Jun, Sep; to 11pm Jul–Aug). 🎫 🛗 📷
📱 **aquariumbcn.com**

Populated by over 11,000 organisms belonging to 450 different species, Barcelona's aquarium is one of the biggest in Europe. Occupying three levels of a glass building, the aquarium focuses particularly on the local Mediterranean coast. Two nature reserves, for instance, the Delta de L'Ebre and the Medes isles off the Costa Brava, are given a tank

apiece. Tropical seas are also represented and moving platforms ferry visitors through a glass tunnel under an "ocean" of sharks, rays and sunfish. A large hall of activities for children includes an irregularly shaped tank of rays built around an island that is reached through crawl-through glass tunnels.

ⓥ Museu d'Història de Catalunya

Plaça Pau Vila 3. **Map** 5 A4.
🚇 Barceloneta, Drassanes. **Tel** 93 225 47 00. **Open** 10am–7pm Tue & Thu–Sat, 10am–8pm Wed, 10am–2:30pm Sun & public hols. **Closed** 1 & 6 Jan, 25 & 26 Dec. 🎫 free last Tue of the month Oct–Jun. 🛗 📷 noon & 1pm Sun & public hols. 📱 **mhcat.cat**

This museum charts the history of Catalonia, from Lower Palaeolithic times through to

Café-lined façade of the Museu d'Història de Catalunya

the region's heydays as a maritime power and industrial pioneer. Second-floor exhibits include the Moorish invasion, Romanesque architecture, medieval monastic life and the rise of Catalan seafaring. Third-floor exhibits cover the industrial revolution and the impact of steam power and electricity on the economy. There is also a glass floor laid over a relief map of Catalonia that visitors can walk over. The first floor is reserved for temporary exhibits. Some captions are in English; pick up a free guide for the rest.

A *golondrina* tour boat departing from the Portal de la Pau

The Columbus Monument lit by fireworks during La Mercè fiesta

㉗ Monument a Colom

Plaça del Portal de la Pau. **Map** 2 F4. **Tel** 93 302 52 24. Drassanes. **Open** 8:30am–8:30pm daily (to 7:30pm Oct–Feb).

The Columbus monument at the bottom of La Rambla was designed by Gaietà Buigas for the 1888 Universal Exhibition *(see p48)*. At the time, Catalans considered the great explorer a Catalan rather than an Italian.

The 60 m (200 ft) monument marks the spot where Columbus stepped ashore in 1493 after returning from his voyage to the Caribbean, bringing with him six Caribbean Indians. He was given a state welcome by the Catholic Monarchs in the Saló del Tinell of the Plaça del Rei *(see p58)*. The Indians' subsequent conversion to Christianity is commemorated in the cathedral *(see pp60–61)*. A lift leads to a viewing platform at the top of the monument. The bronze statue was designed by Rafael Arché.

㉘ Golondrinas

Plaça del Portal de la Pau. **Map** 2 F5. **Tel** 93 442 31 06. Drassanes. Departures: variable (phone for details). Catamaran Orsom **Tel** 93 441 05 37. lasgolondrinas.com; barcelona-orsom.com

Sightseeing trips around Barcelona's harbour and to the Port Olímpic can be made on *golondrinas* ("swallows") – small double-decker boats that moor at Portal de la Pau in front of the Columbus Monument at the foot of La Rambla.

The half-hour harbour tours are on traditional wooden boats and go out beneath the castle-topped hill of Montjuïc towards the industrial port. There is also a one-and-a-half hour trip on modern catamarans that takes in Barcelona harbour, the local beaches and finally Port Olímpic.

㉙ Museu Marítim and Drassanes

Avinguda de les Drassanes. **Map** 2 F4. **Tel** 93 342 99 20. Drassanes. **Open** 10am–8pm daily. **Closed** 1 & 6 Jan, 25 & 26 Dec. free Sun from 3pm mmb.cat

The great galleys that were instrumental in making Barcelona a major seafaring power were built in the sheds of the Drassanes (shipyards) that now house the maritime museum. These royal dry docks are the largest and most complete surviving medieval complex of their kind in the world. They were founded in the mid-13th century, when dynastic marriages uniting the kingdoms of Sicily and Aragón meant that better maritime communications between the two became a priority. Three of the yards' four original corner towers survive.

Among the vessels to slip from the Drassanes' vaulted halls was the *Real*, flagship of Don Juan of Austria, who led the Christian fleet to the famous victory against the Turks at Lepanto in 1571. The highlight of the museum's collection is a full-scale replica decorated in red and gold.

The *Llibre del Consolat de Mar*, a book of nautical codes and practice, is a reminder that Catalonia was once the arbiter of Mediterranean maritime law *(see p45)*. There are Pre-Columbian maps, including one from 1439 that was used by Amerigo Vespucci.

Stained-glass window in the Museu Marítim

EIXAMPLE

Barcelona claims to have the greatest collection of Art Nouveau buildings of any city in Europe. The style, known in Catalonia as Modernisme, flourished after 1854, when it was decided that the medieval walls should be torn down to allow the city to develop into what had previously been a construction-free military zone.

The designs of the civil engineer Ildefons Cerdà i Sunyer (1815–76) were chosen for the new expansion (eixample) inland. These plans called for a rigid grid system of streets, but at each intersection, the corners were chamfered to allow the buildings there to overlook the junctions or squares. The few exceptions to this grid system include the Diagonal, a main avenue running from the wealthy area of Pedralbes down to the sea, and the Hospital de la Santa Creu i de Sant Pau by Modernista architect Domènech i Montaner (1850–1923). He hated the grid system and deliberately angled the hospital to look down the diagonal Avinguda de Gaudí towards Antoni Gaudí's church of the Sagrada Família, the city's most spectacular Modernista building (see pp82–5). The wealth of Barcelona's commercial elite, and their passion for all things new, allowed them to give free rein to the age's most innovative architects in designing their residences, as well as public buildings.

Sights at a Glance

Museums and Galleries
3 Fundació Antoni Tàpies

Churches
7 Sagrada Família pp82–5

Modernista Buildings
1 Casa Batlló
2 Illa de la Discòrdia
4 La Pedrera
5 Casa Terrades, "Casa de les Punxes"
6 Hospital de la Santa Creu i de Sant Pau

See also Street Finder maps 3, 4 and 5

◀ A dizzying view into La Pedrera's interior courtyard

For keys to symbols see back flap

Street-by-Street: Quadrat d'Or

The hundred or so city blocks centering on the Passeig de Gràcia are known as the Quadrat d'Or, "Golden Square", because they contain so many of the best Modernista buildings *(see pp26–7)*. This was the area within the Eixample favoured by the wealthy bourgeoisie, who embraced the new artistic and architectural style with enthusiasm, not only for their residences, but also for commercial buildings. Most remarkable is the Mansana de la Discòrdia, a single block with houses by Modernisme's most illustrious exponents. Many interiors can be visited by the public, revealing a feast of stained glass, ceramics and ornamental ironwork.

Diagonal Metro

Vinçon home decor store
(see p155)

Passeig de Gràcia, the Eixample's main avenue, is a showcase of highly original buildings and smart shops. The graceful street lamps are by Pere Falqués (1850–1916).

RAMBLA DE CATALUNYA

PASSEIG DE GRÀCIA

❸ **Fundació Tàpies**
Topped by Antoni Tàpies' wire sculpture *Cloud and Chair*, this 1879 building by Domènech i Montaner houses a wide variety of Tàpies' paintings, graphics and sculptures.

Passeig de Gràcia Metro

Ⓜ

❷ ★ **Illa de la Discòrdia**
In this city block, three of Barcelona's most famous Modernista houses vie for attention. All were created between 1900 and 1910. This ornate tower graces the Casa Lleó Morera by Domènech i Montaner.

Casa Lleó Morera

Casa Ramon Mulleras

Museu del Perfum

Casa Amatller

To Plaça de Catalunya

❶ **Casa Batlló**
(see pp78-9)

Palau Baró de Quadras was designed by Puig i Cadafalch in 1904 in a neo-Gothic style. The ornate façade is riddled with grotesque sculptures including this one, which adorns the doorway

Locator Map
See Barcelona City Centre map pp16–17

AVINGUDA DIAGONAL

CARRER DE PAU CLARIS

CARRER DE PROVENÇA

CARRER DE LLÚRIA

Casa Thomas

CARRER DE MALLORCA

To Sagrada Família

CARRER DE ROUGER DE

CARRER DEL BRUC

CARRER DE VALÈNCIA

CARRER D' ARAGÓ

Palau Ramon de Montaner

5 Casa Terrades "Les Punxes"
Built in red brick with carved-stone ornamentation, this 1905 house by Puig i Cadafalch echoes the Gothic buildings of northern Europe.

4 ★ La Pedrera
Gaudí put all his architectural daring into this, his most famous house. The result is a remarkable wave-like façade and a roofscape of chimneys and vents resembling abstract sculptures.

| 0 metres | 100 |
| 0 yards | 100 |

Key

— Suggested route

For keys to symbols *see back flap*

❶ Casa Batlló

Unlike Gaudí's other works, this block of flats on the prestigious Passeig de Gràcia – commissioned by Josep Batlló i Casanovas – involved the conversion of an existing building. With its reworked façade in stunning organic forms and its fantastic chimneys and rooftop, it remains as bold and convention-defying today as it did when it was finished in 1906. The building has been said to symbolise the legend of St George killing the dragon, whose scaly back arches above the main façade. It was designated a UNESCO World Heritage Site in 2005.

View of façade and Dragon's Back

★ **The Chimneys**
Extraordinary chimneys, usually the unseen and functional parts of a building, have become Gaudí's trademark. These fine examples are tightly packed and covered in abstract patterns.

KEY

① **Stairs to main floor**

② **The Dining Room** ceiling ripples with bulbous forms that are thought to represent the splash caused by a drop of water.

③ **The light-well**, created by enlarging the orginal patio, provides maximum light to interior windows.

④ **The ceramic cross** was made in Mallorca and damaged in transit. Gaudí liked the cracked effect and refused to send it back for repair. The arms point to the four cardinal points of the compass.

⑤ **Dragon's belly room**

⑥ **The iron balconies** have been likened to the masks worn in carnival processions.

⑦ *Trencadis* decorations

⑧ **Fireplace room** Josep Batlló's office has a mushroom-shaped fireplace tiled in earthy colours.

Patio and Rear Façade
This outdoor space at the back of the house allows a view of the rear façade, which has cast-iron balconies and superbly colourful *trencadis* work at the top.

Attics
The closely packed brick arches supporting the roof are plastered and painted white, giving the sensation of being inside the skeleton of a large animal.

◀ Inspired by the sea, the extraordinary inner courtyard of Casa Batlló is decorated with thousands of blue azulejo tiles

★ The Dragon's Back
One of the most extra-
ordinary innovations to
the house is this steep,
narrow, colourfully tiled
cap above the façade
that it is difficult to see as
anything other than
the spine of a reptile.
Inside it is a white domed
room that was used as a
water deposit.

VISITORS' CHECKLIST

Practical Information
Passeig de Gràcia 43.
Map 3 A4.
Tel 93 216 03 06.
Open 9am–9pm daily. ♿ 📷
📷 W casabatllo.cat

Transport
🚇 Passeig de Gràcia.

Façade
Salvador Dalí saw the curving walls and
windows as "representing waves on a
stormy day". The spindly, individually
shaped columns across the first-floor
windows were also compared to
tibias, earning Casa Batlló the
nickname "House of Bones".

Entrance

★ Main Drawing Room
One side of this room is formed by stained-
glass windows looking out over the Passeig de
Gràcia. The ceiling plaster is moulded into a
spiral and the doors and window frames
undulate playfully.

Sumptuous interior of the Casa Lleó Morera, Illa de la Discòrdia

❷ Illa de la Discòrdia

Passeig de Gràcia, between Carrer d'Aragó and Carrer del Consell de Cent. **Map** 3 A4. Ⓜ Passeig de Gràcia. Casa Lleó Morera: 🕙 11am Mon–Sat in English. 🔲 **casalleomorera.com** Institut Amatller d'Art Hispànic: **Tel** 93 467 01 94. 🎟️ 🔲 **amatller.org**.

Barcelona's most famous group of Modernista *(see pp26–7)* buildings illustrates the wide range of styles used by the movement's architects. They lie in an area known as the Illa de la Discòrdia (Block of Discord), after the startling visual argument between them. The three finest were remodelled in the Modernista style from existing houses early in the 20th century. No. 35 Passeig de Gràcia is Casa Lleó Morera (1902–6), the first residential work of Lluís Domènech i Montaner. A shop was installed in the ground floor in 1943, but the Modernista interiors upstairs, with their magnificent stained-glass bay windows, still exist. Tours can be booked through the website or at the Palau de la Virreina *(see p62)*;

high heels or other shoes that might damage the mosaic floors are not permitted. Beyond the next two houses is Casa Amatller, designed by Puig i Cadafalch in 1898. Its façade, under a stepped-gable roof, features a harmonious blend of Moorish and Gothic windows. The ground floor contains a shop. The entrance patio, with its spiral columns

and staircase covered by a stained-glass skylight, can be peeked at at any time; the rest of the building, including the beautiful wood-panelled library, can only be seen on a guided tour. The third house in the block is Antoni Gaudí's Casa Batlló *(see pp78–9)*, with its fluid façade evoking marine or natural forms. The bizarrely decorated chimneys became a trademark of Gaudí's later work.

❸ Fundació Antoni Tàpies

Carrer d'Aragó 255. **Map** 3 A4. **Tel** 93 487 03 15. Ⓜ Passeig de Gràcia. **Open** 10am–7pm Tue–Sun & public hols. **Closed** 1 & 6 Jan, 25 Dec. 🎟️ 🎟️ by appointment (93 207 58 62). ♿ 🔲 **fundaciotapies.org**

Antoni Tàpies *(see p31)*, who died in 2012, was one of Barcelona's best-known artists. Inspired by Surrealism, his abstract work is executed in a variety of materials, including concrete and metal *(see pp74–5)*. Although perhaps difficult to appreciate at first, the exhibits should help viewers obtain a clearer perspective of Tàpies' work. The collection is housed in Barcelona's first domestic building to be constructed with iron (1880), designed by Domènech i Montaner for his brother's publishing firm.

Antoni Gaudí (1852–1926)

Born in Reus (Tarragona) into an artisan family, Antoni Gaudí i Cornet was the leading exponent of Catalan Modernisme. After a blacksmith's apprenticeship, he studied at Barcelona's School of Architecture. Inspired by a nationalistic search for a romantic medieval past, his work was supremely original. His first major achievement was the Casa Vicens (1888) at No. 24 Carrer de les Carolines *(see p28)*. But his most celebrated building is the church of the Sagrada Família *(see pp82–5)*, to which he devoted his life from 1914. When he had put all his money into the project, he went from house to house begging for more. He was killed by a tram in 1926.

Decorated chimneypot, Casa Vicens

The rippled façade of Gaudí's apartment building, La Pedrera

❹ La Pedrera

Passeig de Gràcia 92. **Map** 3 B3.
Tel 902 202 138. Diagonal.
Open Mar–Oct: 9am–8pm daily; Nov–
Feb: 9am–6:30pm daily. **Closed** 25
Dec. Night guided visits
Wed–Sat. **lapedrera.com**

Also known as Casa Milà, La
Pedrera (which translates as
"The Stone Quarry") is Gaudí's
greatest contribution to
Barcelona's civic architecture,
and his last work before he
devoted himself entirely to the
Sagrada Família *(see pp82–85)*.

Built between 1906 and
1910, La Pedrera departed from
established principles of
construction and, as a result,
was ridiculed by Barcelona's
intellectuals. Gaudí designed this
eight-floor apartment block
around two circular courtyards.
The ironwork balconies, by Josep
Maria Jujol, are like seaweed
against the wave-like walls of
white stone. There are no straight
walls anywhere in the building.

The Milà family had an
apartment on the fourth floor,
which now features a typical
Modernista interior. The
museum, "El Espai Gaudí", on the
top floor, includes models and
explanations of Gaudí's work.
From here, visitors can access
the extraordinary roof. The
sculptured ducts and chimneys
have such a threatening
appearance they are known as

espantabruixes, or witch-scarers.
Free temporary exhibitions are
held on the first floor.

❺ Casa Terrades

Avinguda Diagonal 416. **Map** 3 B3.
Diagonal. **Closed** to public.

This free-standing, six-sided
apartment block by
Modernista architect Josep
Puig i Cadafalch gets its
nickname, Casa de les
Punxes (House of the
Points), from the spires
on its six corner turrets.
It was built between
1903 and 1905 by
converting three
existing houses on the
site and was Puig's
largest work. It is an
eclectic mixture of

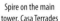

Spire on the main
tower, Casa Terrades

medieval and Renaissance
styles. The towers and gables
are influenced in particular by
the Gothic architecture of
northern Europe. However, the
deeply carved, floral stone
ornamentation of the exterior,
in combination with red brick
used as the principal building
material, are typically Modernista.

❻ Hospital de la Santa Creu i de Sant Pau

Carrer de Sant Antoni Maria Claret
167, 08025 Barcelona. **Map** 4 F1.
Tel 93 291 90 00. **Open** 10am–
6:30pm Mon–Sat (to 4:30pm Nov–
Mar), 10am–2:30pm Sun. free
1st Sun of month. noon, 1pm in
English. **santpaubarcelona.org**

Lluís Domènech i Montaner
began designing a new city
hospital in 1902. His innovative
scheme consisted of 26
attractive Mudéjar-style
pavilions set in large gardens,
as he believed that patients
would recover better among
fresh air and trees. All the
connecting corridors and
service areas were hidden
underground. Also
believing art and colour
to be therapeutic, he
decorated the pavilions
profusely. The roofs are
tiled with ceramics, and
the reception pavilion
has mosaic murals
and sculptures by
Pau Gargallo. After his
death, the project was
completed in 1930 by
his son, Pere.

Statue of the Virgin, Hospital de la Santa Creu i de Sant Pau

⊙ Sagrada Família

Europe's most unconventional church, the Basílica de la Sagrada Família, is an emblem of a city that likes to think of itself as individualistic. Crammed with symbolism inspired by nature and striving for originality, it is the greatest work of Gaudí *(see pp26–7)*. In 1883, a year after work had begun on a Neo-Gothic church on the site, the task of completing it was given to Gaudí, who changed everything, extemporizing as he went along. It became his life's work and he lived like a recluse on the site for 14 years. He is buried in the crypt. At his death only one tower on the Nativity façade had been completed, but work resumed after the Civil War and several more have since been finished to his original plans. Work continues today, financed by public subscription.

Bell Towers
Eight of the 12 spires, one for each apostle, have been built. Each is topped by Venetian mosaics.

The Finished Church

Gaudí's initial ambitions have been kept over the years, using various new technologies to achieve his vision. Still to come is the central tower, which is to be encircled by four large towers representing the Evangelists. Four towers on the Glory (south) façade will match the existing four on the Passion (west) and Nativity (east) façades. An ambulatory – like an inside-out cloister – will run round the outside of the building.

★ Passion Façade
This bleak façade was completed between 1986 and 2000 by artist Josep Maria Subirachs. A controversial work, its sculpted figures are angular and often sinister.

Main entrance

KEY

① **The altar canopy** was designed by Gaudí.

② **The apse**; stairs lead down from here to the crypt below.

③ **The bell tower**, with a lift to reach the upper galleries.

Spiral Staircases
Steep stone steps – 370 in each staircase – are closed to the public, but visitors can reach the upper galleries by lift to enjoy the majestic views.

★ Nativity Façade
The most complete part of Gaudí's church, finished in 1930, has doorways representing Faith, Hope and Charity. Scenes of the Nativity and Christ's childhood are embellished with symbolism, such as doves representing the congregation.

★ Crypt
The crypt, where Gaudí is buried, was begun by the original architect, Francesc de Paula Villar i Lozano, in 1882. On the lower floor, a museum traces the careers of both architects and the church's history.

Nave
In the nave, which was inaugurated in 2010, a forest of fluted pillars supports four galleries above the side aisles, while skylights let in natural light.

Passion Façade

It has been said that the Sagrada Família is like a book in stone: meant to be read in the same way as a medieval cathedral, with each element representing a Biblical event or aspect of Christian faith. This was certainly Gaudí's intent: his architecture was inseparable from the profound Catholicism that inspired it. The temple is dedicated to the Sagrada Família, the Holy Family. The two existing façades are detailed, visual accounts of two key Bible passages. The Glory façade (yet to be built) will address the theme of judgement of sinners.

Detail on brass door of the Passion façade

Main entrance to the Passion façade

Christ's Passion

The Passion façade depicts the sufferings and execution of Jesus, and its style reflects its subject matter. The statuary by Catalan sculptor Josep Maria Subirachs has attracted much criticism for its chunky, angular, "dehumanised" carving, but Gaudí would probably have approved. He is known to have favoured an Expressionist style to give the story of Christ's Passion maximum impact.

A great porch, whose roof is held up by six inclined buttress-like swamp tree roots, shades the 12 groups of sculptures, arranged in three tiers and to be viewed from bottom to top, left to right in an inverted "S". The first scene, bottom left-hand corner, is the Last Supper at which Jesus (standing) announces his impending betrayal. Next to this is the arrest in the Garden of Gethsemane. An olive trunk's grain mimics the shape of the

high priest's servant's ear that Peter cut off. The kiss of betrayal by Judas follows. The numbers of the cryptogram to the side of Jesus add up to 33 in every direction: his age at the time of his death.

The Flagellation

In the flagellation (between the central doors) Jesus is shown

Knights sculpture on the Passion façade

tied to a column at the top of a flight of three steps representing the three days of the Passion. Peter denying Christ is indicated by the cock that will crow three times in fulfilment of Jesus' prophecy. Behind this group of figures is a labyrinth, a metaphor for the loneliness of Jesus' path to the cross.

The sculptural group on the bottom right is in two parts. First is Ecce Homo (Christ bound with ropes and crowned with thorns). Pilate, overlooked by the Roman eagle, is shown washing his hands, freeing himself of responsibility for Jesus' death. Above, the "Three Marys" weep as Simon the Cyrene, a passer-by, is compelled by the Romans to pick up Christ's cross.

The Holy Shroud

The central sculpture depicts an event not described in the Bible, but added to the story of the Passion by later tradition. A woman named Veronica holds up her head cloth, which she has offered to Jesus to wipe the blood and sweat from his face. It has been returned, impressed with his likeness.

Next comes the solitary figure of the Roman centurion on horseback piercing the side of Jesus with his sword. Above him, three soldiers beneath the cross cast lots for Jesus' tunic. The largest sculpture (top centre) shows Christ hanging from a horizontal cross. At his feet is a skull referring to the place of the Crucifixion, Golgotha. Above him is the veil of the Temple of Jerusalem. The final scene is the burial of Jesus. The figure of Nicodemus, who is anointing the body, is thought to be a self-portrait of the sculptor Subirachs.

Nativity Façade

The northern, Nativity façade (overlooking Carrer Marina), finished according to Gaudí's personal instructions before his death, is far more subdued than the Passion façade – so much so that many of the sculptures barely rise out of the surface of the wall, making them difficult to identify. A great many natural forms are incorporated into the work, confusing interpretation further. Gaudí intended the whole work to be coloured, but his wishes are unlikely ever to be carried out.

Detail of sculpture on Nativity façade

Faith, Hope and Charity

The lavish ornamentation of the façade is arranged around three doors dedicated to Hope (left), Faith (right) and Charity, or Christian Love, in the middle. The two columns between the doorways rest on a turtle and a tortoise, signifying the permanence and stability of Christianity. In contrast, the two chameleons on either extreme of the façade represent forces of change. The four angels on top of the columns are calling to the four winds and announcing the proximity of the end of the world.

Detail of a spire, Nativity façade

Hope Doorway

The lowest carvings of the Hope Doorway show the Flight into Egypt (left) and the Slaughter of the Innocents (right). Above the door are Joseph and the child Jesus watched over by Mary's parents (Jesus's grandparents), St Ann and St Joachim. The lintel of the door is composed of a woodcutter's two-handled saw and various other tools, such as a hammer, axe, square and mallet – all indicative of Joseph's profession as a craftsman. Further above is a triangular grouping showing the betrothal of Mary and Joseph. The spire above the doorway is in the form of an elongated boulder, which is an allusion to the holy Catalan mountain of Montserrat (see pp124–5). At the base of this boulder sits Joseph in a boat; he bears a close resemblance to Gaudí himself and is very likely a posthumous homage by the masons who put the final touches to the façade after the master's death.

Faith Doorway

The Faith Doorway illustrates passages from the gospels and Christian theology. The heart of Jesus can be seen set into the lintel above the door. The scene on the lower left is the Visitation by Mary to Elizabeth, her cousin and mother of John the Baptist. On the right, Jesus wields a hammer and chisel in his father's workshop. Above the door is Jesus in the temple with John the Baptist (left) and John's father Zachariah (right). Higher up, the baby Jesus is presented in the temple, held by Simeon. As it rises, the stonework forms an intricate pinnacle recording the fundamentals of Catholicism, including a lamp with three wicks for the trinity, bunches of grapes and ears of wheat for the Eucharist, and a hand set with an eye, showing God's omniscience and infinite care.

Charity Doorway

The double doors of the central Charity Doorway are separated by a column recording Jesus's genealogy. The three Magi are on the lower left of the door, with the shepherds opposite them. Out of the nativity emerges the spiky tail of a many-pointed star (or comet). Around it are a children's choir and musicians. Above the star is the Annunciation and the Coronation of the Virgin Mary by Jesus. Above is a pelican sitting on a crown next to a glass egg bearing the JHS monogram of Jesus.

The lavish Nativity façade entrance

Street-by-Street: Montjuïc

Montjuïc is a spectacular vantage point from which to view the city. It has a wealth of art galleries and museums, as well as theatres. Many of the buildings were designed for the 1929 International Exhibition, and the 1992 Olympics were held on its southern slopes. Montjuïc is approached from the Plaça d'Espanya between brick pillars based on the campanile of St Mark's in Venice. They give a foretaste of the eclecticism of building styles from the Palau Nacional, which houses magnificent Romanesque art, to the Poble Espanyol, which illustrates the architecture of Spain's regions.

6 Pavelló Mies van der Rohe
This elegant statue by Georg Kolbe stands serenely in the steel, glass, stone and onyx pavilion built in the Bauhaus style as the German contribution to the 1929 International Exhibition.

AVINGUDA DE FRANCESC FERRER I GUARDIA

AVINGUDA DELS MONTANYANS

PASSEIG DE

7 ★ Poble Espanyol
Containing replicas of buildings from many regions of Spain, this "village" provides a fascinating glimpse of vernacular styles.

AVINGUDA DE L'ESTADI

To Montjuïc castle and Olympic stadium

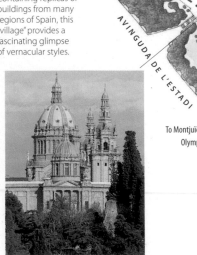

4 ★ Museu Nacional d'Art de Catalunya (MNAC)
On show in the Palau Nacional (National Palace), the main building of the 1929 International Exhibition, is Europe's finest collection of Romanesque frescoes. These were a great source of inspiration for Joan Miró.

5 Font Màgica
Fountains and cascades descend in terraces from the Palau Nacional. Below is the Font Màgica (Magic Fountain), whose jets are programmed to "perform" to a music and light show as darkness falls. Sometimes the spectacle is accompanied by the twin columns of fountains that lead up the hill in a particularly fine display.

Locator Map
See Barcelona City Centre map pp16–17

Plaça d'Espanya

Museu Etnològic displays artifacts from Oceania, Africa, Asia and Latin America.

Mercat de les Flors theatre (see p162)

3 Museu Arqueològic
The museum displays important finds from prehistoric cultures in Catalonia and the Balearic Islands. The *Dama d'Evissa*, a 4th-century sculpture, was found in Ibiza's Carthaginian necropolis.

Teatre Lliure is a prestigious Catalan theatre.

2 Teatre Grec
(see p90)

1 ★ Fundació Joan Miró
This tapestry by Joan Miró hangs in the centre he created for the study of modern art. In addition to Miró's works in various media, the modern building by Josep Lluís Sert is of architectural interest.

To Montjuïc castle and cable car

Key

— Suggested route

| 0 metres | 100 |
| 0 yards | 100 |

Flame in Space and Naked Woman (1932) by Joan Miró

❶ Fundació Joan Miró

Parc de Montjuïc. **Map** 1 B3. **Tel** 93 443 94 70. Pl. Espanya, then bus 150 or 55; or Paral·lel, then funicular to Montjuïc. **Open** Jul–Sep: 10am–8pm Tue–Sat (to 9:30pm Thu); Oct–Jun: 10am–7pm Tue–Sat (to 9:30pm Thu), 10am–2:30pm Sun & public hols. **Closed** 1 Jan, 25 & 26 Dec. **fundaciomiro-bcn.org**

Joan Miró (1893–1983) went to La Llotja's art school *(see p65)*, but from 1919 spent much time in Paris. Though opposed to Franco, he returned to Spain in 1940 and lived mainly in Mallorca, where he died. An admirer of Catalan art *(see p31)* and Modernisme *(see p26–7)*, Miró remained a Catalan painter but invented and developed a Surrealistic style, with vivid colours and fantastical forms. Indefatigable and endlessly creative, he concentrated on ceramics in the 1950s, but also created remarkable tapestries, as well as book illustrations and works in a range of other media.

Miró began to consider establishing a museum in the late 1960s, but it was not until 1975, after the return of democracy to Spain, that the Miró Foundation became a reality. His friend, the architect Josep Lluís Sert, designed the stark, white building, a remarkable Rationalist construction arranged around courtyards and drenched with natural light that pours in through ingeniously angled skylights. It houses an

enormous permanent collection (which currently numbers more than 14,000 works). Miró himself donated the works, and some of the best pieces on display include his Barcelona Series (1939–44), a set of 50 black-and-white lithographs. Other highlights include early works like the *Hermitage, Sant Joan d'Horta* (1917), painted in the beautiful Catalan town that would feature prominently in Miró's early work.

By the 1930s, Miró had found his own unique language, displayed in remarkable paintings like *Man and Woman in Front of a Pile of Excrement* (1935) – Miró's reaction to the simmering violence that would erupt in the Spanish Civil War. Many of the later works are colourful and exuberant, such as *Caress of a Bird* (1967), one of the sculptures that adorn the Foundation's terrace.

The Foundation also has a small but exquisite collection of artworks by other celebrated artists. These include Alexander Calder's mesmerising *Mercury Fountain*, in which gleaming liquid mercury flows instead of water. There are also works by Basque sculptor Eduardo Chillida, and paintings by Mark Rothko and Antoni Tàpies.

When Miró first conceived of the museum, he wanted to create a space in which young artists could experiment, and the Espai 13 gallery showcases the work of emerging artists. The Foundation also hosts blockbuster exhibitions, which attract such huge crowds that the queues snake down the hill.

After your visit, you can relax in the small adjacent sculpture garden, with its wonderful panoramic views. This garden links into the neighbouring Jardins de Laribal, some of the oldest and most beautiful gardens on Montjuïc. The shady paths, dotted with fountains and tiled benches, wind gently down the hill towards a park information office that also contains a café-restaurant.

❷ Teatre Grec

Parc de Montjuïc. **Map** 1 C3. **Tel** 93 316 10 00. Plaça Espanya, then 55 bus **Open** daily dawn to dusk, except during the Barcelona El Grec Festival in summer when opening is restricted to ticket holders. **grec.bcn.cat/**

This remarkable outdoor amphitheatre is hidden away amid greenery at the foot of Montjuïc. Originally a quarry, it was converted into an open-air theatre in 1929, when Montjuïc was remodelled as part of the International Exhibition. It is said to have been inspired by the ancient Greek theatre at Epidaurus, and it is the epicentre of Barcelona's biggest performing arts festival – "El Grec".

This is easily one of the most atmospheric venues in the city, set amid extensive gardens, with groves of orange trees, pretty pavilions and a series of terraces and viewing points that frame beautiful views of the gardens themselves and the city beyond. During the Grec Festival, there is an open-air bar and a restaurant in the gardens.

The open-air Teatre Grec, modelled on ancient Greek amphitheatres

The Museu Nacional d'Art de Catalunya, in the imposing National Palace

❸ Museu Arqueològic

Passeig Santa Madrona 39–41. **Map** 1 B3. **Tel** 93 423 21 49. Espanya, Poble Sec. **Open** 9:30am–7pm Tue–Sat, 10am–2:30pm Sun & public hols. **Closed** 1 Jan, 25 & 26 Dec. except last Sun of month; under 16s & over 65s free. **mac.cat**

Housed in the 1929 Palace of Graphic Arts, this fascinating archaeology museum contains artifacts from prehistory to the Visigothic period (AD 415–711). The mysterious Bronze Age megaliths called *talayots* from the Balearics are described here, and there are beautiful collections of Hellenic Mallorcan jewellery and Iberian silver treasures. Among the highlights of the collection is the Dama d'Eivissa ("The Lady of Ibiza"), a remarkable 4th-century sculpture in the form of an elaborately dressed goddess, and the startling Priapus of Hostafrancs, a 2nd-century Roman fertility symbol.

The museum boasts a superb collection of artifacts gathered from the Greco-Roman town of Empúries *(see p122)*, once the most important Greek colony on the entire Spanish peninsula. The displays include exquisite mosaics, coins, everyday items such as oil lamps and amphorae, and several statues, including a copy of the famous Asclepius (the original remains in situ). The collection concludes with ornate, gem-encrusted Visigothic jewellery, belt buckles, helmets and armour.

❹ Museu Nacional d'Art de Catalunya (MNAC)

Parc de Montjuïc, Palau Nacional. **Map** 1 A2. **Tel** 93 622 03 60. Espanya. 150, 55. **Open** 10am–6pm Tue–Sat (until 8pm May–Sep), 10am–3pm Sun & public hols. **Closed** Mon, 1 Jan, 1 May, 25 Dec. except Sun from 3pm and 1st Sun of month; under 16s & over 65s free. by appointment (93 622 03 75). **mnac.cat**

The austere Palau Nacional was built for the 1929 International Exhibition, but since 1934 it has housed the city's most important art collection. The artworks span 1,000 years, ranging from paintings and sculpture to furniture, photographs, drawings, prints and coins.

The museum has probably the world's greatest display of Romanesque items *(see pp24–5)*, centered on a series of magnificent 12th-century frescoes. The most remarkable are the wall paintings from Sant Climent de Taüll and La Seu d'Urgell *(see pp115–16)*. These have been arranged in sets specially designed to recall the remote mountain churches high in the Pyrenees from which they came.

There is also a superb Gothic collection, which includes notable works by the 15th-century

Catalan artists Bernat Martorell, Lluís Dalmau and Jaume Huguet *(see p30)*. These impressive, often richly gilded works reflect Catalunya's growing wealth and power in this period.

The Cambó Bequest, a fine collection of paintings chosen to complement the medieval artworks, was donated by the collector and politician Francesc Cambó. This bequest, along with remarkable paintings on permanent loan from the Thyssen-Bornemisza collection in Madrid, ensures that the museum boasts an impressive Renaissance and Baroque collection, including works by El Greco, Zurbarán, Velázquez, Titian, Tiepolo, and Rubens.

The museum also boasts a good selection of 19th- and early 20th-century artworks and decorative objects, including beautiful curving furniture designs by Gaudí for the Casa Batlló. Also here is the famous painting by Ramon Casas of himself and Pere Romeu on a tandem, which once hung in the Els Quatre Gats tavern.

The photography collection runs the gamut from early 19th-century portraits to gritty photo-journalism from the Spanish Civil War. The numismatic collection contains more than 100,000 coins, the earliest dating back to the 6th century BC.

12th-century *Christ in Majesty*, Museu Nacional d'Art de Catalunya

Part of the evening show put on by the Font Màgica, or "Magic Fountain"

❺ Font Màgica

Plaça Carles Buïgas **Map** 1 B2
🚇 Espanya **Shows** Apr–Oct: every 30
minutes 9–11pm Thu–Sun; Nov–Mar:
every 30 minutes 7–8:30pm Fri & Sat.
Closed 6 wks Jan and Feb ♿ 🅿 free.

This marvel of engineering was
built by Carles Buigas (1898–
1979) for the 1929 International
Exhibition. The flamboyant Art
Deco fountain shoots jets of
multicoloured water to music
in exuberant sound-and-light
shows held every weekend.
The musical themes vary, but
the show often culminates with
Freddie Mercury and Montserrat
Caballé's hugely popular duet
Barcelona, performed at the
1992 Olympics.

The four columns just behind
the Font Màgica were originally
erected by Modernista architect
Puig i Cadafalch at the turn of
the 20th century. Designed to
represent the stripes on the
Catalan coat-of-arms, they were
destroyed in 1928 as part of a
ban on Catalan symbols. Now
rebuilt, they are once again a
potent symbol of Catalan pride.

❻ Pavelló Mies van der Rohe

Avinguda Francesc Ferrer i Guàrdia 7.
Map 1-B2. **Tel** 93 423 40 16. 🚇
Espanya. 🚌 50. **Open** 10am–8pm
daily (to 6pm winter). **Closed** 1 Jan, 25
Dec. 🅿 free to under 16s. 🎫 noon Sat
or by appointment. 🅆 **miesbcn.com**

If the simple lines of this glass
and polished stone pavilion
look modern today, they must
have shocked visitors to the
1929 International Exhibition.

Designed by Ludwig Mies van
der Rohe (1886–1969), director
of the Bauhaus school, it was
deemed an exhibit in its own
right; its cool halls were left
virtually empty, containing only
one item – van de Rohe's world-
famous Barcelona Chair. The
building was torn down after the
exhibition, but an exact replica
was built for the centenary of
the designer's birth.

Morning by Georg Kolbe (1877–1945),
Pavelló Mies van der Rohe

❼ Poble Espanyol

Avinguda Francesc Ferrer i Guàrdia.
Map 1 A2. **Tel** 93 508 63 00. 🚇
Espanya. **Open** 9am–8pm Mon, 9am–
midnight Tue–Thu & Sun, 9am–3am
Fri, 9am–4am Sat. 🚌 🅿 free 24th
Sep for the La Mercé Festival. 🎭 🎫
🅆 **poble-espanyol.com**

The idea behind the Poble
Espanyol (Spanish Village) was
to illustrate and display local
Spanish architectural styles
and crafts. It was laid out for
the 1929 International
Exhibition, but has proved to
be enduringly popular and

now attracts well over a million
visitors a year. More than 100
buildings, streets and squares
from across Spain have been
recreated – from whitewashed
Andalusian homes to arcaded
Castilian squares, and from
Catalan villages to Basque
farmhouses. Replicas of the
towers in the walled city of
Ávila in central Spain form the
impressive main entrance.

Resident artisans produce
crafts including hand-blown
glass, sculpture, ceramics, Toledo
damascene, leather goods and
musical instruments. There is
plenty more to entertain visitors,
including shops, restaurants,
bars, a flamenco show, a
museum of modern art, a
children's theatre and a varied
programme of family-oriented
craft and music workshops.

❽ CaixaForum

Avinguda de Francesc Ferrer i
Guàrdia 6–8, Montjuïc. **Tel** 93 476
86 00. 🚇 Espanya. 🚌 13, 150.
Open 10am– 8pm daily (Jul & Aug
to 11pm Wed). **Closed** 1 & 6 Jan,
25 Dec. ♿ 🅿

Barcelona grows ever-stronger
in the field of contemporary art
and this exhibition centre can
only enhance its reputation.
The "La Caixa" Foundation's
collection of 700 works by
Spanish and international artists
is housed in the Antiga Fàbrica
Casaramona, a restored textile
mill in Modernista style.

The mill was built by Josep
Puig i Cadafalch after he had
completed the Casa de les
Punxes. Opened in 1911, it was
intended to be a model factory
– light, clean and airy – but had
only a short working life until
the business closed down in
1920. The building became a
storehouse and, after the Civil
War, stables for police horses.

There are a series of galleries
dedicated to temporary displays
(often major international
touring exhibitions), plus a
permanent collection of
contemporary art. Look out
for family workshops, concerts,
talks, film screenings and other
cultural events – often free.

9 Plaça d'Espanya

Avinguda de la Gran Via de les Corts Catalanes. **Map** 1 B1. Espanya.

The fountain in the middle of this junction, the site of public gallows until 1715, is by Josep Maria Jujol, one of Gaudí's most faithful collaborators. The huge 1899 bullring to one side is by Font i Carreras, and boasts a dazzling red-brick façade. It has been converted into Las Arenas, a spectacular shopping and entertainment centre, with an observation deck on the roof where you can enjoy fantastic views of Montjuïc.

On the Montjuïc side is the Avinguda de la Reina Maria Cristina, flanked by two 47 m (154 ft) campaniles modelled on the bell towers of St Mark's in Venice and built as the entry to the 1929 International Exhibition. The avenue leads up to the Font Màgica *(see facing page)*.

10 Castell de Montjuïc

Parc de Montjuïc. **Map** 1 B5. **Tel** 93 256 44 45. Paral·lel, then funicular & cable car. 150 from Plaça Espanya. **Open** Apr–Sep: 10am–8pm daily; Oct–Mar: 10am–6pm daily. free for under 16s and from 3pm Sun.

Crowning the very summit of Montjuïc is a huge, 18th-century

castle, which boasts spectacular views over the entire city, the port and a vast stretch of coastline. The first fortress here was built in 1640, and became the site of numerous battles during the War of the Spanish Succession in the early 1700s, when the Catalans fought the Bourbon king, Felipe V.

After Felipe V's success, the Bourbon rulers rebuilt the Montjuïc fortress in order to ensure that the local populace was kept under control. It became infamous as a prison and torture centre, a role it continued to play until after the Civil War. Notable Catalan leaders were imprisoned and executed here in the aftermath of the Civil War, including Lluís Companys *(see p48)*.

The castle contained a military museum for several decades, but when, in 2008, it was formally restored to the Catalan authorities by the Spanish government, it was decided to close the military museum and create a centre dedicated to peace. Exhibits describe the development of Montjuïc and the castle's turbulent history, and special activities for families are held at weekends. There's a café with a terrace on the Pati d'Armes, and in summer, outdoor cinema in the gardens.

Entrance to the Olympic Stadium, refurbished in 1992

11 Estadi Olímpic Lluís Companys

Passeig Olímpic. **Map** 1 A3. **Tel** 93 292 53 79. Espanya, Poble Sec. 55. **Open** for concerts & football matches. Museum: **Open** 10am–6pm (to 8pm Apr–Sep) Tue–Sat, 10am–2pm Sun. **Closed** 1 Jan, 1 May, 25 & 26 Dec.

The Estadi Olímpic Lluís Companys is the centrepiece of the so-called Anella Olímpica (Olympic Ring), the string of superb sports facilities erected for the 1992 Olympics. The stadium was built in 1929 for the International Exhibition, and was then remodelled in order to host the Olímpiad Popular in 1936. This event (conceived as a protest against the Olympics being held in Berlin under Hitler) never took place because of the outbreak of the Spanish Civil War. However, the stadium got its chance to take a starring role in the 1992 Olympics, for which it was dramatically enlarged and modernised, although the original façade was preserved.

Next door is the glassy, modern Museu Olímpic i de l'Esport with interactive exhibits dedicated to sport. Nearby are the steel-and-glass Palau Sant Jordi stadium, Barcelona's biggest venue for concerts by the likes of Muse, Madonna and Bruce Springsteen; the Piscines Picornell, which includes a gym and fantastic indoor and outdoor swimming pools; and the diving pools used in the 1992 Olympics. These are open in summer to the delight of kids and they offer extraordinary views over the entire city.

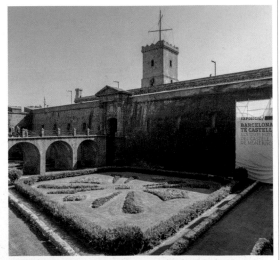

Formally laid-out gardens carpeting the former moat of the Castell de Montjuïc

FURTHER AFIELD

Radical redevelopments throughout the city in the late 1980s and 1990s gave Barcelona a wealth of new buildings, parks and squares. Sants, the city's main station, was rebuilt and the neighbouring Parc de l'Espanya Industrial and Parc de Joan Miró were created containing futuristic sculpture and architecture. In the east, close to the revitalized area of Poblenou, the city has a modern national theatre and concert hall. In the west, where the streets climb steeply, are the historic royal palace and monastery of Pedralbes, and Gaudí's Torre Bellesguard and Park Güell. Beyond, the Serra de Collserola, the city's closest rural area, is reached by two funicular railways. Tibidabo, the highest point, has an amusement park, the Neo-Gothic church of the Sagrat Cor and a nearby steel-and-glass communications tower. It is a popular place among *barcelonins* for a day out.

Sights at a Glance

Museums and Galleries
- ❸ Camp Nou Tour and Museum
- ❹ CosmoCaixa
- ⓫ Museu Can Framis
- ⓬ Disseny Hub Barcelona (DHUB)
- ⓮ Museu de Ciències Naturals – Museu Blau

Historic Buildings
- ❺ Monestir de Pedralbes
- ❾ Torre Bellesguard

Modern Buildings
- ❻ Torre de Collserola

Parks and Gardens
- ❶ Parc de Joan Miró
- ❷ Parc de l'Espanya Industrial
- ❼ Park Güell
- ❿ Parc del Laberint d'Horta

Squares and Districts
- ⓭ Estació del Nord
- ⓯ Poblenou

Theme Parks
- ❽ Tibidabo

Key
- Central city area
- Motorway (highway)
- Main road
- Other road

0 km 1
0 miles 1

Sights Outside the City Centre

◀ The Neo-Gothic Temple Expiatori del Sagrat Cor dominates the summit of Tibidabo

Dona i Ocell (1983) by Joan Miró in the Parc de Joan Miró

❶ Parc de Joan Miró

Carrer d'Aragó 1. 🚇 Tarragona.
Open 10am until dusk daily.

Barcelona's 19th-century slaughterhouse *(escorxador)* became this unusual park in the 1980s, hence its alternative name, Parc de l'Escorxador.

It is constructed on two levels: the lower level, fringed with shady paths and studded with palm trees, is popular with dog walkers and for football kick-abouts; the upper is paved and dominated by a magnificent 1983 sculpture by the Catalan artist Joan Miró *(see p31)*, entitled *Dona i Ocell (Woman and Bird)*. Standing 22 m (72 ft) high, its surface is covered with colourful glazed tiles. The park has several play areas for children.

❷ Parc de l'Espanya Industrial

Carrer Muntades 37. 🚇 Sants-Estació.
Open 10am until dusk daily.

This modern park, designed by Basque architect Luis Peña Ganchegui, owes its name to a textile mill that once stood on the 5 hectare (12 acre) site.

Laid out in 1986 as part of Barcelona's policy to provide more open spaces within the city, the park has canals and a rowing lake – with a Classical statue of Neptune at its centre. Tiers of steps rise around the lake like an amphitheatre and on one side a row of ten futuristic watchtowers dominates the entire area. Their only function is to serve as public-viewing platforms and lamp standards.

Six contemporary sculptors are represented in the park, among them Andrés Nagel, whose enormous metal dragon incorporates a children's slide.

❸ Camp Nou Tour and Museum

Avda de Arístides Maillol (7, 9). **Tel** 90 218 99 00. 🚇 Maria Cristina, Collblanc. **Open** late March–mid-Oct, and Christmas and Easter holidays: 9:30am–7:30pm daily; mid-Oct–late Mar: 10am–6:30pm Mon–Sat, 10am–2:30pm Sun. **Closed** 1 & 6 Jan, 25 Dec. 🅿️ ♿ 📷 stadium only (reduced hours on match days). 🌐 **fcbarcelona.com/camp-nou/museo**

Camp Nou, Europe's largest football stadium, is home to the city's famous football club, FC Barcelona (known as Barça).

Line of watchtowers in the Parc de l'Espanya Industrial

Founded in 1899, it is one of the world's richest soccer clubs, with some 100,000 members.

The stadium is a magnificent, sweeping structure, built in 1957 to a design by Francesc Mitjans. An extension was added in 1982 and it can now comfortably seat 100,000 fans.

The club's museum displays memorabilia and trophies. The second floor has a multimedia presentation on the history of the club. There are also paintings and sculptures of famous club footballers commissioned for the Blaugrana Biennial, an exhibition held in 1985 and 1987. *Blaugrana* (blue-burgundy) are the colours of Barça's strip. The club's flags were used as an expression of nationalist feelings when the Catalan flag was banned during the Franco dictatorship.

As well as hosting its own high-profile matches (mainly at weekends), Camp Nou also accommodates affiliated local soccer clubs and promotes other sports in its sports centre, ice rink and mini-stadium.

View across Camp Nou stadium, prestigious home of FC Barcelona

❹ CosmoCaixa

C/Isaac Newton 26. **Tel** 93 212 60 50.
🚇 Avinguda del Tibidabo. 🚌 17, 22,
58, 60, 73, 75, 196. **Open** 10am–8pm
Tue–Sun (daily Jul–Aug and bank
holidays). **Closed** 1 & 6 Jan, 25 Dec.
🔲 free 1st Sun of month. ⬛ 🔲

Barcelona's revamped science
museum is even more stimulating and interactive than its
popular predecessor, which was
housed in the Modernista
building that still stands on site.
Beside it now is a new glass-
and-steel building, with six of its
nine storeys set underground.
Exhibits covering the history of
science, from the Big Bang to
the computer age, are housed
in this modern museum. One of
its most important pieces is a
glasshouse containing a recreated section of flooded
Amazon rainforest inhabited by
fish, amphibians, insects, reptiles,
mammals, birds and plant
species. Elsewhere, an interactive
tour through Earth's geological
history explains processes such
as erosion and sedimentation,
with a Geo-logical Wall that
examines different types of rock.

Other exhibits include the
Matter Room, taking a look at
the Big Bang theory; "Tecno-
révolució", an interactive
exploration of cutting-edge
technological and scientific
developments, such as nano-
technology and robot eyes; and
a dazzling 3-D planetarium.
There are also innovative
temporary exhibitions on
environ-mental issues and
family activities.

Madonna of Humility, Monestir
de Pedralbes

❺ Monestir de Pedralbes

Baixada del Monestir 9. **Tel** 93 256 34
34. 🚇 Reina Elisenda. **Open** Apr–Sep:
10am–5pm Tue–Fri, 10am–7pm Sat,
10am–8pm Sun; Oct–Mar: 10am–
2pm Tue–Fri, 10am–5pm Sat & Sun.
Closed 1 Jan, 1 May, 24 Jun, 25 Dec.
🔲 free under 16s, Sun from 3pm
and first Sun of month. ⬛ by
appointment (Tel 93 256 21 22)
🔲 **monestirpedralbes.bcn.cat**

Approached through an arch
in its ancient walls, the lovely
monastery of Pedralbes
retains the air of an enclosed
community. This ambiance is
heightened by the good state
of preservation of its furnished
kitchens, cells, infirmary and

refectory. But the nuns of
the Order of St Clare moved
to an adjoining property in
1983, when the building was
opened to the public. The
monastery was founded in
1326 by Elisenda de Montcada
de Piños, fourth wife of
Jaume II of Catalonia and
Aragón. Her alabaster tomb
lies in the wall between church
and cloister. On the church
side, her effigy is dressed in
royal robes; on the other, in a
nun's habit.

The monastery is built around
a three-storey cloister. The main
rooms include a dormitory, a
refectory, a chapterhouse, an
abbey and day cells. Numerous
works of art, as well as liturgical
ornaments, pottery, furniture,
altar cloths and gold and silver
work, are on display here.

The most important room
in the monastery is the Capella
(chapel) de Sant Miquel, with
murals of the *Passion* and the
Life of the Virgin, both painted
by Ferrer Bassa in 1346.

❻ Torre de Collserola

Carretera de Vallvidrera al Tibidabo.
Tel 93 211 79 42. 🚇 Peu del Funicular,
then Funicular de Vallvidrera & bus
211. **Open** check the website or
phone to confirm opening times.
Closed 1 & 6 Jan, 25, 26 & 31 Dec. 🔲
⬛ 🔲 **torredecollserola.com**

In a city that enjoys thrills,
the ultimate ride is offered by
the communications tower
near Tibidabo mountain *(see
p100)*. A glass-sided lift swiftly
reaches the top of this 288 m-
(944 ft-) tall structure standing
on the summit of a 445 m
(1,460 ft) hill. The tower was
designed by English architect
Norman Foster for the 1992
Olympic Games. Needle-like
in form, it is a tubular steel
mast on a concrete pillar,
anchored by 12 huge steel
cables. There are 13 levels. The
top one has an observatory
with a telescope and a public-
viewing platform with a 360°
view of the city, the sea and
the mountain chain up on
which Tibidabo sits.

Barcelona v Real Madrid

FC Barcelona

Més que un club is the motto of FC Barcelona: "More
than a club". It has above all, however, been a symbol of
the struggle of Catalan nationalism against the central
government in Madrid. To fail to win the league is one
thing. To come in behind Real Madrid is a
complete disaster. Each season the big
question is which of the two teams
will win the title. Under the Franco
regime, in a memorable episode in 1941, Barça
won 3–0 at home. At the return match in Madrid,
the crowd was so hostile that the police and
referee "advised" Barça to prevent trouble.
Demoralized by the intimidation, they lost 11–1.
Loyalty is paramount: one Barça player who left
to join Real Madrid received death threats.

Real Madrid

❼ Park Güell

In 1910, the industrialist Eusebi Güell commissioned Gaudí to lay out a private housing estate on a hillside above Barcelona. The plan was to create a mini-garden city with common amenities, leisure areas and decorative structures, but only two houses were ever built. What was left after the project fell through was one of the most original public spaces ever conceived. Gaudí's layout makes ingenious use of the contours to create arcades and viaducts, all of natural stone. The most striking features are those covered with *trencadís* – mosaics made up of broken tiles, largely the work of the architect Josep Maria Jujol. The so-called "Monumental Area" requires an admission ticket, but the green expanses surrounding it are free to explore.

Hypostyle Hall
A total of 84 Classical columns – unusually conventional in style for Gaudí's work – support the weight of the square above. Set into the ceiling are four mosaic representations of the sun.

★ Entrance Pavilions
The two fairytale-like gatehouses have oval ground plans and intricately tiled *trencadís* exteriors. Inside one is a museum with displays outlining the park's history.

Entrance

0 metres 40
0 yards 40

KEY

① **Hill of the Crosses** is a stone tower reached by a serpentine path, from which there is a panoramic view over the city from the port to the heights of Tibidabo and Collserola.

② **The Güell House** is now a school.

③ **The Trias house** is one of only two houses to have been built of the would-be housing estate.

④ **The perimeter wall** follows the contours around the park. The Carretera El Carmel entry is formed by a swivelling section of wall executed in wrought iron.

★ Double Staircase
Water trickles from the mouth of the park's emblematic multicoloured dragon that presides over this monumental flight of steps. Above is an ornamental brown tripod and below another fountain, this time the head of a snake.

★ The Square

A serpentine bench covered in *trencadís* – the world's first collage – curves all the way around the edge of this elevated square, intended for outdoor theatre performances. From here there are impressive views over Barcelona.

VISITORS' CHECKLIST

Practical Information

Olot 7, Vallcarca. **Tel** 902 200 302.
Open late Mar–early May & early Sep–late Oct: 8am–8pm; early May–early Sep: 8am–9:30pm; late Oct–late Mar: 8:30am–6:15pm.
♿ 🚻 (strictly timed entry; includes gatehouse museum).
🅦 **parkguell.cat**
Casa-Museu Gaudí: **Tel** 93 219 38 11. **Open** Apr–Sep: 9am–8pm daily; Oct–Mar: 10am–6pm daily.
🚻 🅦 **casamuseugaudi.org**

Transport

🚇 Lesseps or Vallcarca, then a walk of about 1 km (with escalators). 🚌 H6, 32, 24, 92.

Upper Viaduct

This is one of three viaducts that carry snaking pathways on the east side of the park.

Casa Museu Gaudí

This house, which Gaudí lived in until he moved to the Sagrada Família, contains furniture designed by the architect, including benches and cupboards from La Pedrera.

Key

━ Monumental Area

Merry-go-round, Tibidabo

❽ Tibidabo

Plaça del Tibidabo 3–4. **Tel** 93 211 79 42. 🚇 Avda Tibidabo, then Tramvia Blau or bus 196 & Funicular; or Peu del Funicular, then Funicular & bus 111; or Bus T2A from Plaça Catalunya. Amusement Park: **Open** May–Sep: daily; Oct–Apr: Sat & Sun. 🚠 Temple Expiatori del Sagrat Cor: **Tel** 93 417 56 86. **Open** 10am–8pm daily. 🚠 🖥 tibidabo.cat

The heights of Tibidabo can be reached by Barcelona's last surviving tram. The name, inspired by Tibidabo's views of the city, comes from the Latin *tibi dabo* (I shall give you) – a reference to the Temptation of Christ when Satan took Him up a mountain and offered Him the world spread at His feet.

The hugely popular Parc d'Atraccions (Amusement Park, *see p163)* first opened in 1908. The rides were renovated in the 1980s. While the old ones retain their charm, the newer ones provide the latest in vertiginous experiences. Their location at 517 m (1,696 ft) adds to the thrill. Also in the park is the Museu d'Autòmats, displaying automated toys, juke boxes and slot machines.

Tibidabo is crowned by the Temple Expiatori del Sagrat Cor (Church of the Sacred Heart), built with religious zeal but little taste by Enric Sagnier between 1902 and 1911. A lift takes you up to the feet of an enormous figure of Christ.

Just a short bus ride away is another viewpoint – the Torre de Collserola *(see p97)*.

❾ Torre Bellesguard

Carrer de Bellesguard 16. 🚇 Avda del Tibidabo. 🚌 22, 58, 60, 75, 123, 196, **Open** 10am–3pm Tue–Sun. **Closed** 1 & 6 Jan, 25 & 26 Dec. 🚠 free for under 8s. 🚠 🖥 bellesguardgaudi.com

Bellesguard means "beautiful spot" and here in the Collserola hills is the place chosen by the medieval Catalan kings as their summer home. Their castle, built in 1408, was a favourite residence of Barcelona's Martí the Humanist *(see p59)*.

The surrounding district of Sant Gervasi was developed in the 19th century, after the coming of the railway. In 1900, Gaudí built the present house on the site of the castle, which had fallen badly into ruin. Its castellated look and the elongated, Gothic-inspired windows refer clearly to the original castle. The roof, with a walkway behind the parapet, is topped by a distinctive Gaudí tower. Ceramic fish mosaics by the main door symbolize Catalonia's past sea power.

❿ Parc del Laberint d'Horta

Germans Desvalls, Passeig Castanyers. **Tel** 010 (from Barcelona). 🚇 Mundet. **Open** Mar & Oct: 10am–7pm; Apr: 10am–8pm; May–Sep: 10am–9pm; Nov–Feb: 10am–6pm. 🚠 free Wed & Sun. 🚠 🖥 bcn.es/parcsijardins

As its name suggests, the centrepiece of the city's oldest public park, created in the 18th century for Joan Antoni Desvalls, Marqués de Llúpia i

Wrought-iron entrance door at Antoni Gaudí's Torre Bellesguard

d'Alfarràs, is a cypress maze. The semi-wild garden slopes steeply uphill from the entrance beside the marquis' semi-derelict palace, which now houses a gardening school. It is a veritable compendium of aristocratic Baroque fantasies. Classical temples dedicated to Ariadne (who helped Theseus escape from the Minotaur's labyrinth) and Danae (mother of Perseus) stand at either side of a broad paseo, which oversees the maze. From here a monumental flight of steps leads up to a Neo-Classical temple.

Elsewhere, there is a "romantic garden", a faux cemetery and, in the woodland into which the garden eventually leads, a hermit's cave.

⓫ Museu Can Framis

C/Roc Boronat 116–126, Poblenou. **Tel** 93 320 87 36. 🚇 Glòries, Poblenou. 🚌 6, 7, 40, 42, 56, 141, 192, B25. **Open** 11am–6pm Tue–Sat, 11am–2pm Sun. **Closed** 1 Aug–15 Sep. 🚠 🖥 noon Sat or by request. 🚠 🖥 fundaciovilacasas.com

The Can Framis museum occupies a renovated 18th-century wool factory, which is a monument to local industry. It is managed by the Vila Casa Foundation and holds a permanent exhibition, called The Existential Labyrinth, of around 300 works dating from the 1960s onwards. These works are by a wide range of artists born or living in Catalonia, like Tàpies, Llimós, Zush and Cuixart. The Espai A0 gallery hosts good temporary exhibitions by local artists and photographers.

⓬ Disseny Hub Barcelona (DHUB)

Plaça de les Glòries Catalanes 37–38. **Tel** 93 256 67 13. 🚇 Glòries. 🚌 7, 92, 192, H12. **Open** check website for opening times. 🖥 dhub-bcn.cat

With more than 70,000 objects, the Design Museum merges two museums that were previously housed at

Catalonia's modern National Theatre, near the Estació del Nord

different sites across the city. The new museum, opened in spring 2014, exhibits pieces from the Decorative Arts, Ceramics, Textile and Clothing Museum and the Graphic Arts Cabinet. The building, clad in glass and zinc, is a design statement in its own right, and was created by architects Josep Martorell, Oriol Bohigas and David Mackay.

The huge collection is organised on broadly historical lines, tracing the development of the objects that surround us in our everyday lives, from the decorative arts of past centuries (some artifacts date back to the Middle Ages) to contemporary design. The collections include furniture, clothing, jewellery, prints and posters, ceramics, glasswork and even vehicles. A varied programme of lectures and workshops is planned.

⓭ Estació del Nord

Avinguda de Vilanova. **Map** 6 D1. 🚇 Arc de Triomf.

Only the 1861 façade and the grand 1915 entrance remain of this former railway station, now remodelled as a sports centre, a police headquarters, and the city's bus station. Two elegant, blue-tiled sculptures, *Espiral arbrada (Branched Spiral)* and *Cel obert (Open Sky)* by Beverley Pepper (1992) sweep through the park. In front of the station, at Avinguda de Vilanova 12, is a carefully restored Modernista building constructed as a power station in 1897 by the architect Pere Falqués. Nearby, on Carrer de Zamora, is the Teatre Nacional de Catalunya, a vast temple to culture by the Barcelona architect Ricardo Bofill. The Museu de la Música is located here.

⓮ Museu de Ciències Naturals – Museu Blau

Plaça Leonardo da Vinci 4–5, Parc del Fòrum. **Tel** 93 256 22 00. 🚇 Maresme–Fòrum (exit Rambla Prim). 🚌 7, 36, 43, 99, H16. **Open** 10am–7pm Tue–Sat, 10am–8pm Sun. Register one day ahead for Science Nest (**Tel** 93 256 22 20) or at the box office on the day. **Closed** Mon; 1 Jan, 1 May, 24 Jun, 25 Dec. 🎟 free 1st Sun of month, Sun after 3pm and under 16s. ♿ 🌐 **museublau.bcn.cat**

The Natural Science Museum is a Barcelona institution that is more than 100 years old and contains 3 million specimens in the fields of mineralogy, palaeontology, zoology and botany. Previously located in the Old Town, it is now housed in the Parc del Fòrum in a modern, innovative building designed by architects Herzog & de Meuron, who also conceived the Planet Life exhibition, a journey through the history of life and its evolution to the present day. The museum uses state-of-the-art interactive and audiovisual displays. There are also temporary exhibitions, a Media Library and a Science Nest for children up to age 6 at weekends, where images and sound effects recreate different natural surroundings.

La Rambla del Poblenou, a good place for a stroll and a cup of coffee

⓯ Poblenou

Rambla del Poblenou. 🚇 Poblenou.

Poblenou is the trendy part of town where artists have built their studios in the defunct warehouses of the city's former industrial heartland. The area is centred on the Rambla del Poblenou, a quiet avenue, that extends from Avinguda Diagonal down to the sea. Here, palm trees back a stretch of sandy beach. A walk around the quiet streets leading from the Rambla will reveal a few protected pieces of industrial architecture, legacies from the time Barcelona was known as "the Manchester of Spain".

Along the parallel Carrer del Ferrocarril is the Plaça de Prim with low, whitewashed houses reminiscent of a small country town. See pages 108–9 for a guided walk through Poblenou.

Blue-tiled sculpture by Beverley Pepper, Parc de l'Estació del Nord

THREE GUIDED WALKS

There is no shortage of good places to take a stroll in Barcelona. Each of the Street-by-Street maps in the book (the Old Town, the Eixample and Montjuïc) has a short walk marked on it that takes in the well-known sights in the area. Other classic walks are down La Rambla *(see pp62–3)* and around Park Güell *(see pp98–9)*. The walks described on the next six pages, however, take you to three less-explored districts, each with a distinct flavour.

The first walk is around El Born, once a run-down area to stay clear of but now an appealing quarter mixing old streets and fashionable shops. Next comes Gràcia, which could be thought of as "village Barcelona": a proud working-class area of low-rise houses, tiny boutiques and charming squares that

host a busy nightlife. The final walk is around the post-industrial heartland of Poblenou whose buildings are being restored and put to new uses, and whose skyline is punctuated by a few surviving slender brick chimneys. Each route avoids heavy traffic as far as possible and makes the most of quiet or pedestrianized streets and squares. While there are monuments to be seen along the way, the appeal here is as much in the atmosphere of the areas and the unusual shops, characterful cafés and architectural oddities encountered. All three walks begin and end with a Metro station. As in any big city, care should be taken with personal belongings and although it is safe to walk at any time, be aware that the character of areas can change when the bars open.

Choosing a Walk

The Three Walks
This map shows the location of the three guided walks in relation to the main sightseeing areas of Barcelona.

Santa Maria del Mar, El Born walk

Market sweet shop, Poblenou walk

Gràcia
(pp106–7)

Eixample

Poblenou
(pp108–9)

El Born
(pp104–5)

Montjuïc

Old Town

0 km 4

0 miles 2

Key

• • • Walk route

◀ The early Gaudí façade of Casa Vicens on Carrer de les Carolines, Gràcia walk

A One-hour Walk around El Born

The tiny district of El Born, across the Via Laietana from the Barrí Gotic, has made a comeback after long years of neglect. Close to the waterfront, this area flourished in Catalonia's mercantile heyday from the 13th century. The narrow streets still bear the names of the craftsmen and guilds that set up here, for instance, hatters in Carrer dels Sombrerers, mirror-makers in Carrer dels Mirallers and silversmiths in Carrer de la Argenteria. While it still has something of a medieval air, El Born has become the hip and arty place to be.

collection of Gothic mansions dating from the 14th century, with later Renaissance refurbishments. Most of the buildings are now museums and galleries. The Casa Cervelló-Guidice at 25 ⑥ is the only building on the street that still has its original façade. Opposite the Casa Cervelló-Guidice, at 20 ⑦, is the Palau Dalmases, whose patio

⑮ Passeig del Born, the main street of the El Born area

The Carrer de Montcada

From Jaume I Metro station in Plaça de l'Angel ①, set off down Carrer de la Argenteria, but turn left almost at once at the tobacconist's (marked "Tabac") into Carrer del Vigatans. After passing the youth hostel on your left, note the carved head protruding from the wall on the right at the corner of Carrer dels Mirallers ②. Before you reach the end of the street, turn right into Carrer dels Mirallers. On your left you will shortly see an old-fashioned bar called

El Nus ③, whose stone walls, chandeliers and dark-wood furniture evoke the atmosphere of Barcelona in days gone by. At the end of the street you meet the side wall of the church of Santa Maria del Mar ④. Turn left along Carrer Sombrerers. On your left at 23 is Casa Gispert ⑤, a famous old shop selling coffee roasted on the premises, and local nuts and dried fruit. When you can go no further, turn left into Placeta de Montcada, which becomes Carrer de Montcada (see p66), an immaculate

has an ornately carved staircase. It is now a somewhat eccentric bar, hosting all manner of live artistic performances, including classical music and live opera some evenings. Its neighbour at 22 is El Xampanyet ⑧, the city's best-known bar for *cava* (Catalan sparkling wine) and tapas. Much of the right-hand side of Montcada is taken up by five palaces including the Museu Picasso ⑨ (see p66). Opposite this are two important medieval palaces, the Palau Nadal at number 14 ⑩ and the Palau Marquès de Lió at number 12, which now houses a new

Tips for Walkers

Starting point: Plaça de l'Angel.
Length: 1.5 km (1 mile).
Getting there: Go to Jaume I Metro station in the Plaça de l'Angel on Line 4.
Stopping off points: There are many bars and eateries along the route including the Café del Born (Plaça de Comercial) and Origens 99,9% (Carrer Vidrieria 6–8), a Catalan restaurant and shop. You'll find lots on Carrer de la Argenteria, notably Xocolateria Xador for hot chocolate (61–3), and Taller de Tapas (51).

⑨ Visitors flocking to the popular Museu Picasso

(16) Enjoying the café culture in Plaça de Comercial in front of Mercat del Born

hieroglyphic-like frieze. Carrer Triangle leads you into Carrer del Rec and before long you meet the Passeig del Born (15). It was the jousts held in this broad avenue from the 13th to 17th centuries that gave the name to the Born quarter of which it forms the heart. To the left, the Passeig opens out into the Plaça de Comercial, dominated by the Mercat del Born (16), the former wholesale market. This old iron and glass building, modelled on Les Halles in Paris, has now been converted into a cultural centre. Excavations on the site have helped archaeologists piece together a clear picture of life in 18th-century Barcelona.

Continue on Carrer del Rec, on the other side of the Passeig del Born, and turn right at the next junction into Carrer de l'Esparteria. Turn left at Carrer de Vidriera to reach Plaça de les Olles. Turn right here and follow the wide pavement that skirts the Plaça del Palau. It also passes an old ironmonger's with giant paella pans. When you reach the corner with Carrer dels Canvis Vells, across the road from La Llotja (see p65) (17), turn right. Bear right into the Carrer de l'Anisadeta, which is so short that it is over almost as soon as it is begun, and you find yourself back in the charming Plaça de Santa Maria (18), facing the church of the same name (see pp66–7), a perfect place to stop for a coffee or a glass of wine on a café terrace. Pop inside to admire the beautiful Catalan Gothic interior. Bear left across the square to the start of Carrer de la Argenteria, the busiest street in El Born, lined with bars and shops. Follow this back to your starting point at the Metro in Plaça de l'Angel.

Key

• • • Walk route

exhibition, The Museum of World Cultures, offering a journey through the cultures of Asia, Africa, America and Oceania. Just after, the Palau del Marquès de Lió (or Mora) (11) was once part of Barcelona's Textiles and Costume Museum, with a fabulous collection now on show at the Disseny Hub (DHUB) building on Plaça de les Glòries Catalanes (see pp100–101). At the end of Montcada turn right along Carrer de la Princesa, where you'll find tempting shops. First you pass the windows of Brunells pastry shop at 22 (12), then the turrón and sweet shop of La Campana (founded in 1890) at 36 (13).

The Passeig del Born

Take the next small street to the right, Carrer de Corretger, which turns a sharp corner. Turn right at the cake shop into Carrer Triangle. Look up into the arch at the start of Carrer de l'Hostal de Sant Antoni (on your right) (14) to see an unusual

(12) Brunells chocolate shop

A 90-minute Walk through Gràcia

When you cross the Avinguda Diagonal and plunge into the maze of sinuous streets and small squares on the other side, it is easy to get the impression that you have left the city behind and entered a village. Since Gràcia became part of Barcelona in 1897, it has never lost its sense of independence and identity. During the day, it feels calmly removed from the pace of modern metropolitan life just a few blocks away. In August and in the evening, however, expect a hullabaloo as the district draws crowds to its exotic shops and nightlife.

quickly right down Carrer de Domènech. Turn left at the end, up Carrer de Francisco Giner, and this will lead you into Plaça de la Vila de Gràcia ⑤, where a 33 m (108 ft) clock tower is overlooked by the sky-blue façade of Gràcia's local government headquarters. A plaque on the

③ The façade of Casa Fuster, a Modernista building, now a hotel

The Passeig de Gràcia

From Plaça Joan Carles I ①, the famous Passeig de Gràcia continues briefly as a modest, plane tree-shaded avenue. On your left, almost immediately, you come to Casa Bonaventura Ferrer ②, a Modernista building by Pere Falqués I Urpi, with stonework sculpted into swirling leaves and a façade finished off with an iron crown. A short way along, the road narrows to go round another Modernista building (although its inspiration is clearly Neo-Gothic).

The last work of architect Lluís Domènech i Montaner, Casa Fuster ③ has been converted into a hotel. The Café Vienés on the ground floor is open to non-residents.

The squares of Gràcia

A few steps beyond Casa Fuster, up the Passeig de Gràcia's well-to-do continuation, Gran de Gràcia, you can see the handsome stained-glass *miradores* (upper-floor bay windows) above La Colmena *patisseria* at 15 ④. Then go back to Casa Fuster and turn down the road behind its rear façade, Carrer Gràcia. Turn left and

Tips for Walkers

Starting point: Plaça Joan Carles I.
Length: 2.5 km (1.5 miles).
Getting there: Diagonal Metro station in Plaça Joan Carles I is on Line 3 or reached by FCG train.
Stopping-off points: Most of Gràcia's squares have bars and restaurants. Try Bo Restaurant (tapas) in Plaça de la Vila de Gràcia; Café del Sol (drinks and music) or Mirasol (classic bar) in Plaça de Sol; Niu Toc (fish) on Plaça Revolució de Setembre de 1868 or Virreina Bar (sandwiches and beer) in Plaça de la Virreina.

⑤ A performance of *castellers* at fiesta time in Gràcia

(6) Nightlife at the Plaça del Sol

Key

••• Walk route

dels Xiquets de Valls, named after a renowned team of *castellers*. This brings you into the Plaça del Sol (6), a nightlife hub popularly known as Plaça dels Encants. Turn left to leave by Carrer de Maspons. Straight ahead, on the other side of Carrer del Torrent l'Olla, is the Plaça Revolució de Setembre de 1868 (7). The name commemorates the *coup d'état* led by General Prim, which unseated Spain's ruling Bourbon dynasty, who were so antagonistic to the Catalans they ushered in the first republican government in Spain's history. Turn left into the square and leave by Carrer de Verdi that sprouts from the top of it. This is a busy but pleasant street of modern shops. After passing Cinemes Verdi (on your right), which often shows original-version foreign films, turn right down Carrer de l'Or. You soon arrive in one of Gràcia's most agreeable squares, the Plaça Virreina (8), where the church of Sant Joan faces downhill towards two fine buildings: one is a residence with a tower and the other a redbrick house in Modernista style with a graphic red and cream façade and wrought-iron balconies.

(4) Stained-glass windows in *miradores*

Casa Vincens

Leave Virreina by the shady Carrer de Astúries and stay on it across the top of Plaça Diamant

(9). This is where a civil war air-raid shelter has been discovered – open at weekends by appointment (call 93 219 61 34). Turn right up Carrer del Torrent l'Olla and left down Santa Agata. When you reach Gran de Gràcia, cross over it into Carrer de les Carolines. At the bottom of this street at 24 is one of Antoni Gaudí's early works, Casa Vicens (10). It is privately owned but well worth admiring from the outside. Commissioned as a summer house by a brick-and tile-maker, it took the inexperienced Gaudí five years to build (1883–8). Inspired by Moorish architecture, the house was a bold break with tradition and the lavish use of colour and ornament clearly indicate where Gaudí's interests lay. The exterior of the house is a checkerboard of green and white tiles and other tiles with a marigold motif. The riotous ironwork shows off with extravagant loops and intriguing beasts. Now retrace your steps to Gran de Gràcia. If you are in the mood for more Gaudí, go uphill to Plaça Lesseps and from there follow the signs to Park Güell (*see pp98–9*). If not, go downhill past pretty Plaça Trilla (11). You can either finish the walk at Fontana Metro station or continue on back to your starting point.

wall here commemorates the achievements of Catalonia's *castellers*, teams of amateur gymnasts who can often be seen building human towers up to eight people high on fiesta days in Gràcia. Cross the square and leave by Carrer Mariana Pineda. Cross Travessera de Gràcia, one of the district's main shopping streets, and stroll along Carrer

(10) The interior and stained-glass windows at Casa Vicens

A Two-hour Walk through Poblenou

It's hard to believe today, but the trendy district of Poblenou once had the highest concentration of smoke-belching factories in Catalonia. By the 1960s, these had gone out of business or moved to the outskirts, leaving their old buildings to decay. With the 1992 Olympic Games came an impetus for recovery and since then, Poblenou's warehouses have been spruced up and converted into chic studios for artists and photographers. New developments brought hotels, clubs and restaurants, creating a fascinating mix of industrial archaeology and contemporary culture.

③ The controversial Torre Agbar

The Avinguda Diagonal

Leave the Metro station in Plaça de les Glòries Catalanes ① (an area of ongoing redevelopment; *see p101*) by the Carrer Badajoz exit, which will lead you on to the wide seaward extension of Avinguda Diagonal ②. This takes you directly beneath a tall, unusual and much-criticised building that breaks up the city skyline, the Torre Agbar ③. A domed cylindrical tower of 33 floors, unkindly described as an

upended blue cigar, it was built by French architect Jean Nouvel for the local water company, Aigües de Barcelona.

Continue on down Diagonal, which has a wide paseo in the middle flanked by traffic lanes, tramways that link Glòries with Sant Adrià del Besòs, as well as cycle tracks. About 700 m (half a mile) down Diagonal, turn right into Rambla del Poblenou ④, the main street of Poblenou that leads eventually to the sea. After crossing Carrer de Pere IV, the Rambla narrows and becomes more attractive. In the middle is a memorial to Doctor Josep Trueta ⑤. This pioneering surgeon was born in Poblenou in 1897 and, after working to save lives during the bombardments of the Civil War, went into a 30-year exile in England on the fall of democracy in 1939.

Rambla del Poblenou

Keep straight on down the Rambla over the next three circular road junctions. Along the way are several buildings worth stopping to look at, such as 51 (on the

right) ⑥, a handsome salmon-coloured building by Josep Masdeu dating from 1914, which is decorated with Modernista floral motifs.

At the next junction with Carrer del Joncar, turn left between El Tio Che ⑦, a well-known shop founded in 1912, selling ice cream and *turrón* (a typical Spanish sweet made of almonds) and, opposite it, the Casino de l'Aliança de Poblenou ⑧, a concert hall (not a gambling enterprise as its name might suggest). Turn right

Tips for Walkers

Starting point: Plaça de Les Glòries Catalanes.
Length: 3.5 km (2 miles).
Getting there: Glòries Metro station is on Line 1.
Stopping off points: There are bars on Rambla de Poble Nou, swish restaurants on Carrer Taulat and a few cheaper bars on Carrer Maria Aguilo. Go for an ice cream at El Tio Che.

⑤ Memorial to civil-war hero Dr Josep Trueta

⑦ El Tio Che, the renowned ice-cream and *turrón* parlour

at the first junction you come to down Carrer de Maria Aguiló, a lively but humanly scaled pedestrianized shopping street. On the left, up a short street, is the district's market, the Mercat de la Unió ⑨. Beside it is a handsome building, 24 Plaça de la Unió, with Art Nouveau white and green ceramic festoons draped over the windows. Just north of the market is the district's public library ⑩ at Carrer del Joncar 35,

housed in a beautiful building dating from 1884 that used to be a textile factory. Cross over Carrer del Taulat (the junction is slightly staggered) into Carrer del Ferrocarril and turn left into the old square of Plaça del Prim ⑪. Here, you'll see gnarled, leaning, fat-rooted ombu trees (an Argentinian species) and low whitewashed houses. Now somewhat lost amid the modernity around it, this square is the original heart of Poblenou, from which all else grew. It is said that among the fishermen and workers who lived on this square, there were many followers of the mid-19th century Icaria Utopian movement, which militated against capitalism and attempted to create a world of "universal brotherhood". Return to Carrer del Taulat and turn right. If you wish to end your walk here, turn left up Carrer de Bilbao to reach Poblenou Metro

⑬ Torre de les Aigües

station. Otherwise, continue along Taulat, a strip of gardens through modern residential developments.

A short detour to the corner of Carrer de Ramon Turró and Espronceda takes you to a garden ⑫ dedicated to the Indian social reformer and philosopher Mahatma Gandhi, with a sculpture of him by the Nobel Peace Prize-winner Adolfo Pérez Esquivel.

Returning to Passeig del Taulat, ahead of you all the while rises the most characteristic surviving industrial building in Poblenou, the Torre de les Aigües ⑬. Turn left into Carrer de la Selva to get to the base of this structure, which stands in the middle of Plaça de Ramon Calsina. This round, red-brick tower, 63 m (207 ft) high, was built to raise and store water from the nearby Besos river. Near the top of it is a vertigo-inducing metal staircase that leads round the brickwork to a balcony. From here, continue up Carrer de la Selva to Selva de Mar Metro station on the corner of Carrer de Pujades. On the way, you might like to wander a few steps to your left along Carrer de Llull. On the corner with Carrer de Provençals rises the highest chimney in Barcelona ⑭. This graceful, flat-topped, 65 m (213 ft) spire used to form part of the now-defunct Macosa steelworks. Return to Carrer de la Selva and end your walk at the Selva de Mar Metro stop.

Fluvià

CARRER DE PALLARS

CARRER DE PUJADES

Selva de Mar

CARRER DE LLULL

⑫

CARRER DE RAMON TURRÓ

PLAÇA DE RAMON CALSINA ⑬

PASSEIG DEL TAULAT

PASSEIG DE CALVELL

| 0 metres | 250 |
| 0 yards | 250 |

Key

••• Walk route

⑪ The unusual ombu trees in the village-like Plaça del Prim

CATALONIA

Lleida • Andorra • Girona • Barcelona Province • Tarragona

There is a wealth of natural beauty in Catalonia's four provinces, plus the small Catalan-speaking country of Andorra. They offer rocky coasts and mountains, fertile plains and sandy shores. Many who visit don't stray far from the coast, but the rewards for venturing further afield are immense.

Lying beyond the constant bustle of Barcelona, Catalonia is essentially a rural region, with no large cities and few industrial blights. Of the four provinces, all named after their principal city, Lleida is the largest and least populated. Among its jewels are the Romanesque churches of the Boí valley and the Aigüestortes National Park.

The province of Girona is blessed with mountains and sea. This eastern end of the Pyrenees has the magical Cerdanya valley and the ancient monasteries of Ripoll and Sant Joan de les Abadesses, as well as medieval villages and a handsome and too-often overlooked capital city. Its coast, the Costa Brava, is rocky and full of delights.

Barcelona province has its own coasts; the Maresme to the north is rather spoiled by the railway running beside the sea, but the Garraf to the south is more exciting – Sitges is a highly fashionable spot. Inland are the Holy Mountain of Montserrat (Catalonia's spiritual heart), the Penedès winelands, and the country town of Vic.

Tarragona, the most southerly of the provinces, has one of the peninsula's former Roman capitals. Here the land rolls more gently, supporting fruit and nut orchards and the monastic communities of Poblet and Santes Creus, before falling away towards the rice lands of the Ebre. The coastline is more gentle, too, with long, sandy beaches.

The Parc Nacional d'Aigüestortes in the central Pyrenees, in the province of Lleida

◀ Rocky outcrops surround the tranquil bay and golden beach of Tossa de Mar, on the Costa Brava

Exploring Catalonia

Catalonia includes a long stretch of the
Spanish Pyrenees, whose green, flower-filled
valleys hide picturesque villages with
Romanesque churches. The Parc Nacional
d'Aigüestortes and Vall d'Aran are paradises for
naturalists, while Baqueira-Beret offers skiers
reliable snow. Sun-lovers can choose between
the rugged Costa Brava or the long sandy
stretches of the Costa Daurada. Tarragona is
rich in Roman monuments. Inland are the
monasteries of Poblet and Santes Creus and
the well-known vineyards of Penedès.

Isolated houses in the countryside around
La Seu d'Urgell

Key

━━━ Motorway (highway)
━━━ Other highway
━━━ Main road
╌╌╌ Minor road
━━━ Scenic route
╍╍╍ Main railway
──── Minor railway
━━━ International border
━━━ Regional border
△ Summit

Getting Around

The motorway from
France enters Spain at
La Jonquera and, from
Barcelona, follows the
coast via Tarragona and
Tortosa. Buses connect
most towns. The main
north–south railway hugs
the coast from Blanes
southwards. Other lines
connect Barcelona to
Vic and Lleida (see
inside back cover).

For additional map symbols see back flap

Map labels

Pau, Toulouse, VALL D'ARAN, VIELHA, BAQUEIRA-BERET, Arties, Picu d'Estats 3115m, Esterri d'Àneu, PARC NACIONAL D'AIGÜESTORTES, Boi, Llavorsi, VALL DE BOI, Tossal de l'Orri 2137m, Pont de Suert, Sort, LA SEU D'URGELL, La Pobla de Segur, Coll de Nargó, Tremp, Embassament de Talarn, Embassament d'Oliana, Isona, Embalse de Canelles, El Segre, Ponts, Alfarràs, Artesa de Segre, Balaguer, Agramunt, CAT, Almacelles, Belicaire d'Urgell, Bell-lloc d'Urgell, Tàrrega, LLEIDA, Alcarràs, Bellpuig, Juneda, Belianes, Santa Coloma de Queralt, A2, les Borges Blanques, Seròs, Zaragoza, MONTBLANC, La Granadella, POBLET, SANTES CREUS, Maials, La Bisbal de Falset, Alcover, Valls, Flix, Ascó, Falset, Reus, Torredembarra, Batea, Móra d'Ebre, Móra la Nova, Cambrils, TARRAGONA, Gandesa, Salou, Cap de Salou, Rasquera, COSTA, Xerta, L'Hospitalet de l'Infant, El Perelló, L'Ametlla de Mar, Golf de Sant Jordi, TORTOSA, L'Aldea, Cap Tortosa, Amposta, DELTA DE L'EBRE, Sant Carles de la Ràpita, Ulldecona, Alcanar, La Banya, La Jana, Valencia

0 kilometres 25 / 0 miles 15

Church on the seafront of Sitges

Vineyards outside Gandesa, west of Tarragona

Sights at a Glance

1 Vall d'Aran
2 Vielha
3 Baqueira-Beret
4 Vall de Boí
5 Parc Nacional d'Aigüestortes
6 Andorra
7 La Seu d'Urgell
8 Puigcerdà
9 Ripoll

10 Sant Joan de les Abadesses
11 Olot
12 Besalú
13 Girona
14 Figueres
15 Cadaqués
16 Empúries
17 Peratallada
18 Tossa de Mar

19 Blanes
20 Montserrat pp124–5
21 Vic
22 Cardona
23 Solsona
24 Lleida
25 Poblet pp128–9
26 Montblanc
27 Santes Creus

28 Vilafranca del Penedès
29 Sitges
30 Costa Daurada
31 Tarragona
32 Tortosa
33 Delta de l'Ebre

The Vall d'Aran, surrounded by the snow-capped mountains of the Pyrenees

Butterflies of the Vall d'Aran

A huge variety of butterflies and moths is found high in the valleys and mountains of the Pyrenees. The isolated Vall d'Aran is the home of several unique and rare subspecies. The best time of the year in which to see the butterflies is between May and July.

Chequered Skipper
(*Carterocephalus palemon*)

Clouded Apollo
(*Parnassins mnemosyne*)

Grizzled Skipper (underside)
(*Pyrgus malvae*)

❶ Vall d'Aran

Lleida N230. 🚌 Vielha.
🛈 Vielha (973 64 06 88).

This valley of valleys – *aran* means valley – is a lovely 600 sq km (230 sq mile) haven of forests and meadows filled with flowers, surrounded by towering mountain peaks.

The Vall d'Aran was formed by the Riu Garona, which rises in the area and flows out to France as the Garonne. With no proper link to the outside world until 1924, when a road was built over the Bonaigua Pass, the valley was cut off from the rest of Spain for most of the winter. Snow blocks the narrow pass from November to April, but today access is easy through the Túnel de Vielha from El Pont de Suert.

The fact that the Vall d'Aran faces north means that it has a climate similar to that on the Atlantic coast. Many rare wild flowers and butterflies flourish in the perfect conditions that are created by the shady slopes and damp breezes. It is also a famous habitat for many species of narcissus.

Tiny villages have grown up beside the Riu Garona, often around Romanesque churches, notably at **Bossòst**, **Salardú**, **Escunhau** and **Arties**. The valley is also ideal for outdoor sports such as skiing and is popular with walkers.

❷ Vielha

Lleida. 🚗 5,500. 🚌 🛈 Carrer Sarriulera 10 (973 64 06 88). 🗓 Thu. 🎉 Festa de Vielha (8 Sep), Feria de Vielha (8 Oct).

Now a modern ski resort, the capital of the Vall d'Aran retains its medieval past. The Romanesque church of **Sant Miquel** has an octagonal bell tower and a 12th-century crucifix, the *Mig Aran Christ*. It formed part of a larger carving representing the Descent from the Cross. The **Museu de la Vall d'Aran** is devoted to Aranese culture.

🏛 **Museu de la Vall d'Aran**
Carrer Major 26. **Tel** 973 64 18 15.
Open 10am–1pm (mid-Jun–mid-Sep only), 5–8pm Tue–Sat, 10am–1pm Sun. **Closed** bank hols. 🛇

Mig Aran Christ (12th-century), Sant Miquel church, Vielha

❸ Baqueira-Beret

Lleida. 🏔 2,100. 🚌 🚋 Baqueira-Beret (902 41 54 15). 🎭 Romeria de Nostra Senyora de Montgarri (2 Jul).

This extensive ski resort, one of the best in Spain, is popular with both the public and the Spanish royal family. There is reliable winter snow cover and a choice of over 40 pistes at altitudes from 1,520 m to 2,470 m (4,987 ft to 8,104 ft).

Baqueira and Beret were separate mountain villages before skiing became popular, but they have now merged to form a single resort. The Romans took full advantage of the thermal springs located here, which are nowadays appreciated by tired skiers.

❹ Vall de Boí

Lleida N230. 🚋 La Pobla de Segur. 🚌 Pont de Suert. 🚹 Barruera (973 69 40 00). 🖰 vallboi.com

This small valley on the edge of the Parc Nacional d'Aigüestortes is dotted with tiny villages, many of which are built around magnificent Catalan Romanesque churches.

Dating from the 11th and 12th centuries, these churches are distinguished by their tall belfries, such as the six-storey bell tower of the **Església de Santa Eulàlia** at Erill-la-Vall.

The two churches at Taüll, **Sant Climent** *(see p24)* and **Santa Maria**, have superb frescoes. Between 1919 and 1923, the originals were taken for safekeeping to the Museu Nacional d'Art de Catalunya in Barcelona, where their settings have been recreated *(see p91)*. Replicas now stand in their place. You can climb the towers of Sant Climent for superb views of the surrounding countryside.

Other churches in the area worth visiting include those at **Coll**, for its fine ironwork; **Barruera**; and **Durro**, which has another massive bell tower.

At the head of the valley is the hamlet of **Caldes de Boí**, popular for its thermal springs and nearby ski facilities. It is also a good base for exploring the

The tall belfry of Sant Climent church at Taüll in the Vall de Boí

Parc Nacional d'Aigüestortes *(see below)*, the entrance to which is only 5 km (3 miles) from here.

❺ Parc Nacional d'Aigüestortes

Lleida. 🚋 La Pobla de Segur. 🚌 Pont de Suert, La Pobla de Segur. 🚹 Boí (973 69 61 89); Espot (973 62 40 36). 🖰 parcsdecatalunya.cat

The pristine mountain scenery of Catalonia's only national park is among the most spectacular to be seen in the Pyrenees.

Established in 1955, the park covers an area of 102 sq km (40 sq miles). Its full title is Parc Nacional d'Aigüestortes i Estany de Sant Maurici, named after the lake *(estany)* of Sant Maurici in the east and the Aigüestortes (literally, twisted waters) area in

the west. The main village is the mountain settlement of Espot, on the park's eastern edge, although you can access the park from Boí in the west. Around the park are waterfalls and some 150 lakes and tarns which, in an earlier era, were scoured by glaciers to depths of up to 50 m (164 ft).

The finest scenery is around Sant Maurici lake, beneath the twin shards of the Serra dels Encantats, (Mountains of the Enchanted). From here, there is a variety of walks, particularly along the string of lakes that leads north to the towering peaks of Agulles d'Amitges. To the south is the dramatic vista of Estany Negre, the highest and deepest tarn in the park.

Early summer on the lower valley slopes is marked by rhododendrons, while later on wild lilies bloom in the forests of fir, beech and silver birch.

The park is also home to a variety of wildlife. Chamois (also known as izards) live on the mountain screes and in the meadows, while beavers and otters can be spotted by the lakes. Golden eagles nest on mountain ledges, and grouse and capercaillie are found in the woods.

During the summer, the park is popular with walkers, while in winter, the snow-covered mountains are ideal for cross-country skiing.

A crystal-clear stream at Parc Nacional d'Aigüestortes

Les Quatre Barres

Catalonia's national emblem

The four red bars on the *senyera*, the Catalan flag, are said to represent the four provinces: Barcelona, Girona, Lleida and Tarragona. The design derives from a legend of Guifré el Pelós, first Count of Barcelona (*see p44*). It relates how he received a call for help from Charles the Bald, who was King of the West Franks and grandson of Charlemagne. Guifré went to his aid and turned the tide of battle, but was mortally wounded. As he lay dying, Charles dipped his fingers in Guifré's blood and dragged them across his plain gold shield, giving him a grant of arms.

❻ Andorra

Principality of Andorra. 🏛 84,000. 🚌 Andorra la Vella. 🛈 Plaça de la Rotonda, Andorra la Vella (376 73 00 03). 🌐 andorra.ad

Andorra occupies 464 sq km (179 sq miles) of the Pyrenees between France and Spain. In 1993, it became fully independent and held its first ever democratic elections. Since 1278, it had been an autonomous feudal state under the jurisdiction of the Spanish bishop of La Seu d'Urgell and the French Count of Foix (a title adopted by the President of France). These are still the ceremonial joint heads of state.

Andorra's official language is Catalan, though French and Castilian are also spoken by most residents.

For many years, Andorra has been a tax-free paradise for shoppers, a fact reflected in the crowded shops and supermarkets of the capital, **Andorra la Vella**. Les Escaldes (near the capital), as well as Sant Julià de Lòria and El Pas de la Casa (the towns nearest the Spanish and French borders), have also become shopping centres.

Most visitors never see Andorra's rural charms, which match those of other parts of the Pyrenees. The region is excellent for walkers. One of the main routes leads to the **Cercle de Pessons**, a bowl of lakes in the east, and past Romanesque chapels such as **Sant Martí** at La Cortinada. In the north is the picturesque Sorteny valley, where traditional farmhouses have been converted into snug restaurants.

❼ La Seu d'Urgell

Lleida. 🏛 13,000. 🚌 🛈 Carrer Major 8 (973 35 15 11). 🕤 Tue & Sat. 🎪 Festa major (last week of Aug). 🌐 turismeseu.com

This Pyrenean town became a bishopric in the 6th century. Feuds between the bishops of Urgell and the Counts of Foix over land gave rise to Andorra in the 13th century. The **cathedral** has a Romanesque statue of Santa Maria d'Urgell. The **Museu Diocesà** contains a 10th-century copy of St Beatus of Liébana's *Commentary on the Apocalypse*.

🏛 Museu Diocesà

Plaça del Deganat. **Tel** 973 35 32 42. **Open** 10am–1:30pm, 4–7:30pm Mon–Sat (to 6pm Oct & Mar–May), 10am–1:30pm Sun & Nov–Feb. **Closed** 1 Jan, 25 Dec. 🎨 ♿

Carving, La Seu d'Urgell cathedral

❽ Puigcerdà

Girona. 🏛 9,000. 🚌 🚆 🛈 Carrer Querol 1 (972 88 05 42). 🕤 Sun. 🎪 Festa de l'Estany (third Sun of Aug); Festa del Roser (mid-Jul). 🌐 puigcerda.com

Puig is Catalan for hill. Despite sitting on a relatively small hill compared with the encircling mountains, which rise to 2,900 m (9,500 ft), Puigcerdà nevertheless commands a fine view down the beautiful Cerdanya valley. The town of Puigcerdà was founded in 1177 by Alfonso II as the capital of Cerdanya, an important agricultural region, which shares a past and its culture with the French Cerdagne. The Spanish enclave of **Llívia**, an attractive little town with a medieval pharmacy, lies 6 km (3.75 miles) inside France.

Cerdanya is the largest valley in the Pyrenees. At its edge is the **Cadí-Moixeró** nature reserve (*see p170*), a place for ambitious walks.

Portal of Monestir de Santa Maria

❾ Ripoll

Girona. 🏛 11,000. 🚆 🚌 🛈 Plaça del Abat Oliba (972 70 23 51). 🕤 Sat. 🎪 Festa major (11–12 May), La Llana y Casament a Pagès (Sun after festa major). 🌐 ripoll.cat

Once a tiny mountain base from which raids against the Moors were made, Ripoll is now best known for the **Monestir de Santa Maria** (*see p24*), founded in 879. The town is called the "cradle of Catalonia" as the monastery was the power base of Guifré el Pelós (Wilfred the Hairy), founder of the House of Barcelona (*see p44*). He is buried here. In the later 12th century, the west portal was decorated with what are regarded as the finest Romanesque carvings in Spain. This and the cloister are the only parts of the medieval monastery to have survived.

Environs

In the mountains to the west is **Sant Jaume de Frontanyà** (*see p24*), another superb Romanesque church.

The medieval town of Besalú on the banks of the Riu Fluvià

⑩ Sant Joan de les Abadesses

Girona. 🚇 3,400. 💬 ℹ️ Plaça de Abadia 9 (972 72 05 99). 🚌 Sun. 🎫 Festa major (second week of Sep). 📷 🌐 santjoandelesabadesses.cat

A fine, 12th century Gothic bridge arches over the Riu Ter to this unassuming market town, whose main attraction is its **monastery**.

Founded in 885, it was a gift from Guifré, first count of Barcelona, to his daughter, the first abbess. The church has little decoration except for a wooden calvary, *The Descent from the Cross*. Though made in 1150, it looks modern. The figure of a thief on the left was burnt in the Civil War and replaced so skilfully that it is hard to tell it is new. The museum has Baroque and Renaissance altarpieces.

12th-century calvary, Sant Joan de les Abadesses monastery

Environs

To the north are **Camprodon** and **Beget**, both with Romanesque churches *(see p25)*. Camprodon also has some grand houses, and its region is noted for sausages.

⑪ Olot

Girona. 🚇 34,000. 💬 ℹ️ Carrer Hospici 8 (972 26 01 41). 🚌 Mon. 🎫 Feria de Mayo (1 May), Corpus Christi (Jun), Festa del Tura (8 Sep), Feria de Sant Lluc (18 Oct). 🌐 turismeolot.com

This small market town sits at the centre of a landscape that is pockmarked with extinct volcanoes. But it was an earthquake in 1474 that destroyed its medieval past.

During the 18th century, the town's textile industry spawned the "Olot School" of art *(see p30)*. cotton fabrics were printed with drawings. In 1783, the Public School of Drawing was founded. Much of the school's work, which includes paintings such as Joaquim Vayreda's *Les Falgueres*, is in the **Museu Comarcal de la Garrotxa**. Modernista sculptor Miquel Blay's damsels support the balcony at No. 38 Passeig Miquel Blay.

🏛 Museu Comarcal de la Garrotxa

Carrer Hospici 8. **Tel** 972 27 11 66. **Open** 10am–1pm, 3–6pm Tue–Fri; 11am–2pm, 4–7pm Sat, 11am–2pm Sun. 🎫 ♿

⑫ Besalú

Girona. 🚇 2,400. 🚌 ℹ️ Carrer del Pont 1 (972 59 12 40). 🚌 Tue. 🎫 Sant Vicenç (22 Jan), Festa major (weekend closest to 25 Sep), Music Festival (Aug–Sep). 📷 🌐 besalu.cat

A magnificent medieval town with a striking approach across a fortified bridge over the Riu Fluvià, Besalú has two fine Romanesque churches: **Sant Vicenç** and **Sant Pere** *(see p25)*. The latter is the sole remnant of a Benedictine monastery founded in 977, but pulled down in 1835.

In 1964, a **mikvah**, a Jewish ritual bath, was discovered by chance. It was built in 1264 and is one of only three of that period to survive in Europe. The tourist office has the keys to all the town's attractions.

To the south, the sky-blue lake of **Banyoles**, where the 1992 Olympic rowing contests were held, is ideal for picnics.

Shop selling *llonganisses* in the mountain town of Camprodon

Girona Town Centre

1. Església de Sant Pere de Galligants
2. Banys Àrabs
3. Església de Sant Feliu
4. Catedral
5. Museu d'Art
6. Museu d'Història de la Ciutat
7. Museu d'Història dels Jueus

0 metres 250
0 yards 250

GIRONA NEW TOWN

✈ Airport 13km (8 miles)
🚆 Train station 1km (0.5 mile)

Oficina de Turisme (Oficina de Tourismo) 300m (330 yards)

⑬ Girona

Girona. 🗺 97,000. ✈ 🚆 🚌
ℹ Rambla de la Llibertat 1 (972 22 65 75). 🏪 Tue, Sat. 🎉 Sant Narcís (29 Oct for a week). ⬛
🌐 **girona.cat/turisme**

This handsome town puts on its best face beside the Riu Onyar, where tall, pastel-coloured buildings rise above the water. Behind them, in the old town, the Rambla de la Llibertat is lined with busy shops and street cafés.

The houses were built in the 19th century to replace sections of the city wall damaged during a seven-month siege by French troops in 1809. Most of the rest of the ramparts, first raised by the Romans, are still intact and have been turned into the Passeig Arqueològic (Archaeological Walk), which runs right round the city.

The walk's starting point is on the north side of the town, near the **Església de Sant Pere de Galligants** (St Peter of the Cock Crows) (see p25). The church now houses the city's archaeological collection.

From here, a narrow street goes through the north gate, where huge Roman foundation stones are still visible. They mark the route of the Via Augusta, the road which once ran from Tarragona to Rome. The most popular place of devotion in the town is the **Església de Sant Feliu**. The church, begun in the 14th century, was built over the tombs of St Felix and St Narcissus, both patrons of the city. Next to the high altar are eight Roman sarcophagi.

Despite their name, the nearby **Banys Àrabs** (Arab Baths) were built in the 12th century, 300 years after the Moors had left.

🏛 Museu d'Història dels Jueus

Carrer de la Força 8. **Tel** 972 21 67 61. **Open** Jul–Aug: 10am–8pm Mon–Sat, 10am–2pm Sun, pub hols; Sep–Jun: 10am–6pm Tue–Sat, 10am–2pm Sun, Mon and pub hols. **Closed** 1 & 6 Jan, 25 & 26 Dec. 🈲 ♿

This centre charts the history of Jews in Girona. The buildings it occupies in the maze of alleyways and steps in the old town were once part of El Call, the Jewish ghetto, which was inhabited by the city's Jews from the late 9th century until their expulsion from Spain in 1492.

🏛 Catedral

Pl Catedral s/n. **Tel** 972 42 71 89. **Open** Apr–Oct: 10am–7:30pm daily; Nov–Mar: 10am–6:30pm daily. 🈲 📷

Girona Cathedral's west face is pure Catalan Baroque, but the rest of the building is Gothic. The single nave, built in 1416 by Guillem Bofill, possesses the widest Gothic span in the Christian world. Behind the altar is a marble throne known as "Charlemagne's Chair". It is named after the Frankish king whose troops took Girona in

Painted houses packed tightly along the bank of the Riu Onyar in Girona

785. In the chancel is a 14th-century jewel-encrusted silver and enamel altarpiece. Among the fine Romanesque paintings and statues in the cathedral's museum are a 10th-century illuminated copy of St Beatus of Liébana's *Commentary on the Apocalypse*, and a 14th-century statue of the Catalan king, Pere the Ceremonious.

The collection's 11th- to 12th-century tapestry, *The Creation*, is decorated with lively figures. The rich colours of this large work are well preserved.

Tapestry of *The Creation*

🏛 Museu d'Art

Pujada de la Catedral 12. **Tel** 972 41 27 77. **Open** 10am–7pm (to 6pm Oct–Apr) Tue–Sat, 10am–2pm Sun. **Closed** 1 & 6 Jan, 25 & 26 Dec. 🅿 ♿

This gallery holds works from the Romanesque period to the 20th century. The many items from churches ruined by war or neglect tell of the richness of church interiors long ago.

🏛 Museu del Cinema

Carrer Sèquia 1. **Tel** 972 412 777. **Open** Tue–Sun (Jul–Aug: daily). **Closed** 1 & 6 Jan, 25 & 26 Dec. 🅿 free 1st Sun of month. ♿

Next to Església de Mercadel, this collection includes film and artifacts from the mid-19th century to the present day.

🏛 Museu d'Història de Girona

Carrer de la Força 27. **Tel** 972 22 22 29. **Open** Tue–Sun. **Closed** 1 & 6 Jan, 25 & 26 Dec. 🅿 ♿

The city's history museum is in an 18th-century former convent. Recesses where the decomposing bodies of members of the Capuchin Order were placed can still be seen. Exhibits include old *sardana (see p131)* instruments.

⑭ Figueres

Girona. 🏔 45,000. 🚌 🚏 ℹ Plaça del Sol (972 50 31 55). 🗓 Thu. 🎉 Santa Creu (3 May), Sant Pere (29 Jun). 📧 🌐 visitfigueres.cat

Figueres is the market town of the Empordà plain. Beside the plane-tree-shaded Rambla is the former Hotel de Paris, now home to the **Museu del Joguet** (Toy Museum). At the bottom of the Rambla is a statue of Narcís Monturiol i Estarriol (1819–95) who, it is said, invented the submarine.

Figueres was the birthplace of Salvador Dalí, who in 1974 turned the town theatre into the **Teatre-Museu Dalí**. Under its glass dome are works by Dalí and other painters. The museum is a monument to Catalonia's most eccentric artist.

Environs

The **Casa-Museu Castell Gala Dalí**, 55 km (35 miles) south of Figueres, is the medieval castle Dalí bought in the 1970s. It contains some of his paintings. East of Figueres is the Romanesque monastery, **Sant Pere de Rodes** (see p25).

Rainy Taxi, a monument in the garden of the Teatre-Museu Dalí

🏛 Museu del Joguet

C/ Sant Pere 1. **Tel** 972 50 45 85. **Open** Jun–Sep: daily; Oct–May: Tue–Sun. 🅿 ♿ 🌐 mjc.cat

🏛 Teatre-Museu Dalí

Pl Gala-Salvador Dalí 5. **Tel** 972 67 75 00. **Open** Jun–Sep: daily; Oct–May: Tue–Sun. **Closed** 1 Jan, 25 Dec. 🅿 🌐 salvador-dali.org

🏛 Casa-Museu Castell Gala Dalí

C/Gala Dalí, Púbol (La Pera). **Tel** 972 48 86 55. **Open** mid-Mar–Dec: Tue–Sun (Jun–Sep: daily). 🅿 ♿ 📷

The Art of Dalí

Salvador Dalí i Domènech was born in Figueres in 1904 and mounted his first exhibition at the age of 15. After studying at the Escuela de Bellas Artes in Madrid, and dabbling with Cubism, Futurism and Metaphysical painting, the young artist embraced Surrealism in 1929, becoming the movement's best-known painter. Never far from controversy, the self-publicist Dalí became famous for his hallucinatory images – such as *Woman-Animal Symbiosis* – which he described as "hand-painted dream photographs". Dalí's career also included writing and film-making, and established him as one of the 20th century's greatest artists. He died in his home town in 1989.

Ceiling fresco in the Wind Palace Room, Teatre-Museu Dalí

⓯ Cadaqués

Girona. ♨ 3,000. 🚌 ℹ Carrer
Cotxe 1 (972 25 83 15). 🚭 Mon.
🎭 Festa major d'estiu (first week
of Sep), Santa Esperança (18 Dec).
W visitcadaques.org

This pretty resort is overlooked
by the Baroque **Església de
Santa Maria**. In the 1960s, it was
dubbed the "St Tropez of Spain",
due to the young crowd that
sought out Salvador Dalí in
nearby Port Lligat, where he
lived for six months of the year,
from 1930 until his death in 1989.
Today the much modified house,
which expanded far beyond the
original fisherman's cabin, is
known as the **Casa-Museu
Salvador Dalí**. Managed by the
Gala-Salvador Dalí Foundation,
the museum provides a unique
interpretation of the artist's life.

🏛 **Casa-Museu Salvador Dalí**
Portlligat. **Tel** 972 25 10 15. **Open** Tue–
Sun (daily mid-Jun–mid-Sep). **Closed**
1 Jan, 7 Jan–early Feb, 25 Dec. 🎫
W salvador-dali.org

⓰ Empúries

Girona. 🚌 L'Escala. **Tel** 972 77 59 76.
Open mid-Feb–mid-Nov: 10am–6pm
daily (to 8pm Jun–Sep); mid-Nov–
mid-Feb: 10am–5pm Tue–Sun.
Closed 1 & 6 Jan, 25 Dec. 🎫 ruins;
free last Sun of month. 📷 by appt.
W mac.cat

The extensive ruins of this Greco-
Roman town *(see p43)* occupy
an imposing coastal site. Three
settlements were built between
the 7th and 3rd centuries BC:
the old town (Palaiapolis); the
new town (Neapolis); and the

An excavated Roman pillar in the
ruins of Empúries

Roman town. The **old town** was
founded by the Greeks in 600 BC
as a trading port. It was built on
what was a small island, and is
now the site of the tiny hamlet
of Sant Martí de Empúries. In
550 BC, this was replaced by a
larger new town on the shore
that the Greeks named
Emporion, meaning "trading
place". In 218 BC, the Romans
landed at Empúries and built a
city next to the new town.
   A nearby museum exhibits
some of the site's finds, but the
best are in Barcelona's Museu
Arqueològic *(see p91)*.

⓱ Peratallada

Girona. ♨ 400. ℹ C/Unió 3,
Ajuntament de Forallac, Vulpellac
(972 64 55 22). 🎭 Fira de les Herbes
(last weekend in Apr), Festa Major
(6 & 7 Aug), Medieval Market (first
weekend in Oct). W forallac.cat

This tiny village is the most
spectacular of the many that lie
a short inland trip from the Costa
Brava. Together with Pals and
Palau Sator, it forms part of the
"Golden Triangle" of medieval
villages. Its mountaintop
position gives some dramatic
views of the area. A labyrinth of
cobbled streets winds up to the
well-conserved castle and
lookout tower, whose written
records date from the 11th
century. Peratallada's counts and
kings made doubly sure of
fending off any attackers by
constructing a sturdy wall
enclosing the entire village,
which even today limits the
nucleus from further expansion.

Looking south along the Costa Brava from Tossa de Mar

⓲ Tossa de Mar

Girona. ♨ 6,000. 🚌 ℹ Avinguda
Pelegrí 25 (972 34 01 08). 🚭 Thu.
🎭 Festa Major d'Hivern (22 Jan),
Festa Major d'Estiu (29 Jun).
W infotossa.com

At the end of a tortuous
corniche, the Roman town of
Turissa is one of the prettiest
along the Costa Brava. Above
the modern town is the **Vila
Vella** (old town), a protected
national monument. The
medieval walls enclose
fishermen's cottages, a 14th-
century church and countless
bars. The **Museu Municipal** in
the old town exhibits local
archaeology and modern art.

🏛 **Museu Municipal**
Plaça Roig i Soler 1. **Tel** 972 34 07 09.
Open Tue–Sun. 🎫

⓳ Blanes

Girona. ♨ 40,000. 🚊 🚌 ℹ Plaça
Catalunya (972 33 03 48). 🚭 Mon.
🎭 Santa Ana (26 Jul); Festa Major
Petita (21 Aug). W visitblanes.net

The working port of Blanes has
one of the longest beaches on
the Costa Brava. The highlight of
the town is the **Jardí Botànic
Marimurtra**. These gardens,
designed by Karl Faust in 1928,
are spectacularly sited above
cliffs. Their 7,000 species of
Mediterranean and tropical
plants include African cacti.

🌿 **Jardí Botànic Marimurtra**
Pg Carles Faust 9. **Tel** 972 33 08 26.
Open daily. **Closed** 1 & 6 Jan, 25 & 26
Dec. 🎫 📷 ♿ W marimurtra.cat

◀ The fortified bridge leading into the medieval town of Besalú

The Costa Brava

The Costa Brava ("wild coast") runs for some 200 km (125 miles) from Blanes northwards to the region of Empordà, which borders France. It is a mix of rugged cliffs, pine-backed sandy coves, golden beaches and crowded, modern resorts. The busiest resorts – Lloret de Mar, Tossa de Mar and Platja d'Aro – are to the south. Sant Feliu de Guíxols and Palamós are still working towns behind the summer rush. Just inland there are medieval villages to explore, such as Peralada, Peratallada and Pals. Wine, olives and fishing were the mainstays of the area before the tourists came in the 1960s.

Cadaqués retains an air of seclusion as it is accessible only by a steep road. It has an arty atmosphere and its small, stony beaches are relatively unspoiled and uncrowded.

L'Estartit is a good base for the Illes Medes, a former pirates' lair, which now form a marine reserve with clear waters perfect for skin diving.

Palamós is a working port with modern hotels to the south, and secluded beaches and coves lapped by clear water to the north.

Platja d'Aro's long and sandy beach is lined with modern hotels. It is one of the most popular resorts on the coast.

Tossa de Mar has a golden beach in a small cove beneath the fortified old town.

Roses lies at the head of a sweeping bay. Its sandy beach, the longest on the Costa Brava, has become a mecca for lovers of water sports.

L'Escala is a small resort, popular mainly with local tourists. It has fine beaches and a small port where fishing nets dry in the sun.

Begur is a hilltop town just inland. It has good views of the coast, and small coves are tucked at its feet.

Llafranc, a whitewashed resort with a promenade leading to neighbouring Calella, is one of the coast's most pleasant resorts.

Lloret de Mar has more hotels than anywhere else on the coast. But there are unspoiled beaches nearby, such as Santa Cristina.

Map labels:
Llançà
Port de la Selva
Cap de Creus
Parc Natural del Cap de Creus
Peralada
Cadaqués
Castelló d'Empúries
C260
Roses
Fortià
Empuriabrava
Parc Natural dels Aiguamolls de l'Empordà
C31
L'Escala
Punta del Milà
L'Estartit
Illes Medes
Torroella de Montgrí
Riu Ter
C31
Peratallada
Pals
Begur
C66
Palafrugell
Llafranc
Calella de Palafrugell
Palamós
Llagostera
S'Agaró
Platja d'Aro
C31
Sant Feliu de Guíxols
C35
Tossa de Mar
C63
Tordera
Lloret de Mar
Blanes
Malgrat de Mar

0 kilometres   10
0 miles   5

⑳ Monestir de Montserrat

The "serrated mountain" *(mont serrat)*, its highest peak rising to 1,236 m (4,055 ft), is a superb setting for Catalonia's holiest place, the Monastery of Montserrat, which is surrounded by chapels and hermits' caves. A chapel was first mentioned in the 9th century; the monastery was founded in the 11th century, and in 1409 it became an independent abbey. In 1811, when the French attacked Catalonia in the War of Independence *(see p47)*, the monastery was destroyed. Rebuilt and repopulated in 1844, it was a beacon of Catalan culture during the Franco years. Today, Benedictine monks live here. Visitors can hear the Escolania singing the *Salve Regina* and the *Virolai* (the Montserrat hymn) at various times throughout the day except on Saturdays, in July and August and during the Christmas period (call ahead for details).

Plaça de Santa Maria
The focal points of the square are two wings of the Gothic cloister built in 1476. The modern monastery façade is by Francesc Folguera.

KEY

① **Funicular** to the holy site of Santa Cova.

② **The Museum** has a collection of 19th- and 20th-century Catalan paintings and many Italian and French works. It also displays liturgical items from the Holy Land.

③ **Gothic cloister**

④ **The Black Virgin** – La Moreneta – looks down from behind the altar, protected behind glass; her wooden orb protrudes for pilgrims to touch.

⑤ **The rack railway** from Monistrol de Montserrat follows the course of a rail line built in 1880.

⑥ **Cable car** to Aeri de Montserrat station.

View of Montserrat
The complex includes cafés and a hotel. A second funicular transports visitors to nature trails above the monastery.

The Way of the Cross
This path passes 11 statues representing the Stations of the Cross. It begins near the Plaça de l'Abat Oliba.

★ **Basilica Façade**
Agapit and Venanci Vallmitjana sculpted Christ and the Apostles on the basilica's Neo-Renaissance façade. It was built in 1900 to replace the Renaissance façade of the original church, consecrated in 1592.

VISITORS' CHECKLIST

Practical Information
Montserrat (Barcelona province).
Tel 93 877 77 77.
Basilica: **Open** 7:30am–8pm Mon–Fri, 7am–8:15pm Sat–Sun and throughout Aug 🕐 11am & noon Mon–Fri; 11am, noon & 7:30pm Sat; 9:30am, 11am, noon, 1pm & 7:30pm Sun. 🎫
Museum: **Open** 10am–5:45pm daily. 🅿️ ♿ 🎫
Ⓦ **montserratvisita.com**

Transport
🚡 Aeri de Montserrat, then cable car; Monistrol-Enllaç, then rack railway. 🚌 from Barcelona.

Basilica Interior
The sanctuary in the domed basilica is adorned by a richly enamelled altar and paintings by Catalan artists.

The Virgin of Montserrat

The small wooden statue of La Moreneta (the dark maiden) is the soul of Montserrat. It is said to have been made by St Luke and brought here by St Peter in AD 50. Centuries later, the statue is believed to have been hidden from the Moors in the nearby Santa Cova (Holy Cave). Carbon dating suggests, however, that the statue was carved around the 12th century. In 1881, Montserrat's Black Virgin became patroness of Catalonia.

The blackened Virgin of Montserrat

Inner Courtyard
On one side of the courtyard is the baptistry (1958), with sculptures by Carles Collet. A door on the right leads towards the Black Virgin.

❷❶ Vic

Barcelona. 🚗 41,000. 🚉 🚌 **ℹ** Plaça del Pes (93 886 20 91). 🚌 Tue & Sat. 🎭 Mercat del Ram (Sat before Easter), Sant Miquel (5–15 Jul), Música Viva (5 days mid-Sep), Mercat medieval (6–10 Dec). 📅 **W** victurisme.cat

Market days are the best time to visit this small country town. This is when the local sausages *(embotits)* for which the area is renowned are piled high in the Gothic Plaça Major, along with other produce from the surrounding plains.

In the 3rd century BC, Vic was the capital of an ancient Iberian tribe, the Ausetans. The town was then colonized by the Romans – the remains of a Roman temple survive today. Since the 6th century, the town has been a bishop's see. In the 11th century, Abbot Oliva commissioned El Cloquer tower, around which the cathedral was built in the 18th century. The interior is covered with vast murals by Josep-Maria Sert (1876–1945, *see p31*). Painted in reds and golds, they represent Biblical scenes.

Adjacent to the cathedral is the **Museu Episcopal de Vic** *(see p25)*, which has one of the best Romanesque collections in Catalonia. The large display of mainly religious art and relics includes bright, simple murals and wooden carvings from rural churches. Also on display are 11th- and 12th-century frescoes and some superb altar frontals.

Cardona dominating the surrounding area from its hilltop site

🏛 **Museu Episcopal**
Plaça Bisbe Oliba 3. **Tel** 93 886 93 60. **Open** Tue–Sun. **Closed** 1 & 6 Jan, 25 & 26 Dec. 📷 ♿ 📷 free 1st Thu of month.

❷❷ Cardona

Barcelona. 🚗 5,000. 🚌 **ℹ** Avinguda Rastrillo (93 869 27 98). 🚌 Sun. 🎭 Carnival (Feb), Festa major (second weekend of Sep). **W** cardona.cat

This 13th-century, ruddy-stoned castle of the Dukes of Cardona, constables to the crown of Aragón, was rebuilt in the 18th century and is now a luxurious parador *(see p134)*. Beside the castle is an early 11th-century church, the **Església de Sant Vicenç**.

Set on a hill, the castle gives views of the town and of the Muntanya de Sal (Salt Mountain), a huge salt deposit next to the Riu Cardener that has been mined since Roman times.

❷❸ Solsona

Lleida. 🚗 9,000. 🚌 **ℹ** Carrer Castell 20 (973 48 00 50). 🚌 Tue & Fri. 🎭 Carnival (Feb), Corpus Christi (May/ Jun), Festa major (8–11 Sep). 📅 **W** solsonaturisme.com

Nine towers and three gateways remain of Solsona's fortifications. Inside is an ancient town of noble mansions. The cathedral houses a beautiful black stone Virgin. The **Museu Diocesà i Comarcal** contains Romanesque paintings; a wonderfully preserved ice store, the **Pou de Gel**, is also worth a visit.

🏛 **Museu Diocesà i Comarcal**
Plaça del Palau 1. **Tel** 973 48 21 01. **Open** Tue–Sun. ♿ **Closed** 1 Jan, 25 & 26 Dec.

🏛 **Pou de Gel**
Portal del Pont s/n. **Tel** 973 48 10 09. **Open** Sat–Sun; daily Jul–Aug and Easter. 📷 📷

❷❹ Lleida

Lleida. 🚗 138,500. 🚉 🚌 **ℹ** C / Major 31 (973 70 03 19). 🚌 Thu & Sat. 🎭 Sant Anastasi (11 May), Sant Miquel (29 Sep). **W** turismedelleida.cat

Dominating Lleida, the capital of Catalonia's only inland province, is **La Suda**, a fort taken from the Moors in 1149. The cathedral, founded in 1203, lies within the fort's walls, above the town. It was transformed into barracks by Felipe V in 1707. Today it is desolate, but remains imposing, with magnificent Gothic windows.

A lift descends from La Seu Vella to the Plaça de Sant Joan

Twelfth-century altar frontal, Museu Episcopal de Vic

in the busy, pedestrianized shopping street at the foot of the hill. The new cathedral is here, as is the reconstructed 13th-century town hall, the **Paeria**.

㉕ Poblet

See pp128–9.

㉖ Montblanc

Tarragona. 🏔 7,400. 🚉 🚌 ℹ️
Antigua Església de Sant Francesc (977 86 17 33). 🛒 Tue & Fri. 🎭 Festa Major (8–11 Sep), Festa Medieval (two weeks in Apr). 🗓
🌐 montblancmedieval.cat

The medieval grandeur of Montblanc lives on within its walls – possibly Catalonia's finest piece of military architecture. At the **Sant Jordi** gate, St George allegedly slew the dragon. The **Museu Comarcal de la Conca de Barberà** has displays on local crafts.

🏛 **Museu Comarcal de la Conca de Barberà**
Carrer de Josa 6. **Tel** 977 86 03 49.
Open Tue–Sun & public hols. 🗓

㉗ Santes Creus

Tarragona. 🏔 150. 🚌 ℹ️ Plaça de Sant Bernat 1 (977 63 81 41). 🛒 Sat & Sun. 🎭 Santa Llúcia (13 Dec).

The tiny village of Santes Creus is home to the prettiest of the "Cistercian triangle" monasteries.

The other two, Vallbona de les Monges and Poblet, are nearby. The **Monestir de Santes Creus** was founded in 1150 by Ramon Berenguer IV *(see p44)* during his reconquest of Catalonia. The Gothic cloisters are decorated with figurative sculptures, a style first permitted by Jaume II, who ruled from 1291 to 1327. His tomb is in the 12th-century church, which features a rose window.

🏰 **Monestir de Santes Creus**
Tel 977 63 83 29. **Open** 10am–7pm (to 5.30pm Oct–May) Tue–Sun & public hols. **Closed** 1 & 6 Jan, 25 & 26 Dec. 🎫 ♿ 🗓 by appointment.

㉘ Vilafranca del Penedès

Barcelona. 🏔 39,000. 🚉 🚌 ℹ️ Carrer Cort 14 (93 892 05 62). 🛒 Sat. 🎭 Fira de Mayo (2nd week of May), Festa major (end Aug). 🌐 turismevilafranca.com

This market town is set in the heart of Penedès, the main wine-producing region of Catalonia. The **Vinseum** (Wine Museum) documents the history of the area's wine trade. Local *bodegues* can be visited for wine tasting. **Sant Sadurní d'Anoia**, the capital of Spain's sparkling wine, *cava (see pp34–5)*, is 8 km (5 miles) to the north.

🏛 **Vinseum**
Plaça de Jaume I. **Tel** 93 890 05 82.
Open 10am–2pm, 4–7pm Tue–Sat; 10am–2pm Sun.

Anxaneta climbing to the top of a tower of casters

Human Towers

The province of Tarragona is famous for its *casteller* festivals, in which teams of men stand on each other's shoulders in an effort to build the highest human tower *(castell)*. Configurations depend on the number of men who form the base. Teams wear similar colours, and often have names denoting their home town. The small child who has to undertake the perilous climb to the top, where he or she makes the sign of the cross, is called the *anxaneta*. *Castellers* assemble in competition for Tarragona province's major festivals throughout the year. In the wine town of Vilafranca del Penedès, they turn out for Sant Fèlix (30 August), and in Tarragona city for Santa Tecla, its *festa major* on 23 September. Rival teams in Valls appear on St John's Day (24 June), but strive for their best achievement at the end of the tower-building season on St Ursula's Day (21 October), when teams from all over Catalonia converge on the town square.

Monestir de Santes Creus, surrounded by poplar and hazel trees

㉕ Monestir de Poblet

The monastery of Santa Maria de Poblet is a haven of tranquillity and a resting place of kings. It was the first and most important of three monasteries, known as the "Cistercian triangle" *(see p127)*, that helped to consolidate power in Catalonia after it had been recaptured from the Moors by Ramon Berenguer IV. In 1835, due to the Ecclesiastical Confiscation law, and during the Carlist upheavals, it was plundered and damaged by fire. Restoration of the impressive ruins began in 1930 and monks returned in 1940.

View of Poblet
The abbey, its buildings enclosed by fortified walls that have hardly changed since the Middle Ages, is in an isolated valley near the Riu Francolí's source.

★ Cloisters
The evocative vaulted cloisters were built in the 12th–13th centuries and were the centre of monastic life. The capitals are beautifully decorated with carved scrollwork.

KEY

① Museum

② Royal doorway

③ Former kitchen

④ Wine cellar

⑤ **The 12th-century refectory** is a vaulted hall with an octagonal fountain and a pulpit.

⑥ **The dormitory** is reached by stairs from the church. The vast 87 m (285 ft) gallery dates from the 13th century. Half of it is still in use by the monks.

⑦ Parlour cloister

⑧ Sant Esteve cloister

⑨ New sacristy

⑩ **The Abbey Church**, large and unadorned, with three naves, is a typical Cistercian building.

⑪ Baroque church façade

Library
The Gothic scriptorium was converted into a library in the 17th century, when the Cardona family donated its book collection.

Chapterhouse
This perfectly square room, with slender columns, has tiers of benches for the monks. It is paved with the tombstones of 11 abbots who died between 1312 and 1623.

VISITORS' CHECKLIST

Practical Information
Off N240, 10 km (6 miles) from Montblanc. **Tel** 977 87 00 89. **Open** 10am–12:30pm, 3–5:25pm Mon–Sat (to 5.55pm mid-Mar–mid-Oct); 10:30am–12:25pm, 3–5:25pm Sun. **Closed** 1 Jan, 25 & 26 Dec. 🅿 📷 by appointment. 🛈 10am (summer only), 1pm & 6pm Sun & public hols. 🚻 ♿

Transport
🚉 L'Espluga de Francolí, then walk or taxi. 🚌

★ The Altar Piece
Behind the stone altar, supported by Romanesque columns, an impressive alabaster reredos fills the apse. It was sculpted by Damià Forment in 1527.

★ Royal Tombs
The tombs in the pantheon of kings were begun in 1359. In 1950, they were reconstructed by the sculptor Frederic Marès.

Cloisters

Royal tombs

1150 Santes Creus founded – third abbey in Cistercian triangle

1156 Founding of Cistercian monastery at Vallbona de les Monges

14th century Main cloister finished

1479 Juan II, last king of Aragón, buried here

1812 Poblet desecrated by French troops

1940 Monks return

1100	1300	1500	1700	1900

1196 Alfonso II is the first king to be buried here

1336–87 Reign of Pere the Ceremonious, who designates Poblet a royal pantheon

1835 Disentailment of monasteries. Poblet ravaged (p47)

1952 Tombs reconstructed. Royal remains returned

1150 Poblet monastery founded by Ramon Berenguer IV

Palm trees lining the waterfront at Sitges

❷⁹ Sitges

Barcelona. 🚗 29,000. 🚉 🚌
ℹ️ Plaça Eduard Maristany 2 (93 894 42
51). 🚢 Thu (in summer). 🎭 Carnival
(Feb/Mar), Festa major (22–27 Aug).
🌐 **sitgestur.cat**

Sitges has no less than nine
beaches. It has a reputation as a
gay resort, but is just as popular
with Barceloneses. Lively bars
and restaurants line its main
boulevard, the Passeig Marítim,
and there are many examples
of Modernista architecture
scattered amongst the 1970s
apartment blocks. Modernista
artist Santiago Rusiñol (see p31)
spent much time here and
bequeathed his quirky collection
of ceramics, sculptures, painting
and ornate ironwork to the
Museu Cau Ferrat. It lies next to
Sitges's landmark, the
17th-century church of **Sant
Bartomeu i Santa Tecla**.

🏛️ **Museu Cau Ferrat**
Carrer Fonollar. **Tel** 93 894 03 64.
Open Tue–Sun. 🎨 📷

❸⁰ Costa Daurada

Tarragona. 🚉 🚌 Calafell, Sant Vicenç
de Calders, Salou. ℹ️ Tarragona (977
23 03 12). 🌐 **costadaurada.info**

The long sandy beaches of the
Costa Daurada (Golden Coast)
run along the shores of
Tarragona province. **El Vendrell**
is one of the area's active ports.
The **Museu Pau Casals** in
Sant Salvador (El Vendrell) is
dedicated to the famous cellist.
Port Aventura, south of
Tarragona, is one of Europe's

largest theme parks and has
many exotically themed
attractions, such as Polynesia
and Wild West. **Cambrils** and
Salou to the south are the
liveliest resorts – the others are
low-key, family holiday spots.

🏛️ **Museu Pau Casals**
Avinguda Palfuriana 67. **Tel** 902 10 54
64. **Open** Tue–Sun. 📷

🎡 **Port Aventura**
Avinguda de l'Alcalde Pere Molas
Km 2, Vila-seca. **Tel** 902 20 22 20.
Open mid-Mar–6 Jan. 📷 ♿

❸¹ Tarragona

Tarragona. 🚗 134,000. ✈️ 🚉 🚌
ℹ️ Carrer Major 39 (977 25 07 95).
🚢 Tue, Thu & Sun. 🎭 Sant Magí (19
Aug), Santa Tecla (23 Sep).
🌐 **tarragonaturisme.cat**

Tarragona is now a major
industrial port, but it has
preserved many remnants of
its Roman past. As the capital
of Tarraconensis, the Romans

used it as a base for the
conquest of the peninsula in
the 3rd century BC (see p43).

The avenue of Rambla Nova
ends abruptly on the clifftop
Balcó de Europa, in sight of the
ruins of the **Amfiteatre Romà**
and the ruined 12th-century
church of **Santa Maria
del Miracle**.

Nearby is the Praetorium, a
Roman tower that was converted
into a palace in medieval times.
It now houses the **Pretori i Circ
Romans**. This displays Roman
and medieval finds, and gives
access to the cavernous passage-
ways of the excavated Roman
circus, built in the 1st century AD.
Next to the Praetorium is the
Museu Nacional Arqueològic,
containing the most important
collection of Roman artifacts in
Catalonia. It has an extensive
collection of bronze tools and
beautiful mosaics, including a
Head of Medusa. Among the
most impressive remains are the
huge pre-Roman stones on

The remains of the Roman amphitheatre, Tarragona

which the Roman wall is built. An archaeological walk stretches 1 km (half a mile) along the wall.

Behind the wall lies the 12th-century **cathedral**, built on the site of a Roman temple. This evolved over many centuries, as seen from the blend of styles of the exterior. Inside is an alabaster altarpiece of St Tecla, carved by Pere Joan in 1434. The 13th-century cloister has Gothic vaulting, but the doorway is Romanesque *(see pp24–5)*.

In the west of town is a 3rd- to 6th-century Christian cemetery (ask about its opening times in the archaeological museum). Some of the sarcophagi were originally used as pagan tombs.

Ruins of the Palaeo-Christian Necropolis

Environs

The **Aqüeducte de les Ferreres** lies just outside the city, next to the A7 motorway. This 2nd-century aqueduct was built to bring water to the city from the Riu Gaià, 30 km (19 miles) to the north. The **Arc de Berà**, a 1st-century triumphal arch on the Via Augusta, is 20 km (12 miles) northeast on the N340.

The bustling, provincial town of **Reus** lies inland from Tarragona. Although its airport serves the Costa Daurada, it is often overlooked by holiday-makers. However, there is some fine Modernista architecture to be seen here, notably some early work by Antoni Gaudí, who was born in Reus. The Pere Mata Psychiatric Institute was designed by Domènech i Montaner before his master-piece, the Hospital de la Santa Creu i de Sant Pau *(see p81)*.

🏛 **Museu Nacional Arqueològic de Tarragona**
Plaça del Rei 5. **Tel** 977 23 62 09. **Open** Tue–Sun. 🅿 🔇 **W** mnat.es

🏛 **Pretori i Circ Romans**
Plaça del Rei. **Tel** 977 23 01 71. **Open** Tue–Sun. 🅿 🔲 **W** tarragonaturisme.cat

㉜ Tortosa

Tarragona. 🔼 34,000. 🚶 Rambla Felip Pedrell 3 (977 44 96 48). 🚌 Mon. 🎪 Nostra Senyora de la Cinta (1st wk Sep). **W** turismetortosa.cat

A ruined castle and medieval walls are clues to Tortosa's historical importance. Sited at the lowest crossing point on the Riu Ebre, it has been strategically significant since Iberian times. The Moors held the city from the 8th century until 1148. The old Moorish castle, known as La Suda, is all that remains of their defences. It has now been renovated as a parador *(see p134)*. The Moors also built a mosque in Tortosa in 914. Its foundations were used for the present cathedral, on which work began in 1347. Although it was not completed for two centuries, the style is pure Gothic.

Tortosa was badly damaged in 1938–9 during one of the fiercest battles of the Civil War *(see p49)*, when the Ebre formed the front line between the opposing forces.

㉝ Delta de L'Ebre

Tarragona. 🚏 Aldea. 🚌 Deltebre, Aldea. 🚶 Deltebre (977 48 93 09). **W** deltebre.net

The delta of the Riu Ebre is a prosperous rice growing region and wildlife haven. Some 70 sq km (27 sq miles) have been turned into a nature reserve, the **Parc Natural del Delta de L'Ebre**. In Deltebre there is an information centre and an interesting **Eco-Museu**, with an aquarium containing species found in the delta.

The main towns in the area are **Amposta** and **Sant Carles de la Ràpita**, both of which serve as good bases for exploring the reserve.

The best places to see the variety of wildlife are along the shore, from the Punta del Fangar in the north to the Punta de la Banya in the south. Everywhere is accessible by car except the Illa de Buda. Flamingoes breed on this island and, together with other water birds, such as herons and avocets, can be seen from tourist boats that leave from Riumar and Deltebre.

🏛 **Eco-Museu**
Carrer Martí Buera 22. **Tel** 977 48 96 79. **Open** Tue–Sun. 🅿 🔇 🗂

The Sardana

Catalonia's national dance is more complicated than it appears. The dancers must form a circle and accurately count the complicated short- and long-step skips and jumps. Music is provided by a *cobla*, an 11-person band consisting of a leader playing a three-holed flute *(flabiol)* and a little drum *(tamborí)*, five woodwind players and five brass players. The *sardana* is performed during most *festes* and at special day-long gatherings called *aplecs*. In Barcelona, it is danced on Saturday evenings at 6 in front of the cathedral and usually every Sunday evening at 6 in the Plaça de Sant Jaume.

A group of *sardana* dancers captured in stone

TRAVELLERS' NEEDS

Where to Stay   **134–139**

Where to Eat and Drink   **140–153**

Shopping in Barcelona   **154–161**

Entertainment in
Barcelona   **162–169**

Sports and Outdoor
Activities   **170–171**

WHERE TO STAY

Catalonia has an unrivalled variety of accommodation. The Barcelona and Catalonia tourist authorities have complete listings of hotels, country houses and camp sites, as well as information on a range of other options. In Barcelona you can stay in the modern luxury of one of Spain's highest skyscrapers, while on the coast you can try a self-catering holiday village with all sorts of entertainment provided. Family-run *cases de pagès*, which are stone-built farm or village houses or country manors, are Catalonia's most distinctive alternative. Some of the best hotels in each price range are listed on pages 136–9.

A hotel in Barcelona's Rambla de Canaletes

Hotel Grading and Facilities

The different types of hotels in Catalonia are denoted by the blue plaques near their doors. These show a star-rating that reflects the number and range of facilities available, rather than quality of service. Hotels (H) and *hotel-residències* (HR) are graded from one to five stars; *hostals* (H) and *hostal-residències* (HR) from one to three stars; and *pensions* (P), with the simplest accommodation, have one or two stars.

Prices and Paying

Spanish law requires all hotels to display their prices at reception and in every room. As a rule, the higher the star rating, the greater the price. Rates are almost invariably quoted per room (but meal prices per person). A double room in a one-star *hostal* can be as little as €30 a night; one in a five-star hotel will cost more than €180 a night. Prices vary according to region, season, day of the week or a special feature, such as a view or balcony. The prices given on pages 136–9 are based on high-season rates. Prices for rooms and meals are usually quoted without VAT (IVA), currently 21 per cent.

Booking and Check-in

Hotels in Barcelona can be very busy during the many trade fairs held all year round, so booking in advance is advisable. In rural Catalonia, there is rarely any need to book ahead. Resort hotels often close from autumn

A room with a private balcony in Hotel Aiguaclara, Begur *(see p138)*

to spring. You will not normally be asked for a deposit when you book a room, except during peak periods or for a longer stay. Most hotels will honour a booking only until 8pm.

When checking in you will be asked for your passport or identity card to comply with police regulations. It will normally be returned as soon as your details have been copied.

Paradors

There are seven paradors in Catalonia – at Aiguablava, Artíes, Cardona, Seu de Urgell, Vic, Vielha and Tortosa. They form part of Spain's chain of high-quality, government-run hotels in historic buildings or in purpose-built, new buildings in spectacular settings.

Reservations can be made through **Paradores de Turismo de España**, **Petrabax** (in the US) and **Keytel International** (UK).

Rural Accommodation

Cases de pagès (also called *cases rurales*) are Catalan *masies* (farmhouses) that accept visitors. Some offer bed and breakfast, some an evening meal or full board, and many are self-catering. They are listed in the *Guía de Establecimientos de Turismo Rural*, available at the tourist office. You can book directly or through the websites of agencies such as **Rural Catalunya**, **Top Rural** and **Cases Fonda**.

The **Xarxa d'Albergs de Catalunya** runs youth hostels, which also cater for adults and families, and the **Federació d'Entitats Excursionistes de Catalunya** runs mountain refuges for hikers.

Solid, stone-built architecture typical of traditional Catalan farmhouses

Self-Catering

Villas and apartments let by the week are plentiful on the Costa Daurada and Costa Brava. *Apart hotels* (or *hotels-apartament*) and *residències-apartament* are a type of self-catering accommodation. Ranked from one to four stars, each apartment has a kitchen, but each complex also has a restaurant and often a swimming pool and other facilities. Generalitat de Catalunya *(see p174)* tourist offices and most travel agents have details of all types of villas and apartments.

Ciutats de vacances (holiday villages) are similar, but accommodation is in bungalows and includes entertainment and sports facilities.

Gites de Catalunya are superior country houses rented out on a week-by-week basis by **Villas 4 You**. Many *cases de pagès* are also self-catering.

Camp Sites

Catalonia has over 300 camp sites, classified as deluxe (L), one-star, two-star, three-star, or farm (M, *càmpings-masia*). All have basic amenities, guards and a safe. *Catalunya Càmpings*, published by the Generalitat de Catalunya, is available from the tourist offices. Many sites in Barcelona are grouped under the **Associació de Càmpings de Barcelona**. Camping is permitted only at official sites.

Sign for a camp site

Disabled Travellers

Few hotels are well equipped for disabled guests, although some youth hostels are. The **Federació ECOM** and Viajes 2000 *(see p175)* will advise on hotels throughout Catalonia for visitors with special needs.

Recommended Hotels

The hotels listed in this book cover a wide range of price categories and have been selected for their excellent facilities and good value for money. The listings cover a vast variety of accommodation, from simple farmhouses and family-run guesthouses to mountain retreats and extravagant luxury palaces. To make it easier for you to choose your hotel, the establishments have been labelled as boutique, historic, luxury, modern or pensions. Many of the hotels have a good reputation for hospitality and offer a warm welcome to guests.

Among the listings, hotels and pensions that are outstanding in some way have been designated as DK Choice. They have been chosen for their exceptional features, for example, they may be set in beautiful surroundings or in a historically important building, offer excellent service, have a romantic atmosphere, be particularly charming, environmentally friendly or have a great spa. Whatever the reason, it is a guarantee of a memorable stay.

DIRECTORY

Paradors

Keytel International
The Foundry,
15 Blackfriars Rd,
London SE1 8EN.
Tel 027 953 3020 in UK.
ⓦ keytel.co.uk

Paradores de Turismo de España
Calle José Abascal 2–4,
28003 Madrid.
Tel 902 54 79 79.
ⓦ parador.es

Petrabax
37–18 Northern Boulevard, Suite 412,
Long Island City,
NY 11101.
Tel 800 634 1188.
ⓦ petrabax.com

Rural Accommodation

Cases Fonda
ⓦ casafonda.com

Federació d'Entitats Excursionistes de Catalunya
La Rambla 41, 08002
Barcelona.
Tel 93 412 07 77.
ⓦ feec.cat

Rural Catalunya
ⓦ ruralcatalunya.com

Top Rural
ⓦ toprural.com

Xarxa d'Albergs de Catalunya
Carrer Calàbria 147, 08015
Barcelona. **Tel** 93 483 83 41.
ⓦ xanascat.cat

Self-Catering

Villas 4 You
P O Box 1310,
Maidstone,
Kent
ME14 9QH, UK
Tel 0800 096 3439.
ⓦ villas4you.co.uk

Camp Sites

Associació de Càmpings de Barcelona
Gran Via Corts,
Catalanes 608, 3a,
08007 Barcelona.
Tel 93 412 59 55.
ⓦ campingsbarcelona. com

Disabled Travellers

Federació ECOM
Gran Via de les Corts
Catalanes 562, principal
2a, 08011 Barcelona.
Tel 93 451 55 50,
ⓦ ecom.cat

Spanish Tourist Offices

UK
6th Floor, 64 North Row,
London W1K 7DE.
Tel 0207 317 2011.
ⓦ spain.info

US
60 E 42nd St, Suite 5300,
New York, NY 10165.
Tel (212) 265 8822.
ⓦ spain.info

Where to Stay

Old Town

Bonic Barcelona €
Pension Map 5 A3
C/Josep Anselm Clavé 9, 08002
Tel 62 605 34 34
Ⓦ bonic-barcelona.com
Charming B&B in the Gothic
Quarter. Delightful staff.

Chic & Basic Born €
Boutique Map 5 C2
C/Princesa 50, 08003
Tel 93 295 46 52
Ⓦ chicandbasic.com
With its mood lighting and
white-on-white chic, this is a firm
favourite with fashionistas.

Hotel Banys Orientals €
Boutique Map 5 B3
C/Argenteria 37, 08003
Tel 93 268 84 60
Ⓦ hotelbanysorientals.com
Stylish and great value accom-
modation in the Born district,
with a choice of rooms or suites.

La Ciudadela Hotel €
Pension Map 5 C2
Passeig de Lluís Companys 2, 08010
Tel 93 309 95 57
Ⓦ ciudadelaparc.com
Family-run establishment with
modest rooms and a restaurant.

Montecarlo €
Historic Map 5 A1
La Rambla 124, 08002
Tel 93 412 04 04
Ⓦ montecarlobcn.com
Located in the heart of the city.
Rooms are modern, well
appointed and reasonably priced.

Barceló Raval €€
Boutique Map 5 A1
Rambla del Raval 17, 08001
Tel 93 320 14 90
Ⓦ barcelo.com
Contemporary hotel in a glassy,
conical building with a
panoramic rooftop terrace.

Casa Camper €€
Boutique Map 2 F2
C/Elisabets 11, 08001
Tel 93 342 62 80
Ⓦ casacamper.com
Eco-friendly hotel in the multi-
cultural Raval neighbourhood.

Duquesa de Cardona €€
Boutique Map 5 A3
Passeig Colom 12, 08002
Tel 93 268 90 90
Ⓦ hduquesadecardona.com
Stylish place with roof terrace
overlooking Port Vell.

Grand Hotel Central €€
Boutique Map 5 B1
Via Laietana 30, 08003
Tel 93 295 79 00
Ⓦ grandhotelcentral.com
Elegant hotel with accommodating
staff. Boasts a fitness centre,
infinity pool and a restaurant
with a Michelin-starred chef.

Hotel Barcelona Catedral €€
Boutique Map 5 A2
C/Capellans 4, 08002
Tel 93 304 22 55
Ⓦ barcelonacatedral.com
Elegant rooms, great location
and service, and a panoramic
roof terrace with plunge pool.

Hotel Denit €€
Boutique Map 5 B1
C/Estruc 24–26, 08002
Tel 93 545 40 00
Ⓦ denit.com
Stylish small hotel in the
Gothic Quarter: great value for
its central location. Rooms are
light, modern and welcoming.

DK Choice

Hotel España €€
Historic Map 2 E3
C/Sant Pau 9–11, 08001
Tel 93 550 00 00
Ⓦ hotelespanya.com
This beautifully restored
Modernista gem dates back to
1859, and now combines
contemporary furnishings with
beautiful early 20th-century
details, including superb
frescoes by Montaner. There is a
fabulous restaurant, a bar with a
swirling Modernista fireplace
and a gorgeous roof terrace.

Beautiful Modernista decor in the dining
room of the Hotel España

Price Guide

Prices are based on one night's stay in
high season for a standard double room,
inclusive of service charges and taxes.

€	up to €125
€€	€125–275
€€€	over €275

Mesón Castilla €€
Historic Map 2 F1
C/Valldonzella 5, 08001
Tel 93 318 21 82
Ⓦ mesoncastilla.com
Old-fashioned, traditional and
welcoming, with comfortable,
good-value rooms.

Musik Boutique Hotel €€
Boutique Map 5 B2
C/Sant Pere mes Baix 62, 08003
Tel 93 222 55 44
Ⓦ musikboutiquehotel.com
Welcoming hotel with an 18th-
century façade. Minimalist rooms
have iPod docks and Wi-Fi.

Hotel 1898 €€€
Luxury Map 5 A1
La Rambla 109, 08002
Tel 93 552 95 52
Ⓦ hotel1898.com
Rooms have colonial decor. Relaxed
atmosphere, central location.

Hotel Bagués €€€
Luxury Map 5 A1
La Rambla 105, 08002
Tel 93 343 50 00.
Ⓦ hotelbagues.com
Barcelona's most celebrated
firm of jewellers are the guiding
force behind this sumptuous,
5-star hotel.

Hotel DO €€€
Boutique Map 5 A3
Plaça Reial 1, 08002
Tel 93 481 36 66
Ⓦ hoteldoreial.com
Gourmet hotel featuring three
outstanding restaurants in an
exquisite 19th-century building.

DK Choice

Hotel Mercer €€€
Luxury Map 5 B3
C/Lledó 7, 08002
Tel 93 310 74 80
Ⓦ mercerbarcelona.com
Chic, exclusive and intimate, this
small hotel occupies a sump-
tuously restored historic mansion that incorporates a section
of the ancient Roman walls.
The old façade belies a contemporary interior; there's a roof
terrace with plunge pool, and a
patio shaded by orange trees.

Hotel Neri €€€
Boutique Map 5 A2
C/Sant Sever 5, 08002
Tel *93 304 06 55*
W hotelneri.com
Enchanting hideaway in an 18th-
century palace with a superb
restaurant and plush interiors.

Ohla €€€
Luxury Map 5 B1
Via Laietana 49, 08003
Tel *93 341 50 50*
W ohlahotel.com
A flamboyant 5-star option, with
a Michelin-starred restaurant.

Eixample

DK Choice

**Close to Passeig de
Gràcia B&B** €
Pension Map 3 A5
C/Diputació 327, 08008
Tel *696 53 14 39*
Named simply for its great
location, this charming, family-
run B&B in an exquisite Modernista building has four huge
rooms featuring a stylish mix of
furnishings. The largest suite has
its own glassed-in gallery and a
fireplace. Guests enjoy breakfast
in the delightful shared kitchen.

Hostal L'Antic Espai €
Pension Map 3 5B
Gran Via de les Corts Catalanes 660,
08010
Tel *93 304 19 45*
W anticespai.com
Breakfast is served on a flower-
filled terrace at this delightful B&B.

Hotel Praktik Bakery €
Boutique Map 3 A3
C/Provença 279, 08037
Tel *93 488 00 61*
W hotelpraktikbakery.com
The smell of freshly baked goods
from the lobby bakery wafts
through this stylish, small hotel.

Room Mate Emma €
Boutique Map 3 A3
C/Rosselló 205, 08008
Tel *93 238 56 06*
W emma.room-matehotels.com
Futuristic design and small but
stylish rooms. Great value.

Circa 1905 €€
Historic Map 3 A3
C/Provença 286, 08008
Tel *93 505 69 50*
W circa1905.com
Exquisite guest rooms in a
beautiful Modernista mansion
at this stylish boutique B&B.

The elegantly decorated interior of Hotel Arts

Hotel Casa Fuster €€
Luxury Map 3 A3
Passeig de Gràcia 132, 08008
Tel *93 255 30 00*
W hotelescenter.es/casafuster
Beautifully restored Modernista
mansion with lavish rooms and
wonderful old-fashioned service.

Hotel Jazz €€
Modern Map 2 F1
C/Pelai 3, 08001
Tel *93 552 96 96*
W hoteljazz.com
One of the best bargains in
the city centre, with spacious,
modern rooms and a rooftop
plunge pool.

Hotel Majestic €€
Luxury Map 3 A3
Passeig de Gràcia 68, 08007
Tel *93 488 17 17*
W hotelmajestic.es
Features elegant rooms and a
roof terrace with plunge pool.

Hotel Omm €€
Luxury Map 3 A3
C/Rosselló 265, 08008
Tel *93 445 40 00*
W hotelomm.es
Boasting one of the most sought-
after addresses in town, with a
restaurant and spa.

DK Choice

Alma €€€
Boutique Map 3 A4
C/Mallorca 271, 08008
Tel *93 216 44 90*
W almabarcelona.com
A fashionably decorated
town house near Gaudí's
La Pedrera, this hotel oozes
understated elegance and is
famed for its excellent service.
Some original 19th-century
details have been preserved,
but the rooms are chic and
minimalist. The glorious secret
courtyard and stylish roof
terrace are ideal for relaxing
after a hard day's sightseeing.

Hotel El Palace €€€
Luxury Map 3 5B
Gran Via de les Corts Catalanes 668,
08010
Tel *93 510 11 30*
W hotelpalacebarcelona.com
This opulent hotel is the grande
dame of Barcelona's hotel scene.

Mandarin Oriental Hotel €€€
Luxury Map 3 A3
Passeig de Gràcia 38-40, 08007
Tel *93 151 88 88*
W mandarinoriental.com
A classy white and gold interior
and a Michelin-starred restaurant.

Further Afield

ABaC €€€
Luxury
Av. Tibidabo 1, 08022
Tel *93 319 66 00*
W abacbarcelona.com
Ultra-chic hotel attached to one
of the finest restaurants in Spain.

DK Choice

Hotel Arts €€€
Luxury Map K9
C/Marina 19–21, 08005
Tel *93 221 10 00*
W hotelartsbarcelona.com
A stunning hotel in a glassy
skyscraper right on the beach.
Outstanding service and
amenities including a Six Senses
Spa, superb restaurants and
bars, and a fabulous collection
of contemporary art.

Catalonia

BAQUEIRA: Hotel Val de Ruda €€
Modern
Urb. Baqueira-Beret Cota 1500, 25598
Tel *973 645 811*
W hotelvalderudabaqueira.com
Traditional hotel with rustic rooms
in Spain's poshest ski resort.

For more information on types of hotels *see page 135*

BEGUR: Hotel Aiguaclara €€
Boutique
C/Sant Miquel 2, 17255
Tel *972 62 29 05*
🅦 **hotelaiguaclara.com**
Romantic getaway in a beautiful
village, with just a handful of rooms.

CADAQUÉS: Hotel Llané Petit €€
Boutique
Platja Llane Petit s/n, 17488
Tel *97 225 10 20*
🅦 **llanepetit.com**
Peaceful, beachfront location
with crisp blue-and-white rooms.

**CAMPRODON: Hotel de
Camprodon** €
Historic
Plaça Doctor Robert 3, 17867
Tel *97 274 00 13*
🅦 **hotelcamprodon.com**
An early 20th-century gem, with
charming Modernista details.

**CANOVES I SAMALUS:
Hotel Can Cuch** €€
Historic
Can Cuch de Muntanya 35, 08445
Tel *93 103 39 80*
🅦 **hotelcancuch.com**
Farmhouse set in the hills of
Montseny, with exquisite guest-
rooms and a fine restaurant.

CARDONA: Hotel Bremon €
Historic
C/Cambres 15, 08261
Tel *938 68 49 02*
🅦 **hotelbremon.com**
Elegantly converted convent, with
a choice of rooms or apartments.

CORÇÀ: Casa Matilda B&B €
Pension
C/Major 31, 17121
Tel *661 03 02 57/972 63 03 61*
🅦 **casamatilda.es**
Enchanting little B&B that serves
home-made cakes at breakfast.

DELTEBRE: Delta Hotel €
Pension
Av. del Canal, Camí de la Illeta, 43580
Tel *977 48 00 46*
🅦 **deltahotel.net**
Family-run rural hotel, a great
base for exploring the Ebro delta.

ERILL LA VALL: Hostal La Plaça €
Pension
Plaza Iglesia s/n, 25528
Tel *973 69 60 26*
🅦 **hostal-laplaza.com**
This old-fashioned guesthouse in
the lovely Vall de Boí occupies a
traditional stone building.

FIGUERES: Hotel Duran €
Modern
C/Lasauca 5, 17600
Tel *972 50 12 50*
🅦 **hotelduran.com**
Comfortable rooms, gardens and
a pool. Famous for its restaurant.

FIGUERES: Hotel Plaza Inn €
Boutique
Pujada del Castell 14, 17600
Tel *972 51 45 40*
🅦 **plazainn.es**
Very near the Dalí museum; Dalí-
themed rooms and great service.

GIRONA: Bellmirall €
Historic
C/Bellmirall 3, 17004
Tel *972 20 40 09*
🅦 **bellmirall.eu**
Simple rooms in an ancient stone
building hidden away in the Call.

**GIRONA: Hotel Ciutat de
Girona** €
Modern
C/Nord 2, 17001
Tel *972 48 30 38*
🅦 **hotelciutatdegirona.com**
Boasts stylish, airy rooms, a great
restaurant and a fabulous central
location. Superb value.

GIRONA: Hotel Peninsular €
Pension
Av. Sant Francesc 6, 17001
Tel *97 220 38 00*
🅦 **novarahotels.com/es/hotel-
peninsular**
Modern hotel with clean and
bright rooms.

**GRANOLLERS: Casa Fonda
Europa** €€
Historic
C/Anselm Clavé 1, 08402
Tel *938 70 03 12*
🅦 **casafondaeuropa.com**
Classic inn with elegant rooms
and a smart restaurant serving
Catalan cuisine.

**LLAFRANC: El Far de Sant
Sebastià** €€
Boutique
Muntanya de Sant Sebastià, 17211
Tel *972 30 16 39*
🅦 **hotelelfar.com**
Charming hotel on a clifftop over-
looking one of the most beautiful
stretches of the Costa Brava.

LLEIDA: Finca Prats Golf & Spa €€
Luxury
N-240, 25198
Tel *902 44 56 66*
🅦 **fincaprats.com**
Five-star hotel with an 18-hole
golf course and impressive spa.

**LLORET DE MAR:
Hotel Maremagnum** €
Pension
C/Areny 29, 17310
Tel *972 36 44 26*
🅦 **maremagnumlloret.com**
Welcoming, family-run budget
option close to the beach, with
simple but comfortable rooms.

**LLORET DE MAR: Sant Pere del
Bosc Hotel & Spa** €€€
Luxury
Paratge Sant Pere del Bosc s/n, 17310
Tel *972 36 16 36*
🅦 **santperedelboschotel.com**
Lavish suites and a spectacular spa
in a rural Modernista villa.

MONTBLANC: Fonda Cal Blasi €
Historic
C/Alenyá 11, 43400
Tel *97 786 13 36*
🅦 **fondacalblasi.com**
Spacious, rustic rooms in a
19th-century building. Wonderful
little restaurant.

MONTSERRAT: Abat Cisneros €€
Modern
Plaça de Montserrat s/n, 08199
Tel *938 77 77 01*
🅦 **montserratvisita.com**
Modest place with comfortable
rooms and spectacular mountain
and valley views.

A well-furnished room in the Hotel Aiguaclara, Begur

Key to Price Guide *see page 136*

OLOT: Les Cols Pavellons €€€
Luxury
Av. de les Cols 2, 17800
Tel *699 81 38 17*
W lescolspavellons.com
Unique contemporary hotel with rooms in glassy cube-shaped pavilions in the garden, and an award-winning restaurant.

PALS: Hotel Restaurante Sa Punta €€
Boutique
Platja de Pals, 17256
Tel *972 63 64 10*
W hotelsapunta.com
In a rural setting near the beach, with an excellent restaurant and lots of luxurious extras.

DK Choice

PLATJA D'ARO: Silken Park Hotel San Jorge €€
Boutique
Av. Andorra 28, 17251
Tel *972 65 23 11*
W hoteles-silken.com
Friendly and relaxed, this elegant hotel on the Costa Brava has comfortable rooms with balconies overlooking the sea from the hotel's clifftop location. Steps lead down the cliff to a perfect little cove fringed with rocks and pine trees.

PRATDIP: Mas Mariassa €€
Boutique
Carretera T-311, Km 30, 43320
Tel *977 26 26 01*
W masmariassa.com
Stylish rural hideaway about 30 minutes' drive from Tarragona, ideal for exploring the Priorat wine area.

REGENCÓS: Hotel Can Casi €€
Boutique
Veinat Puigcalent 7, 17214
Tel *872 00 60 95*
W hotelcancasi.com
Enchanting little country hotel in a pretty village just 10 minutes' drive from the Costa Brava.

RUPIT: Hostal Estrella €
Pension
Plaça Bisbe Font 1, 08569
Tel *938 52 20 05*
W hostalestrella.com
A cosy option in the picture-postcard village of Rupit, with plenty of rustic charm.

S'AGARÓ: Hostal de la Gavina €€€
Luxury
Plaça de la Rosaleda, 17248
Tel *972 32 11 00*
W lagavina.com
Set on a beautiful peninsula between two coves, this handsome hotel oozes Golden Age glamour.

The magnificent façade of Sant Pere del Bosc Hotel & Spa, Lloret de Mar

SANT LLORENÇ DE MORUNYS: El Monegal €
Modern
C/ Monegal s/n, 25282
Tel *973 49 23 69*
W monegal.com
Warm and welcoming country farmhouse with stylish rooms and delicious organic cuisine.

SANTA CRISTINA D'ARO: Mas Tapiolas €€
Boutique
Carretera C-65, Km 7, Veinat de Solius s/n, 17246
Tel *932 83 70 17*
W hotelmastapiolas.com
Gorgeous accommodation in an 18th-century Catalan farmhouse.

SITGES: Hotel Noucentista €
Historic
C/Illa de Cuba 21, 08870
Tel *93 811 00 70*
W hotelnoucentista.com
Gay-friendly hotel in the heart of town, in a Modernista villa with a garden and a pool.

SITGES: Hotel Galeon €€
Boutique
C/Sant Francesc 46, 08870
Tel *93 894 13 79*
W hotelsitges.com
Offers cozy rooms, many with terraces overlooking the sea, and a small pool.

SITGES: Hotel Platjador €€
Modern
Passeig de la Ribera 35–36, Sitges
Tel *938 94 13 79*
W hotelsitges.com
Airy, spacious rooms on the seafront. The rooftop bar has wonderful views out to sea.

TARRAGONA: Hotel Lauria €
Pension
Rambla Nova 20, 43004
Tel *977 23 67 12*
W dormicumhotels.com
Great-value hotel with classically decorated rooms and a pool.

TARRAGONA: Hotel Husa Imperial Tarraco €€
Modern
Passeig Palmeras s/n, 43003
Tel *977 23 30 40*
W hotelhusaimperial.com
Rooms may be a tad dated at this chain hotel, but the panoramic views make it a winner.

TORRENT: Mas de Torrent Hotel & Spa €€€
Historic
Afueras de Torrent s/n, 17123
Tel *902 55 03 21*
W mastorrent.com
A handful of exquisite rooms and an outstanding restaurant in a country *masia*.

TOSSA DE MAR: Hotel Cap d'Or €
Pension
Passeig del Mar 1, 17320
Tel *972 34 00 81*
W hotelcapdor.com
Small hotel in an 18th-century building right on the seafront, with its own bar and waterfront terrace.

TOSSA DE MAR: Hotel Diana €€
Historic
Plaça Espanya 6, 17320
Tel *97 234 18 86*
W hotelesdante.com
Elegant hotel in the town centre, with charming Modernista details.

TRÈDOS: Hotel de Trèdos €€
Boutique
Carretera de Baqueira, Km 177.5, 25598
Tel *973 64 40 14*
W hoteldetredos.com
Mountain-lodge hotel near the Baqueira-Beret ski resort, with charming staff and large rooms.

VALLCLARA: Ca L'Estruch €
Pension
Raval de Vimbodí 8, 43439
Tel *977 05 60 09*
W www.actiweb.es/calestruch
Lovely, family-run rustic B&B with rustic rooms, stone walls, tiled floors and home-cooked food.

For more information on types of hotels *see page 135*

A Glossary of Typical Dishes

Catalan cuisine at its best, using fresh food, is known as *cuina de mercat* (market cuisine) and there is nowhere better to see produce laid out than at Barcelona's La Boqueria market *(see p155)*. Peppers glisten, fish sparkle and no meat is wasted – even cocks' combs are sold for the pot. Olives come in all sorts of varieties. Spring brings *calçot* onions and broad (fava) beans, while strawberries, from Easter onwards, are eaten with *cava*. In autumn, heaps of wild mushrooms spill across the stalls.

Tapes (Tapas – Snacks)

Bar-hopping around Barcelona is a delightful way to spend an evening, and a good way to try the many local dishes laid out on the counters.
Anxoves: anchovies.
Bunyols de bacallà: salt-cod fritters.
Calamars a la romana: fried squid rings.
Escopinyes: cockles.
Pa amb tomàquet: bread rubbed with tomato, garlic and olive oil – a good filler.
Panadons d'espinacs: small spinach pasties or pies.
Patates braves: potato chunks in spicy tomato sauce.
Peixet fregit: small fried fish.
Pernil: ham – leg of pork seasoned and hung to dry.
Popets: baby octopus.
Truita: omelette.
Truita de patates: traditional potato and onion omelette.

Pa amb tomàquet (bread with tomato), often served with ham

Entrants (Starters)

These are often unusual dishes and two may be enough for a meal. Some may appear as main courses.
Amanida catalana: Catalan mixed salad.
Arròs negre: squid-ink rice. Can be a main course.

Produce at La Boqueria, Barcelona's huge covered market on La Rambla

Cargols a la llauna: snails in a spicy sauce.
Empedrat: salad of salt cod and white beans.
Escalivada: chargrilled or roasted aubergines (eggplant) and peppers, all drizzled with olive oil.
Espinacs a la catalana: spinach with pine nuts, raisins and ham; sometimes made with chard *(bledes)*.
Esqueixada: raw salt-cod salad.
Faves a la catalana: a broad (fava) bean stew of black pudding, bacon, onion and garlic.
Fideus: noodles, usually served with fish and meat.
Garotes: raw sea urchins, from the Costa Brava, eaten with bread, garlic or spring onions.
Musclos: mussels.
Ous remenats amb camasecs: scrambled eggs with wild mushrooms.
Pa de fetge: liver pâté.
Sardines escabetxades: pickled sardines.
Xató: salt-cod salad with *romesco* sauce.

Sopes (Soups)

Caldereta de llagosta: spiny-lobster soup.
Escudella i carn d'olla: the liquid from Catalonia's

traditional hotpot; the meat and vegetables *(carn i olla)* are served as a main course.
Gaspatxo: a clear, cold tomato soup with raw vegetables.
Sopa de farigola: thyme soup.
Sopa de bolets: mushroom soup.

Main Dishes

Methods of cooking are: *a la brasa* (over open flames); *bullit* (boiled); *cremat* (crisp-fried or caramelized); *estofat* (stewed); *farcit* (stuffed); *al forn* (in the oven); *a la graella/planxa* (cooked on a griddle, pan-fried or barbecued); *a la pedra* (on a hot stone).

Peix i Mariscos (Fish and Shellfish)

Allipebre d'anguiles: spicy eel stew.
Anfós al forn: baked stuffed grouper.
Calamars farcits: squid stuffed with pork, tomatoes and onions.
Cassola de peix: fish casserole.
Congre amb pèsols: conger eel with peas.
Escamarlans bullits: boiled crayfish.
Gambes a la planxa: prawns cooked on a griddle.
Graellada de peix: mixed seafood grill.
Llagosta a la brasa: lobster cooked over open flames.
Llagostins amb maionesa: king prawns and mayonnaise.
Llobarro al forn: baked sea bass.
Lluç a la planxa: hake cooked on a griddle.
Molls a la brasa: red mullet cooked over open flames.
Orada a la sal: gilthead bream baked in salt, which is removed on serving.
Paella Valenciana: paella with chicken and seafood.
Peix amb romesco: seafood with the famous *romesco* sauce. Tarragona's master *romesco* makers compete each summer.
Rap a l'all cremat: angler fish with crisped garlic.
Sarsuela: fish, shellfish and spices, everything goes into the pot that gives its name to a light Spanish opera.

Sèpia amb pèsols: cuttlefish with peas.

Suquet de peix: Catalonia's principal fish stew, made with various fish, tomatoes, peppers, potatoes and almonds.

Verats a la brasa: mackerel cooked over open flames.

Carn (Meat)

Ànec amb naps: duck with turnips, ideally the "black" turnips of the Empordà region; also sometimes served with pears *(ànec amb peres)*.

Boles de picolat: meatballs in tomato sauce. Meatballs with cuttlefish *(sèpia)* is classic *mar i muntanya* food.

Botifarra amb mongetes: sausage and beans.

Bou a l'adoba: beef casserole.

Costelles a la brasa amb allioli: flame-roast lamb cutlets with garlic mayonnaise.

Costelles de cabrit rostides: roast goat (kid cutlets).

Cuixa de xai al forn: roast leg of lamb.

Estofat de bou: beef stew with sausages, potatoes, herbs and sometimes a little chocolate.

Estofat de quaresma: a filling bean and potato Lenten vegetable stew.

Freginat: calf's liver with onions.

Fricandó: braised veal with wild mushrooms.

Llom de porc: pork chops.

Oca amb peres: goose with pears – traditional village festival fare.

Niu: a huge fish and meat stew from Palafrugell, Costa Brava, with pigeon, cuttlefish, cod tripe, pig's trotters, egg and garlic mayonnaise.

Peus de porc a la llauna: pig's trotters in a spicy sauce.

Pollastre amb samfaina: chicken with *samfaina*.

Pota i tripa: lamb's trotters and tripe.

Tripa a la catalana: tripe in *sofregit* and wine with pine nuts and almonds.

Xai amb pèsols: lamb with peas.

Barcelona's cheese and honey market *(see p155)* in the Plaça del Pi

Caça (Game)

Although the hunting season is from October to February, some game is available all year round, especially rabbit.

Becada amb coc: woodcock in a bread roll.

Civet de llebre: jugged hare.

Conill a la brasa amb allioli: rabbit with garlic mayonnaise.

Conill amb cargols: rabbit with snails.

Conill amb xocolata: rabbit with garlic, liver, almonds, fried bread, chocolate and old wine.

Aubergines (eggplant) and peppers, used in abundance

Estofat de porc senglar amb bolets: wild boar casserole with wild mushrooms.

Guatlles amb salsa de magrana: quail in pomegranate sauce.

Perdiu: partridge.

Perdius amb farcellets de col: partridge with cabbage dumplings.

Verdures (Vegetables)

Albergínies: aubergines (eggplant).

Bledes: chard.

Bolets: mushrooms.

Calçots: leek-sized green onions, roasted on an open fire and dipped in a spicy tomato sauce. A springtime speciality of the Tarragona region.

Carbassó arrebossat: battered courgettes (zucchini).

Carxofes: artichokes.

Julivert: parsley.

Mongetes tendres i patates: French beans and potatoes.

Pastanagues: carrots.

Pebrots: red peppers.

Postres (Desserts)

Although *pastisseria* (pastries) and *dolços* (sweets) are very popular in Catalonia, desserts in restaurants are generally uneventful. The choice may be simply ice cream or fruit: apple *(poma)*, peach *(préssec)*, banana *(plàtan)* or grape *(raïm)*.

Crema catalana: rich egg custard.

Figues amb aniset: figs in anise.

Flam: crème caramel.

Formatge: cheese. There is little local cheese.

Gelat: ice cream.

Mel i mató: fresh goat's cheese, eaten with honey.

Menjar blanc: an almond blancmange.

Peres amb vi negre: pears in red wine.

Postre de músic: a bowl of mixed nuts and dried fruit, once given as a reward to itinerant musicians.

Recuit: curdled sheep's (or cow's) milk in a small pot.

Mel i mató – a traditional dessert of soft cheese served with honey

Once the haunt of artists, Els Quatre Gats (The Four Cats) is an iconic Barcelona rendezvous

Barraca   €€
Mediterranean   **Map** 5 C5
Passeig Marítim de la Barceloneta 1, 08003
Tel *93 224 12 53*
With prestigious chef Xavier Pellicer at the helm, this serves one of the best paellas in the city, and has a fabulous beachfront location to boot.

La Bella Napoli   €€
Italian   **Map** 2 D3
C/Margarit 14, 08004
Tel *93 442 50 56*
Italian-run pizzeria with authentic pizzas cooked to perfection in a wood-burning stove. Popular, so book ahead.

Brasserie Flo   €€
Traditional Catalan   **Map** 5 B1
C/Jonqueres 10, 08001
Tel *93 319 31 02*   **Closed** *Mon*
Elegant brasserie with *fin-de-siècle* decor. Serves classic Catalan cuisine with a French twist and sumptuous home-made desserts.

Ca l'Isidre   €€
Traditional Catalan   **Map** 2 E3
C/Flors 12, 08001
Tel *93 441 11 39*   **Closed** *Sun*
Family-owned tavern, famous

for classic Catalan dishes prepared with superb local produce. Excellent wine cellar.

Cal Pep   €€
Tapas   **Map** 5 B3
Plaça des les Olles 8, 08003
Tel *93 310 79 61* **Closed** *Sat dinner, Sun, Mon lunch*
Long-established, characterful bar serving a selection of freshly made tapas.

Can Majó   €€
Mediterranean   **Map** 5 B5
C/Almirall Aixada 23, 08003
Tel *93 221 54 55* **Closed** *Sun dinner, Mon*
Great seafood restaurant in Barceloneta; the paella is fabulous. The terrace has sea views.

Can Solé   €€
Seafood   **Map** 5 B4
C/Sant Carles 4, 08003
Tel *93 221 50 12* **Closed** *Sun & Mon dinner*
Traditional restaurant with a pretty tiled interior. The menu features classic rice dishes and stews featuring a variety of seafood.

Cuines Santa Caterina   €€
Modern Catalan   **Map** 5 B2
Av. Francesc Cambó 16, 08003
Tel *93 268 99 18*
Tasty cuisine prepared with seasonal ingredients freshly bought from the adjoining market. Try the baby squid and bean salad.

Espai Sucre   €€
Desserts   **Map** 5 C2
C/Princesa 53, 08003
Tel *93 268 16 30* **Closed** *lunch; all day Sun & Mon*
Prestigious cooking school with a restaurant that has menus composed entirely of exquisite sweet and savoury desserts.

Gravin   €€
Italian   **Map** 5 B3
C/Rera Palau 3–5, 08003
Tel *93 268 46 28*   **Closed** *Mon & Tue lunch*
Sophisticated Italian food such as *taglino al limone* (pasta with lemon and hake) from the Puglia region in an elegant dining room.

Llamber   €€
Tapas   **Map** 5 C2
C/Fusina 5, 08003
Tel *93 319 62 50* **Closed** *Mon & Tue*
An outpost of an award-winning Asturian restaurant, this stylish gastro-bar serves beautifully presented tapas prepared with fresh, local ingredients.

The brightly lit contemporary interior at Espai Sucre

Lu de Flor
€€
Mediterranean **Map** 2 E2
C/Carretes 18, 08001
Tel *93 442 38 53*
Romantic, rustic restaurant with minimalist decor and delicious Mediterranean fare. Short but well-chosen wine list.

Mam i Teca
€€
Modern Catalan **Map** 2 F2
C/Lluna 4, 08001
Tel *93 441 33 35* **Closed** *Tue*
Mam i Teca serves fantastic Catalan dishes prepared with superb, locally sourced produce. Excellent wine list and a good range of Scottish single malts.

La Mar Salada
€€
Mediterranean **Map** 2 B5
Passeig Joan Borbó 58–59, 08003
Tel *93 221 10 15* **Closed** *Tue*
Bright, modern seafood restaurant in Barceloneta with views across the port. Fantastic set lunch.

Montiel
€€
Modern Catalan **Map** 5 C2
C/Flassaders 19, Born, 08003
Tel *93 268 37 29*
Charming restaurant with dishes inspired by locally sourced produce. Do not miss the wonderfully tender *garrinet* (suckling pig).

Pez Vela
€€
Mediterranean
Passeig del Mare Nostrum 19, 08039
Tel *93 221 63 17* **Closed** *Sun dinner*
Fashionable spot on the beach serving a range of cuisine but strong on fresh salads and rice dishes. The set paella menu is great value for money.

Pla
€€
Fusion **Map** 2 F2
C/Bellafila 5, 08002
Tel *93 412 65 52* **Closed** *lunch*
Hidden down a narrow street in the Gothic Quarter, this reliable restaurant offers deftly prepared fusion cuisine in stylish surroundings. Tasting menu available.

The intimate and authentic dining area at Suculent

Els Quatre Gats
€€
Traditional Catalan **Map** 5 A1
C/Montsió 3 bis, 08002
Tel *93 302 41 40*
Beautifully restored tavern, decorated with original works of early 20th-century artists. Young Picasso held his first show here. The food is delicious; the pork cheek with prawn is superb.

Quimet i Quimet
€€
Tapas **Map** 2 E4
C/Poeta Cabanyes 25, 08004
Tel *93 442 31 42* **Closed** *Sun; Aug*
Tiny but charming *bodega* with bottles displayed up to the ceiling. Delicious cheeses and canapés.

Senyor Parellada
€€
Mediterranean **Map** S3
C/Argenteria 37, 08003
Tel *93 310 50 94*
Elegant restaurant in a handsome 19th-century townhouse. The creative menu includes trotters with cuttlefish and grilled baby squid pan-fried with chorizo. Reserve in advance.

DK Choice

Suculent
€€
Tapas **Map** 2 F3
Rambla de Raval 43, 08001
Tel *93 443 65 79* **Closed** *Mon, Sun dinner*
A pretty old *bodega* reinvented as a trendy gastro bar by a trio of celebrity chefs. Suculent offers a range of creative tapas, platters of carefully selected cheeses and cured meats, as well as more substantial fare, such as lamb chops and rice dishes.

El Suquet de l'Almirall
€€
Mediterranean **Map** 5 B5
Passeig Joan de Borbó 65, 08003
Tel *93 321 62 33* **Closed** *Sun*
Classic Spanish seafood restaurant offering fresh fish brought in daily from the quays near the restaurant.

Delicious tapas is served at the bar at Dos Palillos

DK Choice

Café de L'Acadèmia
€€€
Modern Catalan **Map** 5 B3
C/Lledó 1, Plaça Sant Just, 08002
Tel *93 319 82 53* **Closed** *Sat, Sun*
A long-established favourite, Café de L'Acadèmia offers tasty, modern Catalan cuisine in a cozy brick-lined dining room. The menu changes regularly based on what is freshly available in the market. Spectacular desserts. Book a table on the atmospheric, candle-lit terrace overlooking the enchanting Gothic square.

Comerç 24
€€€
Modern Catalan **Map** 5 C2
C/Comerç 24, 08003
Tel *93 319 21 02* **Closed** *Sun & Mon*
Tapas bar with daring and sophisticated gastronomy from the Catalan chef Carles Abellán. Reservations necessary.

Dos Palillos
€€€
Tapas **Map** 2 F2
EC/lisabets 9, 08001
Tel *93 304 05 13* **Closed** *Sun & Mon*
Ultra-chic yet relaxed restaurant with a Michelin star. Serves spectacular Asian fusion tapas.

Koy Shunka
€€€
Japanese **Map** 5 B3
C/Copons 7, 08002
Tel *93 412 79 39* **Closed** *Mon, Sun dinner*
Widely regarded as the best Japanese restaurant in the city, this stylish place features a menu that ranges from classic dishes to more inventive fare.

Quo Vadis
€€€
Traditional Catalan **Map** 2 F2
C/Carme 7, 08001
Tel *93 302 40 72*
Long-established and authentic French-Catalan restaurant. A favourite for a pre-opera dinner. Try the house soup.

For more information on types of restaurants *see page 140–41*

The sleek, modern dining area at the popular Saüc restaurant

Saüc   €€€
Mediterranean   **Map** 5 B3
Via Laietana 49, 08003
Tel *93 321 01 89*
Relish award-winning creative cuisine by the Michelin-starred Chef Xavier Franco in the über-chic surroundings of the Ohla Hotel. Reservations essential.

Eixample

Bar Calders   €
Café   **Map** 2 D2
C/Parlament 25, 08015
Tel *93 329 93 49*
Dedicated to the Catalan writer Pere Calders, this place is a great spot for a vermouth. The menu includes delicious tapas, hummus and salads. Small pretty terrace.

La Bodegueta   €
Tapas   **Map** 3 A3
Rambla de Catalunya 100, 08008
Tel *93 215 48 94*   **Closed** *Sun lunch*
A good-value tapas bar with marble-topped tables and wooden cabinets in an antique wine cellar. The menu includes classics such as *patates braves*, Iberian cold cuts and *esqueixada*.

El Filete Ruso   €
Gourmet burgers   **Map** 3 B3
C/Enric Granados 95, 08008
Tel *93 217 13 10*   **Closed** *mid-Aug*
The food here is made with organic and locally sourced produce. The menu features grilled gourmet burgers, including a vegetarian option, and handcrafted desserts.

Can Ravell   €€
Traditional Catalan   **Map** H4
C/Aragó 313
Tel *93 457 51 14*   **Closed** *Sun*
A delicatessen-cum-restaurant where guests share one huge table under a chandelier and dine on Catalan classics. Well-stocked vintage wine cellar.

Casa Alfonso   €€
Traditional Catalan   **Map** 3 B5
C/Roger de Llúria 6, 08010
Tel *93 301 97 83*   **Closed** *Sun*
This cozy restaurant features hanging hams and checked tablecloths. Try the sumptuous sausages, croquettes and tapas on offer. A great spot for lunch.

Ikibana   €€
Japanese/Brazilian   **Map** 2 D2
Av. del Paral.lel 148, 08015
Tel *93 424 46 48*
A striking interior and Japanese-Brazilian fusion cuisine have made this one of Barcelona's hottest restaurants. The menu includes a variety of wines and sake.

Monvínic   €€
Modern Catalan   **Map** 3 A5
C/ Diputació 249, 08007
Tel *93 272 61 87*   **Closed** *Sat & Sun*
A staggering selection of wines in the large, stylish wine bar and delicious modern cuisine in the dining room.

Petit Comitè   €€
Modern Catalan   **Map** 3 A3
Passeig de la Concepció 13, 08008
Tel *93 550 06 20*   **Closed** *Mon*
Modern Catalan fare with a dash of French aplomb is on offer here. Excellent wine list.

Tapas 24   €€
Tapas   **Map** 3 A5
C/Diputació 269, 08007
Tel *93 488 09 77*   **Closed** *Sun*
Inventive selection of fantastic tapas by chef Carles Abellan. Try delicacies such as Bikini Comerç 24 and the Mcfoie burger.

Tickets   €€
Designer tapas   **Map** 1 C2
Av. Paral·lel 164, 08015
Tel *606 22 55 45*   **Closed** *Mon & Tue; mid-Aug, late Dec–early Jan*
An unmissable destination for devotees of the cuisine created by the Adrià brothers, with a quirky, funfair-themed interior.

Booking is essential and must be made online (www.ticketsbar. es); the phone number is just for last-minute cancellations.

Caldeni   €€€
Modern Catalan   **Map** 3 C4
C/València 452, 08013
Tel *93 232 58 11*   **Closed** *Sun & Mon*
Fantastic contemporary cuisine from Dani Lechuga, a rising young chef on Barcelona's culinary scene. Try the "Meat Special Selection" menu, which features dishes prepared with wagyu Kobe and Nebraska Angus beef.

Casa Calvet   €€€
Traditional Catalan   **Map** 3 B5
C/Casp 48, 08010
Tel *93 412 40 12*   **Closed** *Sun*
One of Antoni Gaudí's earliest commissions, this Modernista building now houses a restaurant. A changing menu of modern cooking is executed with panache.

Cinc Sentits   €€€
Modern Catalan   **Map** 2 F1
C/Aribau 58, 08011
Tel *93 323 94 90*   **Closed** *Sun & Mon*
Exquisite Catalan cuisine by Michelin-starred chef Jordi Artal. Your dining choices comprise a trio of set menus: *gastronòmic*, *essència* and *sensaciones*.

Softly lit dining room at Cinc Sentits

Elegant interior of the classy Roca Moo

Fonda Gaig €€€
Modern Catalan
Còrcega 200, 08036
Tel 93 453 20 20
Smart bistro with stylish modern decor, serving sophisticated local cuisine by one of the city's top chefs, Carles Gaig.

Moments €€€
Modern Catalan **Map** 3 A5
Passeig de Gràcia 38–40, 08007
Tel 93 151 87 81 **Closed** Sun & Mon
Glamorous restaurant situated in the Mandarin Oriental hotel. The mouthwatering, multi-award-winning menu is created by superchef Carme Ruscalleda.

L'Olivé €€€
Modern Catalan **Map** 3 A4
Balmes 47, 08007
Tel 93 452 19 90 **Closed** Sun dinner
Classic restaurant offering fine Catalan fare prepared with whatever is freshest at the market. Wide variety of delicious home-made desserts.

Roca Moo €€€
Modern Catalan **Map** 3 A3
Rosselló 265, 08008
Tel 93 445 40 00 **Closed** Sun & Mon
This ultra-chic restaurant in Hotel Omm features a menu overseen by the Roca brothers of El Celler de Can Roca (see p152). Try one of the three fine tasting menus with matching wines.

Tragaluz €€€
Mediterranean **Map** 3 A3
Passatge de la Concepció 5, 08008
Tel 93 487 06 21
Chic uptown restaurant with a huge skylight. Offers a wide-ranging menu of Mediterranean fare. The ground floor features an oyster bar and a Japanese natural charcoal barbecue grill.

Windsor €€€
Modern Catalan
C/Còrsega 286, 08080
Tel 93 237 75 88 **Closed** Sun
Contemporary Catalan haute cuisine is served here. The menu is based on seasonal local produce. Dine in elegant surroundings with chandeliers. There's also a pretty garden for alfresco dining.

Further Afield

Café Adonis 1940 €
Café **Map** 3 C3
C/Bailèn 188, Gràcia, 08037
Tel 93 459 12 92
Wonderfully old fashioned, split level café-bar with a simple menu featuring great burgers, salads and sandwiches.

Cafè Godot €
Mediterranean **Map** 3 B2
C/Sant Domènec 19, Gràcia, 08012
Tel 93 368 20 36
Stylish modern café serving bistro-style food with a contemporary twist, including a great brunch at the weekends.

Cafè Pagès €
Café **Map** 3 C2
C/Torrent de l'Olla 27, 08012
Tel 93 368 09 58
A Gràcia favourite with retro-style decor, Café Pagès offers a tasty and affordable set-lunch menu. Come here for great home-made cakes and coffee.

Café Salambó €
Café **Map** 3 C2
C/Torrijos 51, 08012
Tel 93 218 69 66
This large, split-level café with pool tables is a popular neighbourhood haunt. Serves

everything from a good daily set lunch to cocktails in the evening. Regular live music.

Cal Boter €
Traditional Catalan **Map** 3 C2
C/Tordera 62, 08012
Tel 93 458 84 62 **Closed** Sun dinner, Mon
An excellent place for Catalan comfort food. The menu includes traditional carns a la brasa (grilled meats) and local sausages. Fantastic set lunch.

DK Choice

Gut €
Mediterranean **Map** 3 B2
C/Perill 13, Gràcia, 08012
Tel 93 186 63 60
Arrive early for a seat at this charming, light and airy restaurant, where tasty, healthy food, some Asian-influenced and with vegetarian and gluten-free options, is prepared daily with market-fresh ingredients. They also serve delicious home-made cakes, perfect for an afternoon break.

Kathmandú €
Nepalese **Map** 3 C3
C/Còrsega 421, 08037
Tel 93 459 37 69
Sample tasty, aromatic Nepalese dishes including barbecued meat, thalis and spicy curries. Great-value lunch menu.

Abou Khalil €€
Lebanese
C/Santaló 88, 08021
Tel 93 201 88 30
Barcelona's first Lebanese restaurant is also its best, serving delicious eastern Mediterranean dishes. Live music and dance some nights.

The simple dining area at Tragaluz, chic restaurant in the Eixample

For more information on types of restaurants see page 140–41

Acontraluz €€
Mediterranean
C/Milanesat 19, Sarrià, 08017
Tel *93 203 06 58* **Closed** *Sun dinner*
Well off the tourist trail, this has
an enchanting garden, a
retractable roof and refined
cuisine, redolent of sun and sea.

Casa de Tapes Cañota €€
Tapas **Map** 1 B2
C/Lleida 7, 08004
Tel *93 325 91 71* **Closed** *Sun dinner,
Mon*
The big and bustling Casa de
Tapes Cañota near Montjuïc
serves freshly made gourmet
tapas such as succulent beef with
garlic and a seafood basket.

Envalira €€
Mediterranean **Map** 3 B1
Plaça del Sol 13, 08012
Tel *93 218 58 13* **Closed** *Sun dinner,
Mon; Aug*
A family-run restaurant with a
laid-back ambience. The menu
includes delicious Mediterranean
rice dishes and Galician shellfish.
Attentive service.

Kuai Momos €€
Fusion **Map** 3 B2
C/Martínez de la Rosa 71, Gràcia,
08012
Tel *93 218 53 27* **Closed** *Sun*
A chic, buzzy restaurant serving
Asian tapas such as gyoza, salads,
curries and rice dishes.

Tram-Tram €€
Modern Catalan
C/Major de Sarrià 121, 08017
Tel *93 204 85 18* **Closed** *Sun dinner,
Mon lunch*
A smart, welcoming interior and a
delightful terrace are the setting
for classic Catalan favourites
prepared with a modern twist by
young chef Isidre Soler.

The cool, vaulted dining space of Michelin-starred ABaC

La Venta €€
Traditional Catalan
Plaça del Doctor Andreu s/n, 08035
Tel *93 212 64 55* **Closed** *Sun dinner*
Enjoy flavourful local cuisine
with stunning panaromic views
of the city. This restaurant is
housed in a 19th-century
Modernista building on the
slopes of Tibidabo.

Wagokoro €€
Japanese **Map** 3 A1
C/Regàs 35, 08006
Tel *93 501 93 40* **Closed** *Sun & Mon*
Fantastic, authentic Japanese
food and beverages such as
nihonshu (sake), shochu (spirit)
and umeshu (fruit liqueur) served
in a simple dining room by a
charming couple.

ABaC €€€
Modern Catalan
Av. Tibidabo 1, 08022
Tel *93 319 66 00* **Closed** *Sun & Mon*
Outstanding cuisine from young
chef Jordi Cruz, which has earned
him two Michelin stars. Enjoy
delicacies such as smoked steak
tartare and veil of mustard and
pepper bread brittle.

Alkimia €€€
Modern Catalan **Map** 3 C2
C/Indústria 79, 08025
Tel *93 207 61 15* **Closed** *Sat, Sun,
Easter, 3 weeks in Aug & Christmas*
This small designer restaurant
offers an unforgettable culinary
experience from one of the city's
most popular chefs, Jordi Vilà.
Feast on dishes such as noras
rice with saffron and fresh
langoustine.

La Balsa €€€
Mediterranean
C/Infanta Isabel 4, 08022
Tel *93 211 50 48* **Closed** *Sun dinner,
Mon*
Escape the hustle of the city at
this relaxed garden oasis. Sample
fresh Mediterranean cuisine on a
leafy, plant-filled terrace.

Botafumeiro €€€
Seafood **Map** 3 A2
C/Gran de Gràcia 81, 08012
Tel *93 218 42 30*
Large, traditional restaurant with
white-aproned waiters bearing
platters of ultra-fresh fish to the
crowded tables. Try the tender
pulpo Gallego (Galician octopus).

Con Gracia €€€
European **Map** 3 B2
C/Martínez de la Rosa 8, 08012
Tel *93 238 02 01* **Closed** *Sat dinner,
Sun & Mon; Christmas*
Creative cuisine based on fresh
market produce served in a series
of sophisticated set menus. Try
the wine-tasting menu, where
each course is paired with a wine.

Hisop €€€
Modern Catalan
Passatge de Marimon 9, 08021
Tel *93 241 32 33* **Closed** *Sat lunch,
Sun; early Jan & early Aug*
Minimalist natural-wood decor
ensures the focus is firmly on
food at Hisop, where the
experimental cuisine is always a
treat. Excellent wine list with
Catalan and Spanish vintages.

Els Pescadors €€€
Seafood
Plaça de Prim 1, 08005
Tel *93 225 20 18*
Elegant fish restaurant in Poble
Nou. Reserve a table on the
charming terrace, which over-
looks a picturesque square
and tuck into beautifully fresh
seafood and classic Catalan
rice dishes.

Roig Robí €€€
Modern Catalan **Map** 3 A2
C/Sèneca 20, 08006
Tel *93 218 92 22* **Closed** *Sat lunch,
Sun; late Aug*
Enjoy exquisite Catalan cuisine in
elegant surroundings. Good
selection of bacalà (salt-cod)
dishes. Romantic garden terrace
for summer dining.

Minimalist but intimate dining room
at Wagokoro

Catalonia

ANGLÈS: L'Aliança D'Anglès €€
Modern Catalan
C/Jacint Verdaguer 3, 17160
Tel *972 42 01 56* **Closed** *Mon; Sun, Tue & Wed dinner*
Fantastic, creative cuisine in an early 20th-century villa, surrounded by gardens. Superb selection of Spanish wines.

ARTIES: Casa Irene €€€
Traditional Catalan
C/Major 3, 25599
Tel *973 64 43 64* **Closed** *Mon*
Elegant stone-built hotel and restaurant with an exquisite menu. A perfect place to dine after a day on the nearby ski slopes.

BANYOLES: Ca L'Arpa €€€
Modern Catalan
Passeig Industria 5, 17820
Tel *972 57 23 53*
Excellent Michelin-starred restaurant within a chic hotel in the historic Banyoles quarter. Patrons can see their food being prepared.

BEGUR: Fonda Caner €€
Traditional Catalan
C/Pi i Ralló 10, Costa Brava, 17255
Tel *972 62 23 91*
Traditional restaurant with old-fashioned charm tucked away in Begur's old quarter. Serves seasonal cuisine. Enjoy the mixed seafood stew.

BEGUR: Restaurant Rostei €€
Mediterranean
C/Concepció Pi 8, Costa Brava, 17255
Tel *972 62 42 15* **Closed** *Mon; Tue– Sat lunch; in winter open Fri & Sat lunch only*
Romantic, family-run restaurant that serves tasty seafood and fantastic desserts.

BESALÚ: Cúria Reial €€
Traditional Catalan
Plaça de la Llibertat 14, 17850
Tel *972 59 02 63*
Delicious food is served in a beautiful historic building under stone vaults. Try the duck with foie gras and *coca d'escalivada*.

CALDES D'ESTRAC: Marola €€
Seafood
Passeig dels Anglesos 6, 08393
Tel *93 791 32 00* **Closed** *Tue; Sun– Thu dinner*
Modest yet charming beachfront restaurant in Caldes d'Estrac. The ideal setting to enjoy fresh seafood and paella.

CAMBRILS: Can Bosch €€€
Seafood
Rambla Jaume I 19, 43850
Tel *977 36 00 19* **Closed** *Sun dinner, Mon; late Dec–late Jan*
Smart restaurant overlooking the port. Great seafood prepared with a contemporary twist. Patrons rave about the *arroz negro* (rice cooked in squid ink).

EL BRULL: El Castell del Brull €
Traditional Catalan
Camino el Castell s/n, 08559
Tel *938 84 00 63* **Closed** *Wed; Tue, Thu & Sun dinner*
This rustic country restaurant is set in pretty gardens, and serves classic Catalan dishes such as succulent roast lamb, as well as wild boar in season.

ESCUNHAU: El Niu €€
Traditional Catalan
Deth Pònt 1, 25539
Tel *973 64 14 06*
Traditional mountain inn in picturesque Escunhau. The menu features classic local cuisine, especially grilled meats. Open fireplace in winter.

Elegant interior of the Hotel Emporada's El Motel restaurant in Figueres

FALSET: El Celler de l'Aspic €€
Traditional Catalan
C/Miquel Barceló 31, 43730
Tel *977 83 12 46* **Closed** *Sun dinner, Wed*
Charming, rustic restaurant with delicious, seasonal dishes made using locally sourced organic produce. Extensive selection of regional wines.

FIGUERES: El Motel €€€
Traditional Catalan
Av. Salvador Dalí 170, 17600
Tel *972 50 05 62*
Located in the Hotel Emporada, this elegant restaurant enjoys a fine reputation for serving classic regional cuisine. Great wine list. Excellent fixed-price menu.

GARRAF: La Cúpula €€
Seafood
Platja de Garraf, 08871
Tel *936 32 00 15* **Closed** *Mon & Tue*
With a splendid clifftop setting overlooking the pretty Garraf beach, La Cúpula is a great place for a fish lunch.

The brightly lit simple dining area at El Celler de l'Aspic in Falset

For more information on types of restaurants *see page 140–41*

GIRONA: Divinum €€
Tapas
C/Albereda 7, 17004
Tel *872 08 02 18* **Closed** *Sun, Mon dinner*
Chic, contemporary restaurant serving inventive tapas, accompanied by an excellent selection of wines.

DK Choice

GIRONA: El Celler de Can Roca €€€
Modern Catalan
C/Can Sunyer 48, 17007
Tel *972 22 21 57* **Closed** *Sun, Mon, Easter, mid-Aug & Christmas*
Voted regularly as one of the world's top restaurants, El Celler de Can Roca is a temple to molecular gastronomy and boasts three Michelin stars. The place is run by the three Roca brothers: Joan is head chef, Jordi is dessert chef and Josep is the sommelier. Expect innovative dishes such as caramelized olives served on a bonsai tree and oysters with champagne.

HORTA DE SANT JOAN: Mas del Cigarrer €
Traditional Catalan
Ctra Horta de Sant Joan a Bot, 43596
Tel *977 43 51 53* **Closed** *Mon– Wed & Thu dinner in winter*
Charming country restaurant famous for *calçots* (a barbecued leek-like Catalan spring vegetable) and *cargols* – wild snails.

L'AMETLLA DE MAR: L'Alguer €€
Seafood
C/Trafalgar 21, 43860
Tel *977 45 61 24* **Closed** *Mon; mid Dec–mid Jan*
Enjoy fresh seafood with sea views in this waterfront dining room with door-to-ceiling glass windows. Great value set lunch.

L'ESPLUGA DE FRANCOLÍ: Hostal del Senglar €€
Traditional Catalan
Plaça Montserrat Canals 1, 43440
Tel *977 87 04 11*
Excellent hotel-restaurant near the Monestir de Poblet. Great for flame-grilled meats and hearty country dishes.

LLAGOSTERA: Els Tinars €€€
Modern Catalan
Ctra de Sant Feliu a Girona, 17240
Tel *972 83 06 26* **Closed** *Sun dinner, Mon*
Superb contemporary cuisine by an award-winning young chef in an elegant dining room and shaded terrace. Good set menus.

Diners can watch their food being prepared at La Huerta in Lleida

LLEIDA: La Huerta €€
Traditional Catalan
Av. Tortosa 7, 25005
Tel *973 24 24 13*
Delicious local dishes such as fine winter stews, grilled fresh fish and wild mushrooms in season. Warm and friendly service.

LLEIDA: L'Estel de la Mercè €€
Modern Catalan
C/Cardenal Cisneros 30, 25002
Tel *973 28 80 08* **Closed** *Mon, Sun dinner*
A bright, modern hotel-restaurant with a gastro tapas bar, L'Estel de la Mercè serves fresh, contemporary Catalan cuisine.

MONTSENY: Can Barrina €€
Traditional Catalan
Carretera Palautordera al Montseny, Km. 12, 08469
Tel *93 867 91 44*

Beautiful country restaurant and hotel located in the Montseny Natural Park. Wonderful food.

PERALADA: Cal Sagristà €€
Traditional Catalan
C/Rodona 2, 17491
Tel *972 53 83 01*
Scrumptious Catalan cuisine served in a restored old convent. Save room for dessert.

RIPOLL: Reccapolis €€
Traditional Catalan
C/Sant Joan 68, 17500
Tel *972 70 21 06* **Closed** *Sun–Thu dinner, Wed lunch*
Enjoy savoury country favourites in a handsome 20th-century house with a garden. Excellent set lunch and takeaway menu. Efficient and attentive service.

ROMANYÀ DE LA SELVA: Can Roquet €€
Modern Catalan
Plaça de l'Esglesia, 17246
Tel *972 83 30 81*
A beautiful country restaurant run by two Belgians, this has tasty modern French and Catalan cuisine and a charming terrace.

ROSES: Rafa's €€€
Seafood
C/Sant Sebastià 56, 17480
Tel *972 25 40 03*
Informal, convivial and immensely popular seafood restaurant. A favourite with the chef Ferran Adrià of El Bulli fame. The menu changes daily.

SANT CARLES DE LA RÀPITA: Miami Ca Pons €€
Seafood
Passeig Marítim 18–20, 43540
Tel *977 74 05 51*
Classic seafront restaurant in the Hotel Miami Mar offering great-value and quality seafood.

The airy, modern interior of El Celler de Can Roca

SANT FELIU DE GUÍXOLS:
Bahía €€
Seafood
Passeig del Mar 17–19, 17320
Tel *972 32 02 19*
Beachfront restaurant serving local specialities from this region of the Costa Brava, such as *brandada de bacallà* (cod pureed with olive oil) and *cim-i-tomba* (fish stew).

SANT FELIU DE GUÍXOLS:
Cau Del Pescador €€
Seafood
C/Sant Doménec 11, 17220
Tel *972 32 40 52*   **Closed** *Mon, and Tue in winter*
Smart, family-run fish restaurant with rustic decor set in an old fisherman's cottage. Do not miss the famous *suquet* (seafood stew).

SANT FELIU DE GUÍXOLS:
Villa Más €€€
Traditional Catalan
Passeig de Sant Pol 95, 17220
Tel *972 82 25 26*   **Closed** *Mon except Jun–Aug; early Dec–early Jan*
Enchanting 19th-century villa overlooking the Sant Pol beach. Serves outstanding Catalan cuisine and a fine selection of wines.

SANT JOAN DE LES ABADESSES:
Casa Rudes €
Traditional Catalan
C/Major 10, 17860
Tel *972 72 01 15*
Established in 1893 and still a popular local favourite for classic Catalan dishes. Children's menu.

SANT POL DE MAR: Sant Pau €€€
Modern Catalan
C/Nou 10, 08395
Tel *93 760 06 62*   **Closed** *Sun, Mon, Thu lunch; also first three weeks of May & Nov*
Top chef Carme Ruscalleda works her magic at one of Spain's best

Warm dining area at Sant Pau in Sant Pol de Mar

restaurants. Marvel at wonderful dishes created from delicate courgette flowers, wild boar and *espardenyes* (sea cucumber).

SANT SADURNÍ D'ANOIA:
La Cava d'en Sergi €€
Modern Catalan
C/València 17, 08770
Tel *93 891 16 16*   **Closed** *Mon, last Sun of the month; 1 Jan, Easter, first three weeks of Aug & Christmas,*
Stylish restaurant serving modernized versions of Catalan classics. Wonderful range of local wines. Friendly service.

SITGES: Cinnamon €
Asian
Passeig de Pujades 2, Vallpineda, 08750
Tel *93 894 71 66*   **Closed** *Mon & Tue; Wed, Thu & Sun dinner*
Delicious Asian-fusion cuisine in an enchanting old farmhouse. All dishes are bursting with flavour, but start with the *tabbouleh* (Middle Eastern salad). Hosts DJ sessions and other music events.

SITGES: El Pou €
Tapas
C/Sant Pau 5, 08770
Tel *93 128 99 21*   **Closed** *Tue; Mon, Wed & Thu lunch*
Located in the old centre of the city, this restaurant has a relaxed vibe and good classic and modern tapas. Try the speciality wagyu beef burgers, steak tartare and carpaccio.

TARRAGONA: La Cuineta €
Mediterranean
C/Nou del Patriarca 2, 43003
Tel *977 22 61 01*   **Closed** *Sun*
A delightful little restaurant in the historic quarter, La Cuineta serves fresh Mediterranean dishes. The sea bream is superb. Great value lunch menu.

Outdoor seating in rustic surroundings at Cinnamon in Sitges

TARRAGONA: Aq €€
Modern Catalan
C/Les Coques 7, 43003
Tel *977 21 59 54*   **Closed** *Sun & Mon*
Exciting contemporary cuisine is executed by chef Ana Ruiz and served in a classy dining room. Perfect for a special occasion.

TARRAGONA: Les Coques €€
Traditional Catalan
C/Sant Llorenç 15, 43003
Tel *977 22 83 00*   **Closed** *Sun*
Long-established, charming restaurant in the old city serving sophisticated regional dishes and scrumptious desserts. Great-value set menus.

TARRAGONA: Sol-Ric €€
Mediterranean
Av. Via Augusta 227, 43007
Tel *977 23 20 32*   **Closed** *Sun dinner, Mon*
This restaurant offers divine seafood and other regional fare in an elegant setting. Enjoy dishes such as *romesco de Tarragona* (nut and red-pepper sauce) and *arròs de conill* (rice with rabbit) on a lovely summer terrace.

TORTOSA: Sant Carles €
Traditional Catalan
Rambla de Felip Pedrell 13, 43500
Tel *977 44 10 48*   **Closed** *Sun*
Family-run restaurant with hearty, Catalan cuisine. The emphasis is on seafood with clam and shrimp dishes and fish *suquet* (stew). Friendly atmosphere.

VIC: Denominació de Origen Vic €€
Modern Catalan
C/Sant Miquel de Sants 16, 08500
Tel *93 883 23 96*   **Closed** *Sun, Mon*
Located in the heart of the city, this small, minimalist restaurant serves outstanding Catalan cuisine with a creative touch.

For more information on types of restaurants *see page 140–41*

SHOPPING IN BARCELONA

Barcelona is sophisticated, stylish and neatly divided into distinctive shopping districts – Passeig de Gràcia for chi-chi designer stores, the Barri Gòtic for more eclectic antiques and boutiques, El Born for serious fashion divas, and El Raval for markets and museum shops. Though these guidelines are by no means fixed, they do provide a useful rule of thumb and help define the city when time is limited.

All shops are closed on Sunday. There are food markets as well – 44 in all – for every *barrio*, and a scattering of flea markets, such as the Parisian-style Els Encants and the antiques fair in Sant Cugat, which has a more Provençal flavour. A convenient way to tour Barcelona's shops and markets is by taxi or public transport. Even though there are many car parks in the city, there's little point in hiring a car.

Some of the beautifully displayed confectionery at Escribà

Food and Drink

Barcelona's pastry shops are sights in themselves and, with its displays of chocolate sculptures, no *pastisseria* is more enticing or spectacular than **Escribà**. Other food stores also have a great deal of character, none more so than **Colmado Múrria** in the Eixample. This wonderful old place stocks a huge range of hams, cheeses and preserves, in addition to a comprehensive selection of Spanish and foreign wines and spirits.

Department Stores and "Galeries"

The branch of **El Corte Inglés**, Spain's largest department-store chain, on Plaça Catalunya is a Barcelona landmark and a handy place to find everything under one roof, including plug adaptors and services like key-cutting. Other branches are located around the city. Barcelona's hypermarkets also sell a wide range of goods. As they are on the outskirts of the

city – south along the Gran Via towards the airport, and on the Avinguda Meridiana to the north – a car is the best way to reach them.

The *galeries* (fashion malls), built mostly during the affluent 1980s, are hugely popular. **Bulevard Rosa** has hundreds of stores selling clothes and accessories. **L'Illa** is a large, lively shopping mall containing chain stores as well as specialist retailers. **Maremagnum** has several shops and restaurants and is open daily, including public holidays.

Fashion

International fashion labels are found alongside clothes by young designers on and around the Passeig de Gràcia. **Adolfo Domínguez** stocks classically styled clothes for men and women; **Armand Basi** sells quality leisure and sportswear; and discount designer fashion is available at **Montana Outlet**. Many

stores offer traditional, fine-quality tailoring skills.

Speciality Stores

A walk around Barcelona can reveal a wonderful choice of stores selling traditional craft items and handmade goods that in most places have now been largely replaced by the production line. **La Caixa de Fang** has a good variety of Catalan and Spanish ceramics, among them traditional Catalan cooking pots and colourful tiles. **L'Estanc** has everything for the smoker, including the best Havana cigars. **La Manual Alpargatera** is an old shoe store that specializes in Catalan-style espadrilles in all colours, handmade on the premises. The city's oldest store, **Cereria Subirà**, sells candles in every imaginable form.

Design, Art and Antiques

If you are interested in modern design, or just looking for gifts,

Menswear department in Adolfo Domínguez

you should pay a visit to **Vinçon**, the city's famous design emporium. Situated in a Modernista town house on the Passeig de Gràcia, it has everything for the home, including beautiful fabrics and furniture. Another good place to find contemporary interior design is **Pilma**, which sells furniture, kitchen and bathroom accessories, upholstery, carpets, curtains, paintings and lighting from both local and international designers and architects.

Most of the commercial art and print galleries are found on Carrer Consell de Cent, in the Eixample, while the Barri Gòtic – especially the Carrer de la Palla and Carrer del Pi –

Mouthwatering fruit stalls in La Boqueria market

The stylishly sparse display of furniture at Vinçon

is the best place to browse around small but fascinating antiques shops. As well as fine furniture and old dolls, **L'Arca de l'Àvia** sells antique silks and lace, all of which are set out in pretty displays.

Books and Newspapers

Most of the city-centre newsstands sell English-language newspapers, but the best stocks of foreign papers and magazines are found at FNAC at **L'Illa** in Plaça Catalunya. **Come In** is an English bookshop that also sells a selection of DVDs and board games.

Markets

No one should miss the chance to look around **La Boqueria** on La Rambla, one of the most spectacular food markets in Europe. Antiques are sold in the Plaça Nova on Thursdays, and cheese, honey and sweets in the Plaça del Pi on the last Saturday and Sunday of each month from October to May. On Sunday mornings, coin and stamp stalls are set up in the Plaça Reial. The city's traditional flea market, **Encants Vells**, takes place on Mondays, Wednesdays, Fridays and Saturdays just north of the Plaça de les Glòries Catalanes.

DIRECTORY

Food and Drink

Colmado Múrria
C/Roger de Llúria 85.
Map 3 B3.
Tel 93 215 57 89.

Escribà Pastisseries
La Rambla 83.
Map 2 F4.
Tel 93 301 60 27.

Gran Via de les Corts
Catalanes 546.
Map 2 E1.
Tel 93 454 75 35.

Department Stores and "Galeries"

Bulevard Rosa
Passeig de Gràcia 55.
Map 3 A4.
Tel 93 215 83 31.

El Corte Inglés
Avinguda Diagonal
617–19. **Tel** 93 366 71 00.

L'Illa
Avinguda Diagonal
545–57. **Tel** 93 444 00 00.

Maremagnum
Moll d'Espanya.
🌐 maremagnum.es

Fashion

Adolfo Domínguez
Passeig de Gràcia 32.
Map 3 A5.
Tel 61 966 02 77.

Armand Basi
Passeig de Gràcia 49.
Map 3 A3.
Tel 93 215 14 21.

Montana Outlet
C/ Rec, 58. **Map** 5 C3.

Speciality Stores

La Caixa de Fang
C/ Freneria 1. **Map** 5 B2.
Tel 93 315 17 04.

Cereria Subirà
Bajada Llibreteria 7.
Map 5 B2.
Tel 93 315 26 06.

L'Estanc
Via Laietana 4. **Map** 5 B3.
Tel 93 310 10 34.

La Manual Alpargatera
C/ d'Avinyó 7. **Map** 5 A3.
Tel 93 301 01 72.

Design, Art and Antiques

L'Arca de l'Àvia
Carrer dels Banys Nous 20.
Map 5 A2.
Tel 93 302 15 98.

Pilma
Avinguda Diagonal 403.
Map 3 A2.
Tel 93 416 13 99.

Vinçon
Passeig de Gràcia 96.
Map 3 B3.
Tel 93 215 60 50.

Books and Newspapers

Come In
C/Balmes 129.
Map 3 A3.
Tel 93 453 12 04.

Markets

La Boqueria
La Rambla 101. **Map** 5 A2.

Encants Vells
C/ Dos de Maig, P de les
Glòries. **Map** 4 F5.

Food and Drink

The locals are proud of their culinary heritage and rightly so. The land produces superlative fruit and vegetables, flavourful meats and an astonishing array of cheeses; the bounty of the sea offers daily fresh fish and seafood, and the wine-growing regions of the Penedès and the Priorat make some of the best-value vintages in the world. Less well known are the sweet-makers, chocolate shops and *patisseries*, all of which add up to a complete and sophisticated cuisine that is fast becoming the envy of the world.

Charcuterie, Cheese and Delicatessens

If you can't join them you can at least take some delicious treats home. Barcelona has several wonderful stores for stocking up on general goodies. La Boqueria, the city's most famous food market on La Rambla, is the obvious place to start, but if you prefer to shop without the hustle and bustle, head for one of the city's many specialist food shops.

Orígens in El Born specialises in strictly Catalan products – jars of small, dusky Arbequina olives, Sant Joan truffle-scented salt, oils and vinegars, home-made preserves and artisan *charcuterie*. Just around the corner, **La Botifarrería de Santa María** is great for artisan *charcuterie* and a lip-smacking array of home-made sausages in many intriguing flavours, such as pork and cuttlefish, beef and beetroot, or lamb and wild mushroom. Then there's **Casa Gispert** for top-grade dried fruit and nuts, as well as coffee, which is toasted on site, and the fabulous **Formatgeria La Seu** (closed in August). This is the only cheese shop in Spain that stocks exclusively Spanish and Catalan cheeses. Prowl around the walk-in dairy and choose from a great seasonal collection of cheeses made by small producers. These range from creamy Catalan goat's cheeses and six-month-old Manchegos to beech-smoked San Simóns that come in the shape of a dunce's cap. A tasting of two cheeses with vermouth is available for the very reasonable price of €2.80. Formatgeria La Seu's owner, Katherine McLaughlin, also stocks a small range of artisan cheese ice creams.

For more general food products and quintessentially Spanish canned goods (many of which come in wonderful packaging), **Colmado Múrria** is a fascinating old place that stocks just about everything, from saffron to ham and sauerkraut. Another interesting store in the Eixample neighbourhood is **Mantequeria Ravell**, Barcelona's first proper delicatessen. Its merchandise isn't strictly Spanish – there are plenty of Italian and French goods as well – but it does boast the best and most expensive of everything, from pink Himalayan salt to explosive pickled *guindilla* peppers from the Basque country. Its restaurant on the first floor, incidentally, is pricey but sublime.

The **Herboristeria del Rei** isn't actually a food store, but it does contain a formidable array of medicinal herbs, teas and honeys. When it opened in 1823, Queen Isabel II decreed that it be supplier to the royal household. The handsome marble fountain that contains a bust of Linneo, the botanist and famous herbalist, was where the leeches were kept.

Chocolate and Candies

Swanky chocolate and cake shops proliferate mainly in the Eixample, with the exception of **Xocoa**, which has branches all over the city, including two in El Born and one in the Barri Gòtic. This is the trendiest of the chocolate-makers in the city, with its retro packaging and fun shapes, including chocolate CDs and giant keys. **Escribà Pastisseries** is more extravagant, sculpting magnificent cakes, pastries and life-size chocolate models of famous personalities. Oriol Balaguer is perhaps the city's most celebrated chocolatier, and creates sublime classic and contemporary pastries and chocolates. Try them at his **La Xocolateria** in El Born, opposite the Mercat del Born. **Cacao Sampaka** is a truly mind-blowing sweet shop offering amazing off-the-wall fillings of anchovy, black olive and blue cheese, as well as the more traditional herb, spice and floral flavours.

Those looking to take home more traditionally Spanish sweets should try **Caelum** for convent-made sweetmeats such as *yemas* (sweetened egg yolks) and *mazapans* (marzipan treats). Award-winning patissier Carles Mampel creates spectacular cakes, desserts and *petit fours* at **Bubó**. They can be taken away or enjoyed at the adjoining café.

In **Papabubble**, a gorgeous wood-panelled, marble-tiled shop, you can still occasionally see the sweets being made.

Bakeries and Patisseries

Almost every street in the city features its very own *panadería*. Usually open all day, these shops are busiest early in the morning and at around 5pm, snack time in Spain, when you will often find mothers indulging their kids with after-school treats.

Amongst the best of these shops is **Cusachs**, open since 1963 and still producing the traditional Catalan *coques*. These can either be sweet or savoury and are eaten on 23 June, the Sant Joan festival (*see p37*) and the longest day of the year. Some of the best croissants (especially those filled with mascarpone) and other refined pastries, as well as cakes and jams, can be found at **Pastelería Hofmann**.

Another great *panadería* is **Foix de Sarriá** on Major de Sarriá, very well known for its excellent pastries and other baked goods. Amongst its specialities are "royal cake", *sachertorte panellets* (round marzipan cakes), *pasta de té* (fruit biscuits) and *saras* (sponge cake covered with butter cream and almonds).

For the best breads in town, visit **Barcelona Reykjavic**, which sells artisan, organic and wholegrain breads. Delicious homemade cakes and pizzas are also available, and all products are baked on the premises. The **L&R Boulangerie** has authentic French baguettes and seasonally flavoured artisan loaves.

Wine and Cigars

On the edge of La Boqueria market is **El Celler de la Boqueria**, a very good shop that stocks a range of about 500 of the very best Spanish and Catalan wines. In the El Born quarter, **Vila Viniteca** sells a formidable range of Spanish and Catalan wines, ranging from cheap, cheerful table wines for around €3 a bottle to decadently expensive Priorats and Riojas that retail in the region of €300. **Celler de Gelida**, established in 1895, complements its immense wine selection with other local tipples, such as brandy from the Penedès or liqueur from Montserrat. Last, but by no means least, to leave Barcelona without a bottle of the nation's beloved Catalan champagne *(cava)* would be verging on the sacrilegious.

The ultimate place for cigar-lovers and pipe-smokers is **Gimeno**. This legendary purveyor of all things tobacco-related also stocks a fine range of Cuban havanas.

DIRECTORY

Charcuterie, Cheese and Delicatessens

La Botifarrería de Santa María
Carrer Santa María 4.
Map 5 B3.
Tel 93 319 91 23.

Casa Gispert
C/Sombrerers 23,
Born.
Map 5 B3.
Tel 93 319 75 35.

Colmado Múrria
C/Roger de Llúria 85.
Map 3 B3.
Tel 93 215 57 89.

Formatgeria La Seu
C/Dagueria 16,
Barri Gòtic.
Map 5 A2.
Tel 93 412 65 48.

Herboristeria del Rei
C/Vidre 1,
Barri Gòtic.
Map 5 A2.
Tel 93 318 05 12.

Mantequeria Ravell
C/Arago 313.
Map 3 A4.
Tel 93 457 51 14.

Orígens
Passeig del Born 4,
Born.
Map 5 B3.
Tel 93 295 66 90.

Chocolate and Sweet Shops

Bubó
C/Caputxes 10,
Map 5 A3.
Tel 93 268 72 24.

Cacao Sampaka
C/Consell de Cent 292,
Eixample.
Map 3 A4.
Tel 93 272 08 33.

Caelum
C/Palla 8,
Barri Gòtic.
Map 5 A2.
Tel 93 301 69 93.

Enric Rovira
Avinguda Josep Tarradellas 113,
Eixample.
Tel 93 419 25 47.

Escribà Pastisseries
La Rambla 83,
Barri Gòtic.
Map 5 A1.
Tel 93 301 60 27.

Papabubble
C/Ample 28,
Barri Gòtic.
Map 5 A3.
Tel 93 268 86 25.

Xocoa
C/Vidrieria 4,
Born.
Map 5 B2.
Tel 93 319 79 05.

C/Princesa 10,
Born.
Tel 93 319 66 40.

C/Petritxol 11–13.
Tel 93 301 11 97.

La Xocolateria by Oriol Balaguer
C/de la Fusina 5, Born.
Map 5 C2.
Tel 93 348 52 67.

Bakeries and Patisseries

Barcelona Reykjavic
Doctor Dou 12.
Map 2 F2.
Tel 93 302 09 21.

C/Astúries 20,
Gràcia.
Map 3 B1.
Tel 93 237 69 18.

C/Princesa 16,
Born.
Map 5 B2.
Tel 93 186 63 36.

Cusachs
Bailén 223,
Eixample.
Map 3 C2.
Tel 93 213 77 29.

Foix de Sarriá
Major de Sarriá 57.
Tel 93 203 07 14.

L&R Boulangerie
C/Mansó 40,
Sant Antoni.
Map 2 D2.
Tel 93 511 30 08.

Pastelería Hofmann
C/Flassaders 44,
Born.
Map 5 C3.
Tel 93 268 82 21.

Wines and Cigars

El Celler de la Boqueria
C/Petxina 9,
Raval.
Map 2 F2.
Tel 902 889 263

El Celler de la Gelida
C/Vallespir 65, Sants.
Tel 93 339 26 41.

Gimeno
La Rambla 100.
Map 5 A1.
Tel 93 318 49 47.

Vila Viniteca
C/Agullers 7–9,
Born.
Map 5 B3.
Tel 902 327 777.

Clothes and Accessories

The streets of Barcelona are paved with clothing outlets, and dedicated followers of fashion may be surprised to learn that the city can hold its own against New York, London or Paris. With cutting-edge, home-grown Catalan designers such as Antonio Miró and Custo, high-street fashion chains such as Mango and Zara, and literally thousands of unique boutiques, Spanish fashion is currently among the most exciting in the world.

Jewellery, Bags and Accessories

Bags, jewellery, hats and other baubles are essential for serious style divas and Barcelona has plenty of tiny, Aladdin's Cave-type shops to help create the perfect outfit. **Fet amb Love** (Made with Love) is a tiny shop in the Passeig del Born that sells colourful, handmade jewellery and accessories that the owners, Ana and Carmen, source from all over the world. They also sell their own designs, which include Japanese silk hairpins and party handbags. **Minu Madhu** makes exquisite embroidered jackets, patch-work scarves, appliqué hand-bags and hand-painted silk kerchiefs in sumptuous fabrics, textures and colours, along with a selection of children's clothes

Take your own piece of Barcelona streetlife home – literally – with a **Demano** handbag from stockists all over town, such as **Vinçon** (see p155). These innovative designs have been produced in conjunction with designers Marcela Manrique, Liliana Andrade, Eleonora Parachini and the City Hall in an endeavour to reclaim and re-use the polyester PVC banners, placards and billboards produced to announce the cultural events in the city. In addition to one-of-a-kind handbags in various sizes, there are laptop bags, bicycle panniers and handlebar bags, wallets, pencil cases and other small accessories.

Ulleres M. Assumpta, on the Carrer Ramalleres, is a tiny shop selling retro-vintage artisan glasses and sunglasses, with its own designs. Another good bet for unique pieces is **Mô Art**,

a gallery shop housed in a 16th-century building. It has locally handmade jewellery, textiles, bags, accessories and other gifts and art objects.

International and Spanish Designer Labels

Sita Murt, one of the most awarded Catalan designers, offers truly unique skirts, dresses and long pants for the elegant female customer. El Born has plenty of stores selling a top range of designer labels, including **M69** for the boys, with seasonal collections from Paul Smith, Bikkembergs and Vivienne Westwood, among others.

Avenida Diagonal and the Passeig de Gràcia, however, are the true homes of fashionistas, with all the big labels, such as **Chanel**, **Carolina Herrera**, **Gucci** and **Yves Saint Laurent**, as well as **Loewe** for luxury luggage and **Pelleteria La Sibèria** for prêt-à-porter and custom-made designers in suede, nappa and fur.

Second-Hand and Vintage Fashion

Diminutive Carrer Riera Baixa in El Raval is Barcelona's answer to London's Carnaby Street, with its own Saturday market (opening times, however, can be erratic) and several wonderful shops. The theatre-turned-vintage-shop **Lailo** sells anything from collectable costumes from the Liceu opera house and vintage dresses to 1950s bathing suits. The Carrer Tallers, also in El Raval, is another vintage store mecca, with several

shops, including **Flamingos**, which has piles of great finds that you buy by weight.

High-Street and Sports Fashion

Ubiquitous Spanish fashion houses **Zara** and **Mango** have stores all over town. Both flagships are on the Passeig de Gràcia and they are great for good-value basics, work-wear and fashionable party dresses. Both also offer a decent range of menswear. For slightly more upmarket tastes, both **Massimo Dutti** and **Adolfo Domínguez** are reliable suppliers of more classical tailoring, smart casuals and practical items such as ties and belts.

More individual fashion is best sought out in the smaller, independent shops of El Born and the Barri Gòtic. Carrer d'Avinyo in the Old Town inspired the young Picasso to paint and is now inspiring a hip young crowd to shop. A lively street with a market ambience, it is particularly good for indepen-dent clothing stores and essential sportswear – Adidas, Puma and Nike. For gorgeous, original women's clothes and footwear by Spanish designers, try **Como Agua de Mayo**. The designs are feminine and floaty yet supremely stylish and contemporary. **Desigual** is good for urban casuals, while **Doshaburi** stocks the largest selection of vintage Levi's in Spain as well as the more quirky Japanese labels. **Custo**, the most famous of Barcelona's local designers, has two shops in the old city; both are piled high with his trademark brightly printed T-shirts and mismatched coats and skirts.

Finally, football fans can head for FC Barcelona's official stores, the **Botiga del Barça**. They stock all kinds of merchandise related to the sport, including stripes, scarves, boots and balls.

Hats and Shoes

Patterned leather shoes and decorative soles from the cult Mallorcan shoe-maker **Camper** can be purchased for around 25 percent less in Barcelona than other places in Spain. **La Manual Alpargatera** is another cult classic, beloved by *sardana* dancers (Catalonia's national dance) and celebrities alike for his exquisite hand made, individually fitted espadrilles and straw hats.

Another shoe shop, **Casas Sabaters**, has several branches around town, all offering a top-

quality range of leading foot-wear brands. They are also a good destination for last-minute sale items and last season's knock-offs. **Cherry Heel**, with several branches around town, has a fantastic selection of luxury footwear, with brands like Lesilla and Rupert Sanderson. Around the corner, **24 Kilates** stocks the latest limited-edition trainers from all the big brands. **Vialis** is

another local brand, the first shop opening in El Born in 1998. The shoes are unusual, beautifully made and very comfortable. The collection of trainers is also popular.

On a corner in the Old Town's Barri Gòtic, the old fashioned hat shop **Sombrereria Obach** sells all the classics, ranging from Basque berets to stetsons, trilbies and hand-woven Montecristi Panamas.

DIRECTORY

Jewellery, Bags and Accessories

Demano
C/Carders 36, Born.
Map 5 C2.
Tel 93 300 48 07.
[w] demano.net

Fet amb Love
Passeig del Born 2, Born.
Map 5 B3.
Tel 93 319 66 42.

Minu Madhu
C/Sta. Maria 18, Born.
Map 5 B3.
Tel 93 310 27 85.

Mô Art
C/Montcada 25, Born.
Map 5 B3.
Tel 93 310 31 16.

Ulleres M. Assumpta
C/Ramalleres 3, Born.
Map 2 F2.
Tel 93 318 29 96.

International and Spanish Designer Labels

Carolina Herrera
Passeig de Gràcia 87, Eixample.
Map 3 A3.
Tel 93 272 15 84.

Chanel
Passeig de Gràcia 70, Eixample.
Map 3 A4.
Tel 93 488 29 23.

Gucci
Passeig de Gràcia 76, Eixample.
Map 3 A3.
Tel 93 416 06 20.

Loewe
Passeig de Gràcia 35.
Map 3 A4.
Tel 93 216 04 00.

M69
C/Rec 28.
Map 5 C3.
Tel 93 310 42 36.
[w] m69barcelona.com

Pelleteria La Sibèria
Rambla de Catalunya 15, Eixample.
Map 3 A5.
Tel 93 317 05 83.

Sita Murt
Passeig de Gràcia 11, Eixample.
Map 3 A5.
Tel 93 301 51 45.

Yves Saint Laurent
Passeig de Gràcia 102.
Map 3 A3.
Tel 93 200 39 55.

Second-Hand and Vintage Fashion

Flamingos
C/Tallers 31, El Raval.
Map 2 F1.
Tel 182 43 87.

Lailo
C/Riera Baixa 20, El Raval.
Map 2 F2.
Tel 93 441 37 49.

High Street and Sports Fashion

Adolfo Domínguez
Passeg de Gràcia 32, Eixample.
Map 3 A5.
Tel 93 487 41 70.

Botiga del Barça
Maremagnum (Moll d'Espanya).
Map 5 A4.
Tel 93 225 80 45.

Como Agua de Mayo
C/Argenteria 43.
Map 5 B3.
Tel 93 310 64 41.

Custo
Plaça de les Olles 7.
Map 5 B3.
Tel 93 268 78 93.

Desigual
C/Argenteria 65, Born.
Map 5 B2.
Tel 93 310 30 15.

Doshaburi
C/Lledó 4–6, Barri Gòtic.
Map 2 F2.
Tel 93 319 96 29.
[w] doshaburi.com

Mango
Passeig de Gràcia 65.
Map 3 A4.
Tel 93 215 75 30.

Massimo Dutti
Passeig de Gràcia (corner Gran Via), Eixample.
Map 3 A5.
Tel 93 412 01 05.

Zara
Passeig de Gràcia 16, Eixample.
Map 3 A5.
Tel 93 318 76 75.

Hats and Shoes

24 Kilates
C/Comerç 29, Born.
Map 3 C5.
Tel 93 268 84 37.

Camper
Plaça Àngels con C/Elizabets, El Raval.
Map 2 F2.
Tel 93 342 41 41.

Casas Sabaters
C/Portaferrissa 25.
Map 5 A2.
Tel 93 302 11 32.

Cherry Heel
Passeig del Born 36, Born.
Map 3 C5.
Tel 93 295 62 64.

La Manual Alpargatera
C/D'Avinyó 7, Barri Gòtic.
Map 5 A3.
Tel 93 301 01 72.

Sombrereria Obach
Carrer del Call 2, Barri Gòtic.
Map 5 A2.
Tel 93 318 40 94.

Vialis
C/Vidreria 15.
Map 5 B3.
Tel 93 313 94 91.

Speciality Stores

Part of the fun of getting to know Barcelona is to meander through the Old Town's rabbit-warren-like streets, or to explore the wide boulevards of the Eixample. Both of these areas have a wonderful choice of stores selling traditional crafts and handmade goods that in many places have been replaced by the production line. The endless array of shops is a dazzling sight itself and even if you are just window-shopping, it's well worth taking a proper look around to see the merchandise on offer.

Art and Antiques

Antiques aficionados and collectors will be richly rewarded by what Barcelona has to offer. The equivalent of an antiques shopping mall, **Bulevard dels Antiquaris** is home to over 70 shops brimming over with relics from the past. These can range from ancient coins and alabaster statues to tin drums, Regency-period candelabras and assorted bric-à-brac. Carrer del Call, the old Jewish quarter in the Barri Gòtic, is another hub for collectors. Its plush shops include **L'Arca de l'Àvia**, which sells antique lace and linens, old dolls and fine furniture, **Heritage**, a purveyor of semi-precious stone jewellery, antique silks and textiles and the odd mink stole, and **Gemma Povo** for decorative antique iron work. Also check out **Artur Ramon** and **Maria Ubach Antigüedades** on Carrer de la Palla for 18th- and 19th-century glassware and ceramics and paintings dating back to the 14th century. **Tandem** specializes in a wonderful range of tawny, old globes.

Barcelona's oldest and most prestigious art gallery is **Sala Parés**, which exhibits serious Catalan artists, both past and present. For keepsake wall hangings that won't break the bank, try the **Boutique Galería Picasso** for prints, lithographs, posters and postcards by the great Spanish masters Miró, Picasso and Dalí. **Siesta**, a cross between boutique and art gallery, used to be a haber-dashery and displays its locally made, contemporary ceramics, jewellery and glassworks in the original glass cabinets.

Books, Music, DVDs and Stationery

Barcelona is a wonderful city for unearthing intriguing knick-knacks and unique, one-of-a-kind gifts that people will treasure forever. **Papirvm** is an old-fashioned stationery store, piled high with beautiful fountain pens, leather-bound and William Morris print notepads, and even feather quills, as well as retro Boqueria waiters' pads. **Altaïr** is arguably Spain's finest specialist travel bookshop, stocking a stup-endous range of armchair reads, maps, travel guides and coffee-table books for anyone who lives and loves to move. But if you're just looking for some holiday reading, try the **Casa del Llibre**, Barcelona's biggest bookstore for English-language novels, magazines, travel guides, maps and glossy coffee-table books.

Thanks to the wide influence of Barcelona's annual electronic music festival, Sónar *(see p163)*, the city has become a hotspot for music collectors. **Wah Wah Records** and El Raval in general are good for stocking up on the latest club tunes and old vinyl, while **Herrera Guitars** is a safe bet for anyone in the market for a handmade classical Spanish guitar. Commissions are accepted.

Unusual Gifts and Knick-Knacks

El Born and the Barri Gòtic are treasure troves, at once delightful and inspiring. **Sabater Hnos. Fábrica de Jabones** sells home-made soaps, which come in all shapes and smells, from traditional lavender to delicious chocolate. **Natura** is ideal for cheap and chic presents, such as groovy candy-striped socks, duvet slippers, Chinese-style notepads and other Oriental toys and trinkets. For the Don Juan in your life, **La Condonería** (the condom emporium) stocks all manner of rubber delights in every shape, size, colour and flavour imaginable. **Cereria Subirà** is a gorgeous shop, and the city's oldest, dating back to 1761. Today, it sells a phenomenal array of decorative and votive candles in numerous shapes and sizes, including some several feet tall for dramatic effect. **El Rei de la Màgia** is another golden-oldie, founded in 1881. It reveals a world of fairy-tale magic for budding magicians. Nearby, **Arlequí Màscares** creates traditional hand-painted folk masks out of papier-mâché, including Italian Commedia dell'arte masks, glossy French party masks, grotesque Catalan *gigantes* (giant heads used in local festivals), Greek tragedy and Japanese Noh masks.

Lingerie and Perfumes

The French chain **Sephora** stocks a wide selection of brand-name perfumes and cosmetics, often cheaper than those at the airport. **La Galería de Santa María Novella** is the Barcelona outlet of the famous, luxury apothecary in Florence, which has produced artisan perfumes and colognes since 1400. Customers are captivated by the scent of flowers, spices and fruits as they enter the store. The shop also sells cosmetics and herbal remedies. This kind of luxury does not come cheap, however.

Catalan designer Totón Comella's lingerie and swim-wear collections are showcased at her flagship **TCN** store on shopping mecca Passeig de Gràcia, with branches across the city. The fabrics are fabulous and the designs relaxed and casual, with more than a nod to the summers Comella spent in St

Tropez in the 1960s. For every-day undies, check out the quality Spanish chain **Women's Secret** for funky candy-coloured bra and pants sets, swimwear and hip pyjamas.

Interiors

L'Appartement is an eclectic gallery and shop that exhibits and sells furniture ranging from funky lamps to cool folding armchairs. The Zara brand started **Zara Home** with four basic styles in its collection: classic, ethnic, contemporary and white, all at very reasonable prices. **Wa Was**, on the other hand, is more quirky, stocking neon coloured lamps, decorative objects and cooking tools. They also sell original postcards of Barcelona. Fans of gizmos and gadgets will enjoy **Vinçon**. This is the mecca of Barcelona's design stores.

Housed in a 1900 upper-class apartment, its vast space is filled with everything from French Le Creuset cookware to Basque *chiquito* straight-edged tumblers, silk bean bags and futons. The old fashioned clientele is more inclined towards **Coses de Casa**. This is a superb place for handmade patchwork quilts, feminine rosebud prints and Laura Ashley-style floral designs for lovers of chintz.

DIRECTORY

Art and Antiques

L'Arca de L'Àvia
C/Banys Nous 20,
Barri Gòtic.
Map 5 A2.
Tel 93 302 15 98.

Artur Ramon Antiquari
C/Palla 23–25,
Barri Gòtic.
Map 5 A2.
Tel 93 302 59 70.

Artur Ramon Mestres Antics Show Room
C/Palla 10,
Barri Gòtic.
Map 5 A2.
Tel 93 301 16 48.

Boutique Galería Picasso
Tapineria 10.
Map 5 B2.
Tel 93 310 49 57.

Bulevard dels Antiquaris
Passeig de Gràcia 55.
Map 3 A2–A5.
Tel 93 215 44 99.

Gemma Povo
C/Banys Nous 7,
Barri Gòtic
Map 5 A2.
Tel 93 301 34 76.

Heritage
C/Banys Nous 14,
Barri Gòtic.
Map 5 A2.
Tel 93 317 85 15.
W **heritagebarcelona.com**

Maria Ubach Antigüedades
C/Palla 10, Barri Gòtic.
Map 5 A2.
Tel 93 302 26 88.

Sala Parés
C/Petritxol 5,
Barri Gòtic.
Map 5 A2.
Tel 93 318 70 20.

Siesta
C/Ferlandina 18.
Map 2 E1.
Tel 93 317 80 41.

Tandem
C/Banys Nous 19,
Barri Gòtic.
Map 5 A2.
Tel 93 317 44 91.

Books, Music, DVDs and Stationery

Altaïr
Gran Via 616,
Eixample.
Tel 93 342 71 71.
W **altair.es**

Casa del Llibre
Passeig de Gràcia 62,
Eixample.
Map 3 A4.
Tel 93 272 34 80.

Herrera Guitars
C/Marlet 6,
Barri Gòtic.
Map 5 A2.
Tel 93 302 66 66.
W **herreraguitars.com**

Papirvm
C/Baixada de la Llibreteria 2, Barri Gòtic.
Map 5 A2.
Tel 93 310 52 42.
W **papirum-bcn.com**

Wah Wah Records
Riera Baixa 14,
El Raval.
Map 2 F2.
Tel 93 442 37 03.

Unusual Gifts and Knick-Knacks

Arlequí Màscares
Plaça Sant Josep Oriol 8.
Map 5 A2.
Tel 93 317 24 29.
W **arlequimask.com**

Cereria Subirà
Baixada Llibreteria 7.
Map 5 A2.
Tel 93 315 26 06.

La Condonería
Plaça Sant Josep Oriol 7,
Barri Gòtic.
Map 5 A2.
Tel 93 302 77 21.

Natura
C/Argenteria 78,
Born.
Map 5 B2.
Tel 93 268 25 25.

El Rei de la Màgia
Carrer de la Princesa 11.
Map 5 B2.
Tel 93 319 39 20.

Sabater Hnos. Fábrica de Jabones
Pl. Sant Felip Neri 1,
Barri Gòtic.
Map 5 B2.
Tel 93 301 98 32.

Lingerie and Perfumes

La Galería de Santa María de Novella
C/Espasería 4.
Map 5 B3.
Tel 93 268 02 37.

Sephora
C/Rambla de Cataluña 121.
Map 3 A3.
Tel 93 368 92 33.

TCN
Passeig de Gràcia 106.
Map 3 B3.
Tel 932 15 60 05.
W **tcn.es**

Women's Secret
C/Portaferrissa 7,
Barri Gòtic.
Map 5 A2.
Tel 93 318 92 42.

Interiors

L'Appartement
C/Enric Granados 44.
Map 3 A4.
Tel 93 452 29 04.

Coses de Casa
Plaça Sant Josep Oriol 5,
Barri Gòtic.
Map 2 F2.
Tel 93 302 73 28.

Vinçon
Passeig de Gràcia 96.
Map 3 A3.
Tel 93 215 60 50.

Wa Was
Carders 14,
Born.
Map 5 B3.
Tel 93 319 79 92.

Zara Home
Rambla de Catalunya 71.
Map 3 A4.
Tel 93 487 49 72.

ENTERTAINMENT IN BARCELONA

Barcelona has one of the most colourful and alternative live-arts scenes in Europe, offering a smörgasbord of entertainment, from the gilded Liceu opera house and the spectacular Modernista masterpiece Palau de la Música Catalana to small independent theatres hosting obscure Catalan comedies and dark Spanish dramas. But there's also much to be seen simply by walking around. Street performance ranges from the human statues on La Rambla to excellent classical, ragtime and jazz buskers in the plazas. In addition, there are a number of weekend-long musical and arts fiestas that run throughout the year, many of which now attract an international audience of people from all over the world.

The magnificent interior of the Palau de la Música Catalana

Entertainment Guides

The most complete guide to what's going on each month in Barcelona is *enBarcelona*, out every Thursday. The Friday *La Vanguardia* also has a good entertainment supplement, *Què Fem?*, and there is a weekly Catalan edition of *Time Out*.

Seasons and Tickets

Theatre and concert seasons for the main venues run from September to June, with limited programmes at other times. The city's varied menu of entertainment reflects its rich multicultural artistic heritage. In summer, the city hosts the Grec Festival de Barcelona *(see p37)*, a showcase of international music, theatre and dance, held at open-air venues. There is also a wide variety of concerts to choose from during September's **Festa de la Mercè** *(see p38)*. The simplest way to get theatre and concert tickets is to buy them at the box office, although tickets for many theatres can also be bought from branches of the Catalunya Caixa and La Caixa savings banks, or from Servi Caixa machines. The Tiquet Rambles central point in the Virreina Palace (Rambla 99) also offers 50 percent discounted theatre tickets from 3 hours before the show. Grec festival tickets are sold at tourist offices.

Film and Theatre

The **Mercat de les Flors** *(see p164)* is an exciting theatre that focuses on contemporary dance and theatre. The adjoining **Teatre Lliure** presents high-quality productions of classic and modern plays in Catalan. The **Teatre Nacional de Catalunya** *(see p101)*, next to the Auditori de Barcelona, is another fine showcase for Catalan drama. The main venue for classical ballet is the **Liceu** opera house.

Music

Barcelona's Modernista **Palau de la Música Catalana** *(see p65)* is one of the world's most beautiful concert halls, with its stunning interior decor and world-renowned acoustics. Also inspiring is the **L'Auditori de Barcelona** *(see p166)*, which gives the city two modern halls for large-scale and chamber concerts. Its reputation was considerably bolstered when it became the home of the Orquestra Simfònica de Barcelona.

The Liceu opera house, known for operatic excellence, came back from a fire that destroyed the building in 1994 and has been operating at full-octave level ever since.

Big names like David Byrne and Paul McCartney have performed at **Razzmatazz** *(see p166)*. Jazz venues include the **Harlem Jazz Club** *(see p166)* and **Jamboree** *(see p166)*, and salsa fans will enjoy a quick slink down to **Antilla Barcelona**.

Outrageous stage show at one of Barcelona's many clubs

Auditorium of the Teatre Nacional de Catalunya

Nightlife

Barcelona's clubs come in and out of fashion, but some, like **Nitsa** at the Apolo and the open-air **La Terrrazza** in the Poble Espanyol, have remained hugely popular through the years. The party moves down to the beachfront in summer, where clubs like **CDLC** and **Shôko** cater to a mixed crowd of tourists and locals.

Two of the best-known bars are in the old city: **Boadas** for cocktails and **El Xampanyet** for sparkling wine and tapas. **El Bosc de les Fades** is the café of the wax museum and is

imaginatively decorated like a fairy's woodland grotto. **The One Barcelona** in the Poble Espanyol is a large nightclub that plays techno music.

Festivals

During the summer, the streets are alive with outdoor festivals, performances and music. The **Festival del Sónar**, in June, began in an experimental manner as a place to showcase the latest musical talents of Southern European youth using new technologies. The **Classics als Parcs**, in June–July, is a good bet for more serene entertainment.

Amusement Park

In summer, Barcelona's giant amusement park on the summit of **Tibidabo** (see p100) is usually open till the early hours at weekends, but also busy on other days. It is even more fun if you travel there by tram, funicular or cable car.

Sports

The undoubted kings of sport in Catalonia are **FC Barcelona**, known as Barça. They have the largest football stadium in Europe, Camp Nou, and a fanatical following (see p97). Barcelona also has a high-ranking basketball team.

Packed house at the gigantic Camp Nou stadium

DIRECTORY

Film and Theatre

Liceu
La Rambla 51–59.
Map 2 F3.
Tel 93 485 99 00.

Teatre Lliure
Passeig de Santa
Madrona, 40–46.
Map 1 B3.
Tel 93 289 27 70.

Teatre Nacional de Catalunya
Plaça de les Arts 1.
Map 4 F5.
Tel 93 306 57 00.

Music

Antilla Barcelona
Carrer de Aragó
141–143.
Tel 93 451 45 64.
w antillasalsa.com

L'Auditori de Barcelona
Carrer de Lepant 150.
Map 6 E1.
Tel 93 247 93 00.

Palau de la Música Catalana
C/Palau de la Música 4.
Map 5 B1.
Tel 90 244 28 82.

Nightlife

Boadas
Carrer dels Tallers 1.
Map 5 A1.
Tel 93 318 95 92.

CDLC
Passeig Marítim 32.
Map 6 5D.
Tel 93 224 04 70.

El Bosc de les Fades
Pasatge de la Banca.
Tel 93 317 26 49.

El Xampanyet
Carrer Montcada 22.

Map 6 5D.
Tel 93 319 70 03.

La Terrrazza
Poble Espanyol, Av de
Francesc Ferrer i Guàrdia 13.
Map 1 A1.
Tel 93 272 49 80.

Nitsa
Apolo, Carrer Nou de la
Rambla 113. **Map** 2 E3.
Tel 93 441 40 01.
w sala-apolo.com

The One Barcelona
Av de Francesc Ferrer i
Guàrdia 13–27. **Map** 1 A1.
Tel 90 290 92 89.

Shôko
Passeig Marítim 36.
Map 3 A1.
Tel 93 225 92 00.

Festivals

Classics als Parcs
Information Parcs i Jardins
Tel 010 (from Barcelona).

Festa de la Mercè
Tel 93 316 11 60
w merce.bcn.cat

Festival del Sónar
Palau de la Virreina.
w sonar.es

Grec Festival de Barcelona
w grec.bcn.cat

ServiCaixa
Tel 90 215 00 25.
w ticketmaster.es

Amusement Park

Tibidabo
Tel 93 211 79 42.
w tibidabo.cat

Sports

FC Barcelona
Avinguda Aristides
Maillol.
Tel 93 496 36 00.
w fcbarcelona.com

Film and Theatre

Large, multiscreen complexes as well as smaller, more intimate venues today screen a variety of films, catering to all tastes. As a result, Barcelona now hosts several film festivals through the year. Theatre, on the other hand, dates back to medieval times and the city's productions have evolved to become the most cutting-edge in Spain. Although language may be a problem, it's well worth seeing a theatrical production. If not, there are always many dinner-shows to interest non-purists.

Film

Directors such as Alejandro Amenábar (*The Others*), Catalan writer and director Isabel Coixet (*My Life Without You*) and, of course, Spain's bad boy of film, Pedro Almodóvar (*All About My Mother*, *Bad Education*, *Volver*) have revitalised Spanish cinema. Today, Barcelona itself has become the venue for independent film festivals and the biggest event of the year is the **Festival Internacional de Cinema de Catalunya**, held in Sitges in October.

Most Spanish cinemas dub films into Spanish or Catalan, but there are an increasing number of VO (original version) venues that screen not only Hollywood blockbusters, but also film noir and independent art-house movies. The **Centre de Cultura Contemporània de Barcelona (CCCB)** has provided a focal point for modern Barcelona since its opening in 1995, and has played an integral part in the rejuvenation of El Raval. The CCCB serves as a crossroads of contemporary culture with cutting-edge art exhibits, lectures and film screenings.

Icària Yelmo Cineplex is the town's biggest multiscreen VO complex, built around an American-style mall with a number of fast-food eateries on the ground floor and shops on the first. One of Barcelona's oldest and most popular cinemas is **Comedia**. All films here are shown in Spanish only, regardless of the original language. At the heart of the city, the imposing building it occupies was a former private palace, then a theatre and now a five-auditorium cinema. Or, try the **Renoir Floridablanca**, on the edge of El Raval and the Eixample. It screens a range of European and international movies (subtitles are usually in Spanish or Catalan). In Gràcia, **Verdi** and **Verdi Park** are also good for more independent movie-making, as well as an interesting selection of foreign films. They also occasionally have small, themed film festivals that include shorts by new local talent. In summer, you can escape the heat at the outdoor film screenings held in the gardens next to the **Castell de Montjuïc** (*see p93*). A band plays before the film, and you can rent deckchairs, or bring a blanket. There are beer stands and many people bring a picnic.

The Catalan government's repertory cinema, the **Filmoteca de la Generalitat de Catalunya** (closed August), screens an excellent range of films over a period of two or three weeks before the schedule changes. The line-up encompasses anything from obscure, bleak Eastern European epics to upbeat modern musicals such as Baz Luhrmann's *Moulin Rouge*. The two-screen **Méliès** is a gem offering art-house movies, Hollywood classics, B&W horrors and anything by Fellini or Hitchcock.

Two film festivals held in the city are the **Festival de Cine Documental Musical In-Edit**, combining music with film and usually scheduled for the end of October–early November, and the **Festival Internacional de Cine de Autor**, which is organised by the Filmoteca at the end of April–early May. There are also an increasing number of small "bar-cinemas", where, for the price of a beer, you can watch a film on a small screen on a hardbacked school playground chair. At the **Phenomena** cinema, you can catch double bills of cult classics, from *Casablanca* to *The Big Lebowski*.

It's worth knowing that all cinemas have a *dia de l'espectador*, usually Monday night, when tickets are reduced. Weekend matinées are also usually cheaper.

Theatre and Dance

Although English-language productions are still in short supply, there are some rather good independent groups that perform at the **Teatre Llantiol** in El Raval. However, many Catalan and Spanish productions are well worth seeing, regardless of the language constraints. Theatre groups Els Comediants and La Cubana, in particular, offer a thrilling mélange of theatre, music, mime and elements from traditional Mediterranean fiestas. The tiny Llantiol stages a weekly changing repertoire of alternative shows, comedy, magic and other off-the-cuff performances designed to attract a mixed crowd, from the city's growing expatriate community to local arts lovers. Similarly, the **L'Antic Teatre**, on the other side of town, is a cultural centre and bar with a scruffy but pleasant summer roof-terrace and small vegetarian restaurant that hosts a number of alternative production companies, such as the Argentinian Company 4D Òptic. Also good for avant-garde performances and music is the **Mercat de les Flors**, a converted flower market in the Montjuïc. It is also host to a handful of different themed film festivals, including a celebration of Asian film in autumn.

La Rambla and Paral.lel are the main hubs of the city's bigger, more mainstream theatres.

The **Teatre Tívoli** is a gargantuan theatre where high-quality productions, dance and musical recitals by Catalan, Spanish and international stars are held. The **Teatre Poliorama** on La Rambla meanwhile goes more for musicals, occasional operas and flamenco performances three times a week. For serious theatre-lovers however, the **Teatre Nacional de Catalunya (TNC)** is an imposing columned affair designed by the Catalan architect Ricard Bofill, with state-of-the-art facilities and a weighty line-up of Spanish and Catalan directors. The **Teatre Apolo** is good for big-bang musicals, such as Queen's

We Will Rock You and ABBA's *Mamma Mia!*. Modern dance is much loved in Barcelona and there's no shortage of productions, often staged at the city's main theatres. The **Teatre Victòria** on Avinguda del Paral.lel is a reasonable bet for ballet and more classical dance productions, as is the Liceu opera house *(see p166)*.

Visitors who want to see flamenco *(see p167)* while in Barcelona can experience reasonably authentic renditions of the sexy, foot-stomping excitement of the *peñas* (folk bars) of Andalusia. However, if you do get a chance to see the Catalan flamenco singer

Mayte Martín, it's well worth snapping up tickets.

There are also a handful of places that put on a reasonable dinner and show for non-purists including **El Tablao de Carmen** *(see p167)*. **Los Tarantos** in Plaça Reial has daily flamenco concerts at affordable prices (usually less than €10).

Salsa, merengue and other sizzling Caribbean moves have a solid following with various clubs playing host to big-name bands from New York, Puerto Rico and Cuba. Join the party (and take part in regular, free dance lessons) at **Antilla BCN Latin Club**, or at the **Mojito Club** in the Eixample.

DIRECTORY

Film

CCCB
C/Montalegre 5.
Map 2 F2.
Tel 93 306 41 00.
w cccb.org

Cine Comedia
Passeig de Gràcia 13,
Eixample.
Map 3 A5. .
Tel 93 301 35 58.
w cinescomedia.com

Festival de Cine Documental Musical In-Edit
w in-edit.beefeater.es

Festival Internacional de Cine de Autor
w cinemadautor.cat

Festival Internacional de Cinema de Catalunya
Sitges.
Tel 938 94 99 90.
w cinemasitges.com

Filmoteca de la Generalitat de Catalunya
Plaça Salvador Seguí 1–9,
Raval.
Tel 93 567 10 70.

Icària Yelmo Cineplex
C/Salvador Espriu 61,
vila Olímpica.
Map 6 E4.
Tel 902 22 09 22.
w yelmocines.es

Méliès
C/Villarroel 102,
Eixample. **Map** 2 E1.
Tel 93 451 00 51.

Phenomena
C/Sant Antoni Maria
Claret 168. **Map** 4 E2.
Tel 93 252 77 43.
w phenomena-experience.com

Renoir Floridablanca
C/Floridablanca 135,
Eixample.
Map 1 C1.
Tel 93 426 33 37.
w cinesrenoir.com

Verdi
C/Verdi 32, Gràcia.
Map 3 B1.
Tel 93 238 79 90.
w cines-verdi.com

Verdi Park
C/Torrijos 49, Gràcia.
Map 3 C2.
Tel 93 238 79 90.

Theatre and Dance

L'Antic Teatre
C/Verdaguer i Callís 12,
La Ribera. **Map** 5 A1.
Tel 93 315 23 54.
w anticteatre.com

Antilla BCN Latin Club
C/Aragó 141, Eixample.
Map 3 A4.
Tel 93 451 45 64.
w antillasalsa.com

Gran Teatre del Liceu (Opera House)
La Rambla 51–59.
Map 5 A1.
Tel 93 485 99 00.
w liceubarcelona.com

Mercat de les Flors
C/de Lleida 59.
Map 1 B2.
Tel 93 426 18 75.
w mercatflors.org

Mojito Club
C/Rosselló 217,
Eixample.
Map 3 A3.
Tel 93 237 65 28.
w mojitobcn.com

Los Tarantos
Plaça Reial 17.
Map 5 A3.
Tel 93 319 17 89.
w masimas.com/tarantos

Teatre Apolo
Av del Paral.lel 59.
Map 1 B1.
Tel 93 441 90 07.

Teatre Llantiol
C/Riereta 7, El Raval.
Map 2 E2.
Tel 93 329 90 09.
w llantiol.com

Teatre Nacional de Catalunya (TNC)
Plaça de les Arts 1.
Map 6 F1.
Tel 93 306 57 00.
w tnc.cat

Teatre Poliorama
La Rambla 115,
Barri Gòtic.
Map 5 A1.
Tel 93 317 75 99.
w teatrepoliorama.com

Teatre Tívoli
C/Casp 8–10,
Eixample.
Map 3 B5.
Tel 902 33 22 11.

Teatre Victòria
Av del Paral.lel 67–69.
Map 1 B1.
Tel 93 329 91 89.
w teatrevictoria.com

Music

Few cities in the world can match the eclectic range of Barcelona's music scene. Stunning world-class venues such as Palau de la Música and L'Auditori de Barcelona play host to mega-stars, while smaller jazz rooms attract smouldering songsters. Then there are also the underground dives for the best in experimental electronica, as well as the dusty, dimly lit flamenco folk clubs. Traditional Catalan music and dancing (sardanes) can be heard in the Cathedral square most weekends.

Opera and Classical Music

Opera and classical music are beloved by Catalans who lap it up with near religious reverence. Indeed, many of the great artists of the 20th century were locals, including the cellist Pablo Casals and opera singers José Carreras and Montserrat Caballé, who performed Barcelona, the dramatic operatic duet with the late Freddy Mercury.

The city is also home to some of the most spectacular venues in the world, including the glamorous, gilded **Gran Teatre del Liceu**, which first opened its doors in 1847. The opera house has been a continuing beacon of Catalan arts for more than a century and a half, with a rich and dramatic history of fire and bomb attacks. It burned down for the third time in 1994, but careful renovations have restored it to its former glory. Despite its misfortunes, it has sustained a stellar repertoire featuring the world's greatest composers. Performers here have included Anna Pavlova, Maria Callas, Diaghilev's Russian Ballets, Pavarotti, Placido Domingo and, of course, Monserrat Caballé.

The whimsical fancy of the **Palau de la Música** is another of Barcelona's architectural triumphs. A jewel-bright vision by the Modernista master Lluís Domènech i Montaner, this sublime concert hall has a dedicated following, and performers who vie to play here. The Palau is the main venue for the city's jazz and guitar festivals and national and international symphony orchestras perform

here regularly. Both of these venues can be visited on daytime guided tours, but booking tickets for a production is the best way to experience the atmosphere.

Modern, but no less important as a shrine to the Catalan arts scene, **L'Auditori de Barcelona** was built to accommodate growing demand for better facilities and to attract ever greater numbers of world-class musicians. It began primarily as a place for classical concerts and orchestral recitals, but has since begun to embrace giants of jazz, pop and rock.

It is also worth keeping your eyes peeled for regular choral music being performed at the city's churches and cathedrals, most notably the Iglesia Santa Maria del Pi and the Iglesia Santa Maria del Mar, particularly around Christmas time and Easter.

Live Music: Rock, Jazz and Blues

In terms of popular music, Barcelona may not have the endless clubs, pubs, stadiums and music emporiums that make London the best place on the planet for live music, but it doesn't do too badly considering its size. The city attracts a star-studded cast that ranges from pop stars such as Kylie Minogue and Madonna, to contemporary jazz prodigies, such as the Brad Mehldau Quartet, hip-hoppers, rappers and world-groove mixers, country and good old-fashioned rock 'n' roll.

Barcelona still has a clutch of tiny, intimate venues. **Jamboree**,

a cellar-like venue on Plaça Reial, attracts a number of jazz heavyweights as well as more experimental outfits and solo artists such as the saxophonist Billy McHenry. Another good bet is the **JazzSí Club Taller de Músics**, a more obscure destination but much beloved by aficionados of the genre. It doubles up as a jam-session space for students from the nearby music school. **Heliogàbal**, a small underground bar in Gràcia, also hosts jazz concerts.

Concerts are generally free, or very cheap. The **Harlem Jazz Club** is narrow, crowded and smoky but it's one of the city's longest-surviving clubs for alternative and lesser-known jazz troupes. **Little Italy** is a boon for those who like the tinkle of the piano keyboard and the soft pluck of the double bass. Enjoy an eclectic mix of blues, jazz and bossa nova over dinner on Wednesdays and Thursdays. The most formal of the jazz venues, however, is Barcelona's "free" theatre – the **Teatre Lliure** in Montjuïc is an excellent source for contemporary jazz masters, modern orchestras and experimental grooves, playing host to a diverse number of musicians, from Eric Mingus, to The Sun Ra Arkestra directed by Marshall Allen. For lovers of the genre, this is the best of the lot.

One of the two major players for pop and rock maestros is **Bikini**, Barcelona's very own Studio 54 – in fact, it opened in 1953, preceding the New York icon by a year. This veteran of the scene, which opens from midnight onwards, is still going strong with a robust line-up of big-name bands and a cocktail of different club nights. The other, **Razzmatazz**, arguably the city's most important live music venue, plays host to the likes of Róisín Murphy, Arctic Monkeys, Air and Jarvis Cocker. Club sessions go until dawn in Lolita, The Loft and three other clubs next door. The Loft is a trendy club that also holds rock and jazz concerts several nights a week. For a touch of unbeatable glam, **Luz de Gas** is a glitzy ballroom that oozes old-fashioned atmosphere with its lamp-lit tables, chandeliers and a programme of bands and shows that enjoyed their heyday in the 1970s and 1980s.

The biggest international stars – including Madonna, Beyoncé, Eric Clapton and Coldplay – take over the huge arenas on Montjuïc, the **Estadi Olímpic** and the **Palau Sant Jordi** (see p93).

If your taste is for the small and subtle, **Bar Pastis** is a minuscule bar, decorated with dusty bottles and yellowing posters from French musicals. Live French love ballads, tango

and coplas can be heard here most nights of the week. Other bars that regularly host live music include **The Philharmonic**, a classic English pub, and the **Sala Monasterio** in the Port Olímpic.

Flamenco

Although flamenco is traditionally an Andalusian artform, originally created by the gypsies of Southern Spain to depict their sufferings and hardship, it has for many years been a popular form of entertainment in Barcelona and throughout Spain. One of the best places to see a live show is **El Tablao de Carmen**, a stylish restaurant serving both Catalan

and Andalucian dishes in the Poble Espanyol. The venue is named after Carmen Amaya, a famous dancer who performed for King Alfonso XIII in 1929, in the very spot where it now stands. Various dinner/show packages are available.

For a less formal ambience, **Los Tarantos**, situated in the Plaça Reial, is a lively atmospheric nightspot with live flamenco and Latin music every night of the week. Although it caters to the tourist trade, the performances are very reasonably priced.

JazzSí Club Taller de Músics (see p166) offers traditional flamenco concerts on Fridays, often accompanied by well-known guest musicians.

DIRECTORY

Opera and Classical Music

L'Auditori de Barcelona
C/Lepant 150,
Eixample.
Map 4 E1.
Tel 93 247 93 00.
W **auditori.cat**

Gran Teatre del Liceu
La Rambla 51,
Barri Gòtic.
Map 5 A1.
Tel 93 485 99 00.
W **liceubarcelona.com**

Palau de la Música Catalana
C/Palau de la
Música 4,
La Ribera.
Map 5 B1.
Tel 902 442 882.
W **palaumusica.cat**

Live Music: Rock, Jazz and Blues

Bar Pastis
C/Santa Mònica 4,
El Raval.
Map 2 F4.
Tel 634 93 84 22.
W **barpastis.com**

Bikini
Deu I Mata 105,
LesCorts.
Tel 93 322 08 00.
W **bikinibcn.com**

Harlem Jazz Club
C/Comtessa de
Sobradiel 8,
Barri Gòtic.
Tel 93 310 07 55.
W **harlemjazzclub.es**

Heliogàbal
Ramón y Cajal 80,
Gràcia.
Map 3 C2.
W **heliogabal.com**

Jamboree
Plaça Reial 17,
Barri Gòtic.
Map 5 A3.
Tel 93 319 17 89.
W **masimas.com**

JazzSí Club Taller de Músics
C/Requesens 2,
El Raval.
Tel 93 329 00 20.
W **tallerdemusics.com**

Little Italy
C/Rec 30,
Born.
Map 5 C3.
Tel 93 319 79 73.

Luz de Gas
C/Muntaner 246.
Map 2 F1.
Tel 93 209 77 11.
W **luzdegas.com**

Razzmatazz
C/Pamplona 88,
Poblenou.
Map 4 F5.
Tel 93 320 82 00.
W **salarazzmatazz.com**

Sala Monasterio
Moll de Mestral 30.
Map 6 A4.
W **salamonasterio.net**

Teatre Lliure
Plaça Margarida Xirgu 1.
Tel 93 289 27 70.
W **teatrelliure.com**

The Philharmonic
C/Mallorca 204.
Tel 93 451 50 43.

Flamenco

El Tablao de Carmen
Arcs, 9, Poble Espanyol.
Map 1 B1
Tel 933 25 68 95.
W **tablaodecarmen. com**

Los Tarantos
Plaça Reial 17.
Map 5 A3.
Tel 933 19 17 89.
W **masimas.com/ tarantos**

Concert Venues

L'Auditori de Barcelona
C/Lepant 150.
Tel 93 247 93 00.
W **auditori.com**

Teatre Lliure
Plaça Margarida Xirgu 1,
Montjuïc.
Tel 93 289 27 70.
W **teatrelliure.com**

Sala Fabià Puigserver
Passeig Santa
Madrona 40-46,
Montjuïc.
Map 1 B3.
Tel 93 289 27 70.

Nightlife

If New York is the city that never sleeps, then Barcelona is the one that never goes to bed and those with energy can party around the clock, all week long. It has one of the most varied scenes, with something for everybody. Old-fashioned dance halls rub shoulders with underground drum-and-bass clubs and trashy techno discos, and club-goers are either glammed-up or grunged-out. Each *barrio* (neighbourhood) offers a different flavour.

Nightlife

In the summer, the beaches become party havens when the *xiringuitos* (beach bars) spring back into life. Wander from Platja de Sant Sebastià in Barceloneta all the way to Bogatell (a few kilometres beyond the Hotel Arts), and you'll find people dancing barefoot on the sand to the tune of Barcelona's innumerable DJs, while the Barri Gòtic – lively at the best of times – becomes one massive street party throughout the summer. Way uptown (above the Diagonal), the city's most glamorous terraces morph into social hubs; many of the city's most upmarket hotels, including the Mandarin Hotel and the 1898, have fabulous rooftop bars.

If you want to hang out with the locals, the demolition of some of El Raval's less salubrious streets has meant that the neighbourhood has become much safer and easier to move about in after dark. The underground vibe, however, remains steadfastly intact, with tiny hole-in-the-wall-style bars where folks drink and boogie till the early hours. Similarly, Gràcia has a bohemian, studenty ambience.

If it's an alternative scene you seek, Poble Sec has a handful of "ring-to-enter" joints in addition to the drum-and-bass club, **Plataforma**. The city also has a thriving and friendly gay scene, most notably within the Eixample Esquerra, also known as the Gay Eixample, boasting numerous late-night drinking holes, discothèques, saunas and cabarets.

Barri Gòtic

On warm summer evenings, the Plaça Reial tends to get overrun with tourists banging on tin drums and whooping it up, but if you're looking for more grown-up fun, check out the **Marula Café**. This slinky club also has a small stage for live concerts, and focuses on danceable funk and R 'n' B. The huge and stylish **Otto Zutz** club has been open since the 1980s, but remains a perennial favourite with a well-dressed uptown crowd. The nightclub **The Apartment** is one of the newest venues on lively Carrer Escudellers, and features big-name DJs and regular live gigs.

El Raval

Designer clubs proliferate in Barcelona these days, but check out the old-school ambience of **Marsella**, founded in 1820 and still famous for its wicked green absinthe (*absenta*). The likes of Picasso, Hemingway and Miró are said to have drunk here, and the 19th-century-styled interior, with marble tables, chandeliers and battered old mirrors evokes a bygone era. Equally historic is **Bar Almirall**, founded in 1860; head for the back of the room, where deep sofas, strong cocktails and smooth sounds create an intimate atmosphere in the early hours.

With its red, black and white decor and a specially designed underlit bar, **Zentraus** is one of the best-looking clubs in the neighbourhood. Doubling up as a restaurant until midnight or so, the tables are cleared away once the DJ sessions get

underway. For the more adventurous, **Moog** is more extreme, with blaring, heart-pumping techno for aficionados of the genre. The stark industrial interior gives it the character of a New York nightclub in the mid-1990s. Likewise, the state-of-the-art sound system ensures a thumping, ear-bleedingly good night out.

Port Vell and Port Olímpic

Beach parties aside, this area continues to be a hub for creatures of the night. The Port Olímpic itself is nothing but bars and boats, while the leisure and shopping complex **Maremagnum** (*see p155*) has a clutch of elegant clubs. Under the Hotel Arts, **Catwalk** is still one of the only places in the city for hip hop and R'n'B. **CDLC** and nearby restaurant and lounge bar **Shôko**, in front of the Hotel Arts, however, still manage to draw the celebrities staying nearby. For a more laid-back atmosphere, **Opium** is a club with a pleasant terrace on the Barceloneta beach. Barcelona's outpost of international mega-franchise **Pacha** – which first opened in 1967 in Sitges – is also by the beach and, unlike many of the city's clubs, is open daily. The poolside Wet Bar at the **Hotel W** is a favourite with celebs.

Eixample

One of the city's best-loved discos, **City Hall** is a multiple space and terrace where you can pick and choose your groove according to your mood. It has different themes every night, from Saturday night-fever discos to Sunday chill-outs. **Luz de Gaz** (*see p167*) is theatrically stylish, with retro sounds from the 1970s and '80s. **Dow Jones** has a unique "Stock Exchange" system for setting the prices of drinks, which rise and fall with demand. For sports fans they also offer Sky coverage.

Poble Sec

The most alternative nightlife has come to roost in the "dry village", though in name only. The bars are wet and the music is happening. **Apolo** is another old-fashioned music hall, though it attracts a more independent breed of DJ and performer. Expect anything here, from soulful gypsy folk singers from Marseille to the legendary purveyor of deep funk, Keb Darge.

Further into the village, **Mau Mau** is an alternative club and cultural centre with a firm eye on what's new and happening. This could mean local DJs, Japanese musicians such as the cultish Cinema Dub Monks, alternative cinema and multimedia art installations. If it's of the here and now, chances are Mau Mau's on it.

For the seriously hardcore and lovers of high-speed garage, **Plataforma** is Barcelona's only serious drum-and-bass club, hosting DJs from far and wide in a huge concrete warehouse.

Gràcia and Tibidabo

Gràcia's bar scene is very varied: relax with the hipster crowd over a *vermut* (locally made vermouth is currently the most fashionable local tipple) and excellent snacks at **Lo Pinyol**, or enjoy one of the dizzying array of gins on offer at **Bobby Gin**. The **Atlantic** club in Tibidabo is set in a beautiful Modernista mansion with its own gardens, and the **Mirablau** offers unparalled views over the city from its perch near the Tramvia Blau stop halfway up Tibidabo.

Montjuïc

There are several mega-clubs located away from the city centre and from anyone trying to sleep, and most of them are only open on Friday and Saturday nights. The big boys are based in Poble Espanyol, where folks can party until the sunrise. **La Terrrazza** is only open in the summer, but is well-known for its all-night rave parties under the stars, and takes its name from the giant terrace it occupies. Nearby, on Plaça Espanya, the Ibiza-style **Privilege** hosts some of the best parties in town, with top national and international DJs..

You can get into the Montjuïc party mood early evening at the Font Màgica (Magic Fountain), watching the jets dance to Freddie Mercury and Montserrat Caballé's *Barcelona (see p92)*.

DIRECTORY

Barri Gòtic

Marula Café
Carrer dels Escudellers 49.
Map 5 A3.
Tel 93 318 76 90.

Otto Zutz
Carrer de Lincoln 15.
Map 3 A1.
Tel 93 238 07 22.

The Apartment
Carrer dels Escudellers 5.
Map 5 A3.

El Raval

Bar Almirall
C/Joaquin Costa 33.
Map 2 F2.
Tel 93 318 99 17.

Marsella
C/Sant Pau 65.
Map 2 F3.
Tel 93 442 72 63.

Moog
C/Arc del Teatre 3.
Map 2 F4.
Tel 93 319 17 89.
W moog-barcelona.es

Zentraus
Rambla de Raval 41.
Map 2 F3.
Tel 93 443 80 78.
W zentraus.cat

Port Vell and Port Olímpic

Catwalk
Ramon Trias Fargas 2–4, Port Olímpic.
Map 6 E4.
Tel 93 221 61 61.
W clubcatwalk.net

CDLC
Passeig Marítim 32, Port Olímpic.
Map 6 E4.
Tel 93 224 04 70.
W cdlcbarcelona.com

Hotel W
Plaça de la Rosa dels Vents 1, Barceloneta.
Tel 932 95 28 00.

Opium
Passeig Marítim de la Barceloneta 34.
Tel 902 26 74 86.
W opiummar.com

Pacha
Passeig Marítim de la Barceloneta 38.
Map 6 D5.
Tel 93 221 56 28.

Shôko
Passeig Marítim 36, Port Olímpic.
Map 6 E4.
Tel 93 225 92 00.
W shoko.biz

Eixample

City Hall
Rambla Catalunya 2–4, Eixample. **Map** 3 A3.
Tel 93 233 33 33.
W cityhallbarcelona.com

Dow Jones
Bruc 97.
Map 3 B4.
Tel 93 420 35 48.

Luz de Gas
C/ Muntaner 246.
Tel 93 209 77 11.
W luzdegas.com

Poble Sec

Apolo
C/Nou de la Rambla 113.
Map 2 D4.
Tel 93 441 40 01.
W sala-apolo.com

Mau Mau
C/Fontrodona 33.
Map 2 D3.
Tel 93 441 80 15.
W maumaubarcelona.com

Plataforma
C/Nou de la Rambla 145.
Map 2 D4.
Tel 93 329 00 29.

Gràcia and Tibidabo

Atlantic
Av. Tibidabo 56, Tibidabo.
Tel 93 511 11 26.

Bobby Gin
C/Francisco Giner 47, Gràcia.
Map 3 B2.
Tel 93 368 18 92.

Lo Pinyol
C/Torrent de l'Olla 7, Gràcia.
Map 3 B3.
Tel 932 17 66 90.

Mirablau
Plaça Doctor Andreu, Tibidabo.
Tel 93 418 58 79.

Montjuïc

Privilege
C/Tarragona 141.
Tel 63 444 99 66.
W privilege barcelona.com

La Terrrazza
Poble Espanyol, Av de Francesc Ferrer i Guàrdia.
Map 1 B1.
Tel 687 96 98 25.
W laterrrazza.com

Sports and Outdoor Activities

From the mountains to the sea, Catalonia provides all manner of terrain for enjoying the outdoor life. The hot summer months can be filled with water activities, from fishing to white-water rafting, while skiers head for the hills with the first snowfalls of winter. Nature lovers will find spectacular wildlife habitats, while Barcelona city offers beaches and numerous sports facilities.

City Facilities

Barcelona has around 30 municipal pools (piscines municipales), including the **Piscines Bernat Picornell** next to the **Estadi Olímpic** and **Palau Sant Jordi** sports stadia on Montjuïc. The pools were the venue for the 1992 Olympic swimming events. The Estadi Olímpic is an athletics stadium and is often used for concerts. The Palau Sant Jordi is used for indoor sports, as well as musical and recreational activities. Tennis fans are well provided for and the **Centre Municipal de Tennis Vall d'Hebron** caters for younger players too. Ice-skating can be fun and the **Pista de Gel del FC Barcelona** offers skate rental and runs an ice-hockey school. Golf courses within easy reach of Barcelona are **Golf Sant Cugat** and **Golf El Prat**. There are several riding stables, and the **Escola Hípica** at Sant Cugat allows day outings over the Collserola hills. Cycle shops hire by the hour, half day and full day. **Bike Tours Barcelona** organizes cycle tours around Barcelona.

Airborne Activities

Catalonia has several small airports where planes can be hired and parachute jumps made. One of the best known flying clubs is **Aeroclub** in Sabadell. **Parapente Biplaza**, which has bases in the Berguedà region of the pre-Pyrenees and in Montsant Castillejos in Tarragona, offers paragliding with an instructor..

Bird Watching

Bird life in Catalonia is a huge attraction for dedicated bird-watchers. Northern European visitors in particular will be thrilled by the sight of hoopoes, bee-eaters, golden orioles and pratincoles. Two major wetland areas, where migratory birds include flamingoes, are **Delta de l'Ebre** (see p131), south of Tarragona, with a visitor centre in Deltebre, and **Aiguamolls de l'Empordà** around Sant Pere Pescador in the Bay of Roses. Both are easy to get to, and their visitor centres supply binoculars and guide services. The best times to visit

Griffon vulture

are early morning and evening. The Pyrenees are home to many raptors, including short-toed, golden and Bonelli eagles, and Egyptian, griffon and bearded vultures. The **Parc Natural del Cadí-Moixeró** (see p116), in the foothills of the Pyrenees, has a visitor centre in Bagà. Look out for alpine choughs, wallcreepers and peregrine falcons, as well as black woodpeckers in the wooded areas.

An angler's paradise – fishing for trout amid spectacular scenery

Field Sports

Sea fishing is free, but a permit (un permís) is required for river fishing. Permits can usually be obtained through local tourist offices.

The Noguera Pallaresa and Segre are fine trout-fishing rivers and the season runs from mid-March to the end of August. The game-hunting season is generally from October to March. Short leases and permits can be obtained from the **Federació Catalana de Caça** in Barcelona or from a local hunting association (associació de caça). Travel agents specializing in hunting and fishing breaks will also readily organise licences.

Hiking

All the national parks and reserves publish maps and walking suggestions. Good areas close to Barcelona are the Collserola hills and the chestnut woods of Montseny. Long-distance GR (Gran Recorrido) footpaths criss-cross Catalonia and the walking possibilities

Paragliding above the Vall d'Aran in the eastern Pyrenees

Shooting the rapids on the white waters of the Noguera Pallaresa

in the **Parc Nacional d'Aigües-tortes** *(see p115)* and the Pyrenees are particularly good, with mountain refuges *(see p135)* for serious hikers. Walkers can obtain information from the **Centre Excursionista de Catalunya**. The **Llibreria Quera**, in Carrer de Petritxol (No. 2) in Barcelona's Barri Gòtic, is the best bookshop for maps and guide books.

All the usual rules apply to those setting off to explore the wilderness – check weather forecasts, wear appropriate clothing, take adequate provisions and let someone know where you are going.

Water Sports

There are around 40 marinas along Catalonia's 580 km (360 miles) of coast, and a very wide range of water sports and activities is available. In Barcelona itself, the **Centre Municipal de Vela Port Olímpic** gives sailing lessons and has a variety of craft. The Costa Brava has long been a good spot for

scuba diving. The best place is around the protected Illes Medes *(see p123)*, from the resort of L'Estartit. There are also diving schools around Cadaqués and Cap Begur, notably at Calella de Palafrugell, launching point for the Illes Ullastres.

The town of Sort on the Riu Noguera Pallaresa is a centre for exciting water sports, such as white-water rafting, canoeing, kayaking and cave diving. Bookings for these and other adventure activities can be made through **La Rafting Company**.

Winter Sports

The Pyrenees offer great winter skiing just 2–3 hours' drive from Barcelona, and at weekends the resorts fill up with city crowds. There are some 20 ski areas. La Molina is good for beginners and Baqueira-Beret *(see p115)* is where Spain's royal family skis. Puigcerdà *(see p116)* in the Cerdanya is a good base for downhill and nordic skiing within reach of 15 ski stations in Catalonia, Andorra and France. The **Associació Catalana d'Estacions d'Esquí i Activitats de Muntanya (ACEM)** supplies resort details, while **Teletiempo**, a weather hotline, provides information on current weather conditions. In Barcelona, a dry ski slope has been installed beside the Piscines Bernat Picornell on Montjuïc.

Skiing at one of the many ski stations in the Pyrenees, within easy reach of Barcelona

DIRECTORY

ACEM
Tel 93 416 01 94. W catneu.net

Aeroclub de Sabadell
Tel 93 710 19 52.
W aeroclub.es

Aiguamolls de l'Empordà
Tel 972 45 42 22.
W castelloempuriabrava.com/
en/natural-park.html

Bike Tours Barcelona
Tel 93 268 21 05.
W bicicletabarcelona.com

Centre Excursionista de Catalunya
Tel 93 315 23 11. W cec.cat

Centre Municipal de Tennis Vall d'Hebron
Tel 93 427 65 00.
W fctennis.cat

Centre Municipal de Vela Port Olímpic
Tel 93 225 79 40.
W velabarcelona.com

Delta de l'Ebre
Tel 977 48 21 81.

Escola Hípica
Tel 93 553 11 83.
W cancaldes.com

Estadi Olímpic/ Palau Sant Jordi
Tel 93 426 20 89.

Federació Catalana de Caça
Tel 93 319 10 66.
W federcat.com

Golf El Prat
Tel 93 728 10 00.
W realclubdegolfelprat.com

Golf Sant Cugat
Tel 93 674 39 08.
W golfsantcugat.com

La Rafting Company
Tel 973 62 14 62.
W laraftingcompany.com

Llibreria Quera
Tel 93 318 07 43.

Parapente Biplaza
Tel 93 823 10 40.
W parapentebiplaza.es

Parc Nacional d'Aigüestortes
Tel 973 69 61 89.

Parc Natural del Cadí-Moixeró
Tel 93 824 41 51.

Piscines Bernat Picornell
Tel 93 423 40 41.
W picornell.cat

Pista de Gel del FC Barcelona
Tel 93 496 36 30.

Teletiempo
Tel 807 17 03 65 (Spain).
W aemet.es

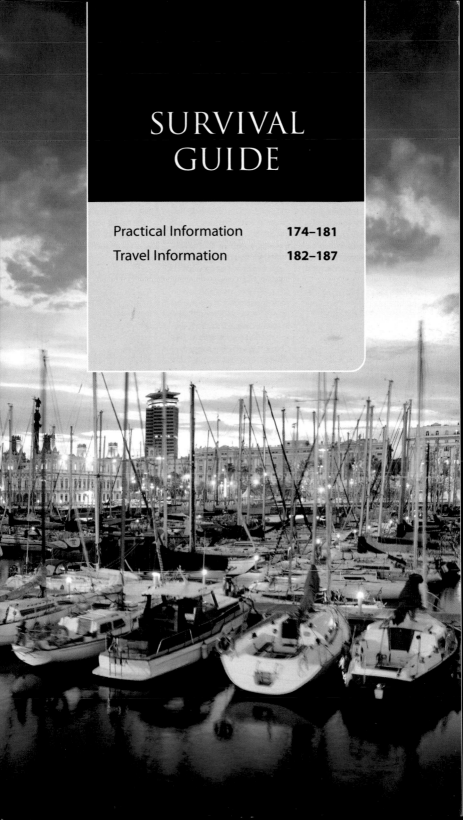

SURVIVAL
GUIDE

Practical Information   174–181

Travel Information   182–187

Personal Security and Health

In Catalonia, as in most parts of Western Europe, rural areas are quite safe, while towns and cities warrant more care. Keep cards and money in a belt, don't leave valuables in your car and avoid poorly lit areas at night. If you feel ill, there will always be a local *farmàcia* (pharmacy) open. In Spain, pharmacists can prescribe some drugs as well as advise. Report lost documents to your consulate *(see p177)* and to the *Mossos d'Esquadra* at the local *comissaria* (police station). Emergency numbers are listed opposite.

Police in Catalonia

In Catalonia, police services are organized into three forces. The *Guàrdia Civil* (paramilitary Civil Guard), dressed in olive-green, polices only borders and airports. In dark blue and red uniforms, the *Mossos d'Escuadra*, the autonomous government's police service, deals with major crime in larger towns and national security, as well as immigration. The *Guàrdia Urbana*, dressed in blue, deals with traffic regulation and the policing of local communities.

If you are a victim of crime, report to the local *comissaria*. There are several dotted around the city, including at Carrer Nou de la Rambla 76–8 (between Montjuïc and the Old Town), at Vía Laietana 43 (in the Barri Gòtic) and at Carrer de l'Almirall Cervera 34 (in Barceloneta). There is also a small office located in Plaça Catalunya.

Crowds strolling on the busy street of La Rambla

What to be Aware of

As in most European cities, pickpocketing in Barcelona is common, so it is wise to take sensible precautions when out and about, especially if travelling during peak season. Always be vigilant with handbags, wallets and cameras, especially in crowds, at major tourist attractions, and in cafés and bars. In particular, keep an eye on your bag at outdoor cafés, as possessions have been known to disappear.

The more common tricks include someone distracting your attention by alerting you to a "stain" on your clothing (this happens a lot in the Metro) or carnation sellers who deftly empty your wallet when you are trying to pay them.

Mosso   Guàrdia
d'Esquadra   Urbana

Never leave valuables in your car and be aware of people hanging around ATMs, since credit-card frauds are also on the increase, especially along the coast.

Barcelona is generally safe for walking, although it is advisable to avoid the Barri Xinès area at night. It should be remembered, however, that violent crime and muggings in Barcelona are rare.

Always take care when using pedestrian crossings, particularly those without lights. Wait until there is a large enough gap to cross safely.

In an Emergency

The national telephone number throughout Spain for all emergency services is 112. After dialling, ask for *policia* (police), *bombers* (fire brigade) or *ambulància* (ambulance). There are also local numbers for the individual emergency services *(opposite)*.

Outside of Barcelona, the largely voluntary *Creu Roja* (Red Cross) often responds to 112 emergency calls for ambulances.

Ambulances transport patients straight to hospital *urgències* (accident and emergency departments).

Red Cross ambulance sign

URGÈNCIES

Accident and Emergency sign

Lost and Stolen Property

Report a loss or theft straight away to the *Guàrdia Urbana*, as many insurance companies give you only 24 hours to make the report. You must make a *denúncia* (written statement) to the police and get a copy for your insurers.

Your consulate can replace a missing passport or issue you with an emergency passport to return to your country of residence, but cannot provide financial assistance, even in emergencies.

Outdoor Hazards

Catalonia's hot summers create the prime conditions for forest fires; extinguish cigarettes and take empty bottles away with you as sun shining on the glass can cause flames. If you go climbing or hill-walking, be properly equipped and let someone know your route. Do not enter a *vedat de caça* (hunting reserve) or *camí particular* (private driveway).

In late spring and throughout the summer, make sure you have some good insect repellent with you to deal with Tiger Mosquitoes, a more virulent strain of irritating, biting insects from Asia that have become prevalent in the area surrounding Barcelona.

Legal Assistance

If you are arrested, you have the right to telephone your consulate which can provide a list of bilingual lawyers. The *Collegi d'Advocats* (Lawyers' Association) can guide you on getting legal advice or representation.

Some holiday-insurance policies cover legal costs and provide a helpline you can call for assistance.

The most common incidents where the law is broken involve alcohol or drugs. It is illegal to drink alcohol in the street, or to purchase alcohol from unlicensed street vendors. If you are caught you may incur a large fine. Driving offences such as speeding and drink driving also result in heavy fines and the possible loss of your licence.

Front of a high-street *farmàcia* (pharmacy) in Catalonia

Medical Treatment

Any EU national who falls ill in Spain is entitled to social-security cover. The Spanish health service is generally efficient and care is of a high standard. To claim medical treatment, UK citizens must apply for a European Health Insurance Card online or at a post office prior to travelling. All basic and emergency treatments are covered by the card at public hospitals, but additional medical insurance is needed for treatment in private hospitals.

For private medical care in Spain ask at a tourist office, or at your consulate or hotel for the name of a doctor. Visitors from the US should make sure their insurance covers medical care abroad. If payment is needed at the time of treatment, ask for an itemized bill. Some insurance companies will ask for an official translation.

For non-emergencies, a *farmacèutic* (pharmacist) can advise and, at times, prescribe without a doctor's consultation for minor infections, but if you have a fever they will direct you to *urgències* (emergencies) at a hospital or, in smaller towns, to an *ambulatori* (medical centre). The sign for a *farmàcia* is an illuminated red or green cross. The addresses of those open at night or at weekends are listed in all pharmacy windows.

Public Conveniences

There are a number of pay-per-use automatic public toilets in the city centre. If you can't find one, simply walk into a bar, café, department store or hotel and ask for *els serveis* or *el lavabo* (in Catalan), or *los servicios* or *los aseos* (in Spanish). On motorways, there are toilets at service stations. Women may have to request *la clau* (the key).

Patrol car of the *Guàrdia Urbana*

Ambulance displaying the Barcelona 061 emergency number

Fire engine displaying the national emergency number

DIRECTORY

In an Emergency

Police (Policia)
Fire Brigade (Bombers)
Ambulance (Ambulància)
Tel 112 (national number).

Police
Policia Nacional
Tel 091.
Guàrdia Urbana
Tel 092.
Mossos d'Esquadra
Tel 088.

Fire Brigade (local numbers)
Tel 080 (Barcelona),
085 (Lleida, Girona, Tarragona).

Ambulance (local numbers)
Tel 061 (Barcelona), use 112 (national number) elsewhere.

Consulates

Canada
Plaça de Catalunya 9, 1°–2°,
08002 Barcelona.
Tel 93 270 36 14.

United Kingdom
Avinguda Diagonal 477, 13°,
08036 Barcelona.
Tel 933 666 221.

United States
Passeig de la Reina Elisenda 23,
08034 Barcelona.
Tel 93 280 22 27.

Banking and Currency

You may enter Spain with an unlimited amount of money, but if you intend to export more than €6,000, you should declare it. Travellers' cheques may be exchanged at banks, bureaux de change (*canvi* in Catalan, *cambio* in Spanish), some hotels and some shops. Banks generally offer the best exchange rates. The cheapest exchange rate may be offered on your credit or debit card, which may be used in cash dispensers displaying the appropriate sign.

A branch of La Caixa, the largest savings bank in Spain

Banks and Bureaux de Change

As a rule of thumb, banks in Catalonia are open from 8am to 2pm on weekdays. Some open until 1pm on Saturdays, but most are closed on Saturdays from July through September. Branches of some of the larger banks in the centre of Barcelona are beginning to extend their weekday opening hours, but this is not yet a widespread practice.

Some city-centre banks have a foreign-exchange desk signed *Canvi/Cambio* or *Moneda estrangera/ extranjera*. Always take your passport as proof of ID to ensure transactions occur.

You can draw cash on major credit and debit cards at a bank. Several US and UK banks have branches in Barcelona, including **Citibank**, **Barclays** and **Lloyds TSB**. If you bank with them, you can cash a cheque there.

A bureau de change, which is indicated by the sign *Canvi/ Cambio*, or the sign "Change", will invariably charge a higher rate of commission than a bank, but will often remain open after hours. *Caixes d'estalvi/ Cajas de ahorro* (savings banks) also exchange money. They open from 8:30am to 2pm on weekdays, and also on Thursdays from 4:30 to 7:45pm.

ATMs

If your card is linked to your home bank account, you can use it with your PIN to withdraw money from cash dispensers/ ATMs. All dispensers take **VISA** or **MasterCard**. Cards with a Cirrus or Maestro logo can also be widely used to withdraw

money from cash machines. Before you enter your PIN, instructions are displayed in Catalan, Spanish, English, French and German. Many dispensers are inside buildings these days, and to gain access customers must run their cards through a door-entry system.

ServiCaixa cash dispensers can also be used to purchase theatre, concert and cinema tickets, a convenient way to beat the queues for the most popular shows. Credit for mobile phones can also be topped up using one of these dispensers.

Credit and Debit Cards

The most widely accepted cards in Spain are **VISA** and **MasterCard**. **American Express** and **Diners Club** are taken in some card locations. Credit cards are usually the cheapest method of payment, as you are not charged commission and are given the official rate of the day. You can also use prepaid VISA, MasterCard and Travel Money Cards, which work like debit cards in shops and restaurants.

All cash dispensers accept most foreign cards, although the commission charged depends on your bank. You may be given the choice to pay the commission in euros or in your home currency. More and more cash machines are closed at night, particularly in the old city, due to crime.

Before you leave home, it is a good idea to phone your credit card provider and your bank to inform them that you will be travelling abroad, otherwise you may find that your credit card

gets blocked by the bank's fraud prevention system when you start using it in Barcelona.

When you pay with a card, cashiers will usually pass it through a card-reading machine. In shops, you will always be asked for additional photo ID or to key in your PIN. As leaving your passport in the hotel safe is preferable, make sure that you have an alternative original document on hand (photocopies will rarely do), such as a driver's licence. Cards are not readily accepted in many smaller bars and restaurants, so it is advisable to check first or carry some cash with you.

DIRECTORY

Banks

Barclays Bank
Passeig de Gràcia 45.
Map 3 A4.
Tel 932 72 54 60.

Citibank
Rambla de Catalunya 12.
Map 3 A4.
Tel 93 344 17 00.

Lloyds TSB Bank
Rambla de Catalunya 123
& Avinguda Diagonal 550.
Tel 902 02 43 65.

Lost Cards

American Express
Tel 900 81 45 00.

Diners Club
Tel 902 40 11 12.

MasterCard
Tel 900 97 12 31 (toll free).

VISA
Tel 900 99 11 24 (toll free).

The Euro

The euro (€) is the common currency of the European Union. It went into general circulation on 1 January 2002, initially for 12 participating countries. Spain was one of those countries, with the Spanish peseta phased out in 2002. EU members using the euro as sole official currency are known as the eurozone. Several EU members have opted out of joining this common currency.

Euro notes are identical throughout the eurozone countries, each one including designs of fictional architectural structures and monuments. The coins, however, have one side identical (the value side), and one side with an image unique to each country. Notes and coins are exchangeable in all participating countries.

Euro Banknotes

Euro banknotes have seven denominations. The €5 note (grey in colour) is the smallest, followed by the €10 note (pink), €20 note (blue), €50 note (orange), €100 note (green), €200 note (yellow) and €500 note (purple).

5 euros

10 euros

20 euros

50 euros

100 euros

200 euros

500 euros

2 euros

1 euro

50 cents

20 cents

10 cents

Coins

The euro has eight coin denominations: €1 and €2; 50 cents, 20 cents, 10 cents, 5 cents, 2 cents and 1 cent. The €2 and €1 coins are both silver and gold in colour. The 50-, 20- and 10-cent coins are gold. The 5-, 2- and 1-cent coins are bronze.

5 cents

2 cents

1 cent

Communications and Media

Public telephones, run by the Spanish telecommunications company Movistar, are easy to find and operate with a card or coins, but international calls have a high charge. Depending on your service provider, you may find it is cheaper to use your mobile phone at roaming rates. The postal service, Correos, is identified by a crown insignia in blue or white on a yellow background. Registered mail can be sent from all Correos offices. These also sell stamps, but it is more usual, and quicker, to buy them from *estancs* (tobacconists). There are a number of Internet cafés based in the city centre.

Logo of the Spanish telecom system

International and Local Telephone Calls

Public telephone boxes *(cabines)* are available throughout the city, and payphones can also be found in some bars and post offices. Both types take coins. There is a high minimum connection charge, especially for international calls, so it is best to ensure that you have plenty of change ready.

Phonecards are a more convenient option and can be bought at *estancs* and newsstands. Some phones have electronic multilingual instruction displays.

Calls can also be made from *locutoris* (public telephone offices) and paid for afterwards. The cheapest offices are those away from the city centre. Private ones, which are often located in shops, are usually much pricier.

The charges for international calls are divided into four bands: EU countries; non-EU European countries and Northwest Africa; North and South America; and rest of the world. With the exception of local calls, using the phone system can be

expensive. Calls from a hotel may also incur a high surcharge.

Reversed-charge (collect) calls made to EU countries may be dialled directly, but most others must be made through the operator.

Spain abolished provincial area codes in 1998, so the full number, including the initial 9, must always be dialled, even from within the area.

Mobile Phones

Spain has several mobile phone operators; the main ones are Movistar, Vodafone, Orange and Yoigo. Roaming rates vary widely depending on agreements between your service provider and the local Spanish provider. Some operators offer special deals for travelling in EU countries. Check with your service provider before leaving. If you plan to make a lot of calls, another good option is to buy a Spanish top-up phone with SIM card and number. A basic phone can be bought for about €30 and SIM cards are sold at most El Corte Inglés and FNAC stores.

When using a mobile phone in Spain, remember to dial 00 followed by your national dialling code (44 for the UK, 1 for the USA) before the number. Most mobile phone operators will charge you to receive calls when using the service outside your home country.

Internet

All hotels, airports and many bars in the centre have Internet hotspots, but often they will charge you a small fee for access and you will usually need to ask for a password. Barcelona has a free, non-user registration Wi-Fi service with 700 **municipal hotspots** in civic centres, museums, sports clubs and libraries. A full list is available online. Cafés with free Wi-Fi are mainly found in the city centre and nearly all

Sign for an Internet hotspot

Useful Spanish Dialling Codes

- When calling within a city, within a province, or to call another province, dial the entire number. The province is indicated by the initial digits: Barcelona numbers start with 93, Lleida 973, Girona 972 and Tarragona 977.
- To make an international call, dial 00, followed by the country code, the area code and the number.
- Country codes are: UK 44; Eire 353; France 33; US and Canada 1; Australia 61; New Zealand 64. When dialling overseas numbers it may be necessary to omit the initial digit of the destination's area code.

- For directory service, dial 11888.
- For an international operator, dial 11825 (English- and French-speaking operators).
- To make a reversed-charge (collect) call to the UK only, dial 900 961682 (from a private landline or telephone box) and you will be asked to dial the number required.
- To report technical faults, dial 1002.
- The speaking clock and wake-up calls can be accessed by dialling 1212 (from Movistar landlines only).

hotels have a computer, or computers, for guests to send emails. Phone centres *(locutorios)* also offer Internet access at a cheaper rate. **Work Centers** office-services stores are useful should you need to print, scan or copy documents.

Postal Service

Correos, Spain's postal service, is rather slow. It is better to send any urgent or important post by *urgente* (express) or *certificado* (registered) mail, or to use a private courier service.

Post can be registered and sent from all Correos offices. However, it is more convenient to buy stamps for postcards and letters from an *estanc* (tobacconists). Postal rates fall into three price bands: Spain, Europe and the rest of the world. Parcels must be weighed and stamped by Correos and must be securely tied with string, or a charge may be made at the counter to have them sealed by a clerk. Smaller packages, like books, can be sent through the yellow post boxes with stamps bought from the *estanc* after weighing.

Main Correos offices open from 8:30am to 8:30pm Monday to Friday and from 9:30am to 2pm on Saturday. Branches in the suburbs and in villages open from 9am to 2pm Monday to Friday and from 9:30am to 1pm on Saturday.

Typical mailbox

Addresses

In Catalan addresses the street name is written first, followed by the building number, the floor number and the number or letter of the apartment. For example, C/ Mir 7, 5è-A means apartment A on floor 5 of building number 7 in Carrer Mir. *Carrer* is often shortened to C/. Floor designations are: *Baixos* (ground floor), *Entresol*, *Principal*, *1r*, *2n* and so on, meaning that *2n* is in fact the

4th level above the ground. Some newer buildings use the less complicated designation of *Baixos* followed by *1r*, *2n* and so on upwards. The postcodes have five digits; the first two are the province number.

Newspapers and Magazines

Some newsagents and kiosks in the city centre stock periodicals in English. Newspapers in English available on the day of publication are the *International Herald Tribune*, the *Guardian International* and the *Financial Times*. Others can be found a day after publication. Weekly news magazines such as *Time*, *Newsweek* and *The Economist*, are readily available. *Catalonia Today*, a monthly newspaper in English, is available at central kiosks and newsstands.

The main Catalan-language newspapers are *El Punt* and *El Periódico*. *La Vanguardia*, in Spanish, is published in Barcelona and is widely respected. The Spanish newspapers *El País*, *El Mundo* and *ABC* are also reliable. Barcelona's best weekly listings magazine in Spanish is *enBarcelona*.

The monthly *Metropolitan* is published in English and can be found in pubs, bars and cinemas. Also available is the Catalan-language *Time Out*.

Television and Radio

In addition to the scores of digital channels, Catalans have a choice of watching TV3 in Catalan, run by the regional government, or TVE1 and TVE2, Spain's two state television channels. There is a Catalan channel, Canal 33, and five main Spanish independents: Antena 3, Tele-5, Canal+ (Canal Plus), Cuatro and La Sexta. A regular foreign-language news

A newsstand on La Rambla in Barcelona

TV3 television station logo

service is provided by Barcelona Televisió (BTV). Most foreign films on television (and in cinemas) are dubbed. Subtitled films are listed as *VO (versión original)*. There are a number of good cinemas in Barcelona that show films exclusively in *VO*. Satellite channels such as CNN, Cine-manía, Eurosport and other European channels are commonly provided in hotels.

The main radio stations are Catalunya Ràdio (102.8FM) and COM Ràdio (100.4FM), the Spanish state Radio Nacional de España (738FM), and the independent stations Radio 2 (93.0FM), broadcasting classical music, and Ser (96.9FM), a Spanish general-interest station.

DIRECTORY

Internet

Municipal Wi-Fi hotspots
🅦 bcn.cat/barcelonawifi/en.

Work Centers
Ronda Universitat 9.
Map 2 F1.
Tel 93 481 41 48.
Roger de Llúria 2.
Map 5 B1.
Tel 93 390 83 50.
🅦 workcenter.es

Postal Service

Central Post Office
Plaça Antonio López s/n.
Map 5 B3.
Tel 934 868302.

TRAVEL INFORMATION

Catalonia's three main airports – El Prat, Girona and Reus – receive international flights from all over the globe. While Barcelona's El Prat mainly handles scheduled services, Girona and Reus deal with package holiday and budget flights. Rail networks and toll highways radiate from Barcelona to serve the region's major towns. Barcelona has a well-developed ringroad *(ronda)* system, and a tunnel through the Collserola Hills brings the inland highways right into the city. Both its Metro system and suburban train links are good, and most rural areas are served by intermittent bus services. For remote areas, a car may be required.

Green Travel

As a tourist-intensive area, Catalonia faces environmental challenges, especially around the busy coastal areas. Trains offer an easy alternative to flying or taking the car, and international and national services are both efficient and economical *(see p184)*.

The local Catalan train network – called *Rodalies* – provides access to most of the region, although to reach some rural areas without direct links, such as the Montseny, the Pyrenean mountain villages and La Garrotxa, you may have to arrange a taxi connection.

Barcelona has a number of cycle-hire shops and a growing network of cycle lanes that provide access to all the major sights of the city. *Bicing*, the municipal government-run free cycle service, can be used with a Bicing card and supplies maps of the city's cycle lanes. Though this is currently open to residents only, commercial operators offer rentals to visitors from around €10 for 2 hours to €60 for a week.

Arriving by Air

Barcelona's El Prat airport is divided into two main terminals: T1 and T2. Most international flights now arrive at T1 (including all flights operated by **Iberia** and **British Airways**). **easyJet** operates from T2. If you need to transfer between terminals, use the free bus shuttle service, which leaves from outside each terminal.

Barcelona is served by many international airlines. The Spanish national carrier, Iberia, offers daily scheduled flights to Barcelona from all west European capitals. It also offers direct flights from several eastern European capitals.

British Airways offers daily flights to Barcelona from Heathrow and Gatwick (also London City airport in summer). easyJet flies to Barcelona from Gatwick, Luton, London Southend, Bristol, Newcastle, Belfast and Liverpool. **Ryanair** flies to Barcelona, Girona and Reus airports from Birmingham, Bristol, Durham, Liverpool, Manchester, Newcastle, Leeds, Stansted, Luton, Doncaster, Bournemouth, East Midlands, Blackpool, Edinburgh, Glasgow and Dublin.

Delta Air Lines offers direct flights to Barcelona from the US. Iberia operates a full service via Madrid from both the United States and Canada.

Catalonia's other two airports mainly handle charter flights: Girona serves the Costa Brava, and Reus, near Tarragona, the Costa Daurada. There are regular buses from Reus and Girona to Barcelona. For passengers arriving from Madrid or other Spanish cities, Spain's domestic flights are operated by Iberia and its associated airlines **Air Nostrum** and **Air Europa**. **Ryanair** and Iberia's low-cost carrier **Vueling** offer services from many Spanish and European destinations to Barcelona.

The most frequent shuttle service between Madrid and Barcelona (El Prat only) is Iberia's **Pont Aeri (Puente Aéreo)**. It flies every quarter of an hour at peak times and passengers can buy tickets just 15 minutes in advance using a self-ticketing machine. The flight takes around an hour.

Other services between Madrid and Barcelona are less frequent but, on the whole, their prices tend to be lower. The major international car rental companies *(see p187)* have desks at both terminals of El Prat airport. Girona also has some rental companies on site and cars can be delivered to Reus from nearby Tarragona. Local firms offer tempting deals; check the small print carefully.

Getting to Barcelona

Barcelona airport is only 16 km (10 miles) away from the city. The express Aerobus service to the

A waiting area in Barcelona's El Prat airport

city centre operates from both terminals from 6am until 1:05am and costs about €8. It takes 25–30 mins from T2 and 35 mins from T1. The final stop is in Plaça Catalunya, but there are also stops in Plaça Espanya and along Gran Vía.

The cheapest way to get to the city is by local (stopping) bus (no. 46) or train. There is a train every 30 minutes. A shuttle bus will take you to the airport train station from T1 and it is a 10-minute walk across the pedestrian flyover from T2. The city centre train stops are at Passeig de Gràcia and Sants.

There are plenty of taxis available from outside of both terminals – join the queue at the taxi rank. Taxis to central Barcelona are metered and the journey should cost between €25 and €32, depending on the volume of traffic, the time of day and which terminal you are using. There is a small supplement added for journeys to and from the airport.

A new Metro line, L-9, which is due to open in 2016, will run from Plaça Catalunya to both airport terminals.

Tickets and Fares

Air fares to Barcelona and the coastal resorts vary through the year, depending on demand. They are generally highest during the summer months. Special deals, particularly for weekend city breaks, are often available in the winter and may include a number of nights at a hotel. Christmas and Easter flights are almost always booked up well in advance.

Charter and Ryanair flights from the UK to Girona and Reus can be very cheap, but tend to be less reliable, and often fly at unsociable hours.

Good deals can be found online to fly to Barcelona from other cities in Spain through Vueling, Air Europa or Iberia.

Sea Travel

Grimaldi Lines has a ferry service between Civitavecchia (near Rome) or Livorno (near Florence) and Barcelona. **Atlas Cruises and Tours** offers transatlantic cruises between the US and Barcelona, as well as cruises around the Mediterranean. **Costa Cruises** offers Mediterranean cruises starting in Barcelona, while **Thomson Cruises**, in the UK, has cruises calling at Barcelona, but starting out from Mallorca.

Travel to the Balearic Islands

Barcelona is the main city on the Spanish mainland from which to reach the Balearic Islands. Flights are run by Iberia, Air Europa and Vueling. **Balearia** runs a hydrofoil (a kind of catamaran) service to Ibiza, which takes 8 hours. It also goes to Majorca, taking 7 hours, and Menorca, taking 4 hours. They also offer car ferry crossings, which take about 8 hours, by **Acciona Trasmediterránea** to Ibiza, Majorca and Menorca. To travel to Formentera you need to take a ferry service from Ibiza. It is wise to book in advance, especially in summer.

Balearia car ferry to the Balearic Islands

DIRECTORY

Airports

Barcelona El Prat
Tel 902 40 47 04.

Girona
Tel 902 40 47 04.

Reus
Tel 902 40 47 04.

Airlines

Air Europa
Tel 902 401 501 (Spain).
W air-europa.com

British Airways
Tel 902 11 13 33 (Spain).
Tel 0844 493 0787 (UK).
W britishairways.com

Delta Air Lines
Tel 902 810 872 (Spain).
Tel (800) 241 41 41 (US).
W delta.com

easyJet
Tel 902 599 900 (Spain).
Tel 0330 365 5000 (UK).
W easyjet.com

Iberia, Air Nostrum
Tel 901 111 500 (Spain).
Tel 02 036 843 774 (UK).
Tel (800) 772 4642 (US).

Ryanair
Tel 0871 246 0000 (UK).
W ryanair.com

Vueling
Tel 807 300 720 (Spain).
W vueling.com

Sea Travel

Atlas Cruises & Tours
Tel (800) 942 3301 (US).
W atlastravelweb.com

Costa Cruises
Tel 902 23 12 31 (Spain).
W costacruceros.es

Grimaldi Lines
Tel 902 531 333 (Spain).
W grimaldi-lines.com

Thomson Cruises
Tel 0871 230 2800 (UK).
W thomson.co.uk/cruise.html

Travel to the Balearic Islands

Acciona Trasmediterránea
Tel 902 45 46 45 (Spain).
W trasmediterranea.es

Balearia
Tel 902 16 01 80 (Spain).
W balearia.com

Travelling by Train and Metro

There are two providers of rail services in Catalonia. The Spanish national RENFE *(Red Nacional de Ferrocarriles Españoles)* operates Spain's intercity services, including first-class fast Talgo and AVE trains and some of Barcelona's commuter services *(Rodalies)*. The Catalan government's FGC *(Ferrocarrils de la Generalitat de Catalunya)* runs some suburban trains in Barcelona and some special-interest services in Catalonia's provinces. Barcelona also has the Metro, an efficient city-wide network of underground (subway) trains.

Trains on the platform at one of Barcelona's major railway stations

Arriving by Train

There are direct international train services to Barcelona from several European cities, including Paris, Montpellier, Geneva, Zurich and Milan. Sleeping compartments can be booked on direct service overnight trains. All trains entering the eastern side of Spain from France go through Port Bou/Cerbère or La Tour de Carol on the Franco-Spanish border. Travelling to Barcelona from departure points not offering a direct service may mean picking up a connection here. International trains arrive at Sants mainline station, located in the centre of Barcelona.

Services from Barcelona to other cities in Spain are fast and frequent. Overnight trains are offered by Estrella (a basic service) to Madrid, and by Trenhotel (a more sophisticated service) to A Coruña and Vigo. AVE runs a high-speed train between Barcelona and Madrid; the journey takes 2, 3 or 5 hours, with around 25 services a day.

Exploring Catalonia by Train

Catalonia has a good network of regional trains *(regionals)* run by **RENFE**. There are three types – the *Media Distancia* and Talgo linking the main towns with few stops in between, and the *Regional* trains, which take longer and stop frequently. A high-speed Euromed service from Barcelona to Tarragona (continuing south to Castelló, València and Alacant/Alicante) leaves from Estació de Sants.

FGC *(Ferrocarrils de la Generalitat de Catalunya)* is a network of suburban trains run by the Catalan government in and around Barcelona. FGC also runs some special services, such as the rack railway (cog railroad) from Ribes de Freser *(see inside back cover)* to Núria in the Pyrenees and La Cremallera, which runs up to Montserrat. It also runs the cable cars and funiculars at the Monastery of Montserrat *(see pp124–5)* and at Vallvidrera, as well as several historic steam trains and an electric train for tourists. Details are available at the FGC station at Plaça de Catalunya or by calling the FGC number listed in the Directory.

Most trains have disabled access – it is worth checking at the time of booking.

renfe

Logo of the Spanish national rail service

Tickets and Reservations

Tickets for Talgo, AVE, Alvia, international trains and all other long-distance travel by train may be bought at any of the major RENFE railway stations from the *taquilla* (ticket office). They are also sold by travel agents, plus a booking fee. Tickets can be purchased on the RENFE website, and long-distance train tickets have a discount if bought online at least 15 days in advance. During the peak months (July to September), many of the most popular intercity routes, particularly to the coasts, are booked up weeks in advance, so it is worth planning ahead. You can also reserve tickets by phone *(see Directory)*. They are held for 48 hours (up to 2 hours before the train leaves) and can be collected at main stations.

Tickets for local and regional services can be purchased from station booking offices. In some larger stations, they can also be bought from ticket machines. Tickets for *Rodalies* (local services) cannot be reserved. A one-way journey in Catalan is *anada* and a round trip is *anada i tornada*.

Train Fares

Fares for rail travel depend on speed and quality. Talgo and

Ticket machines in use at one of Barcelona's Metro stations

AVE trains are more expensive than local and regional trains. RENFE offers discounts to children, people over 60, groups of ten and through travel cards on local, regional and long-distance trains; there are also significant discounts when purchasing online.

Interrail tickets are available for people of all ages from EU member states and Switzerland. Eurail tickets are for residents of non-European countries (you will need to prove your residence status to train staff). These tickets offer discounts on rail travel and can be purchased at Estació de Sants and Estació de França stations. Young Person's cards are available through the **Centre d'Informació i Assessorament de Joves (CIAJ)** and are intended for people under 26, of any nationality. They offer a discount of up to 20 percent on journeys from any point in Spain to Europe. To purchase these, you will need proof of your age and identity.

The Barcelona Metro

There are 11 underground Metro lines in Barcelona, run by **Transports Metropolitans de Barcelona (TMB)**. Lines are identified by number and colour. Platform signs distinguish between trains and their direction by displaying the last station on the line. In the street it is easy to spot a Metro station – look for a sign bearing a red "M" on a white diamond background.

The Metro is usually the quickest way to get around the city, especially as all multi-journey tickets are valid for the Metro and FGC lines (in Zone 1),

as well as on the bus and local RENFE services. A RENFE or FGC sign at a Metro station indicates that it has a RENFE or FGC connection.

Metro trains run from 5am to midnight from Monday to Thursday, to midnight on Sunday and weekday public holidays, from 5am to 2am on Friday and the day before a public holiday, and all night on Saturdays.

Barcelona is in the process of building a new Metro line, the L9, which will eventually reach the airport and pass through the heart of the city. There are currently five new stops on the L9 on the outskirts of the city, with more being added over the coming years. When

A one-way (single) Metro ticket for Barcelona's subway

completed in 2016, the L9 will be the longest Metro line in Europe.

Barcelona Tickets and Travelcards

A range of tickets and money-saving travel cards are available to tourists. Some cover train, bus and Metro. Combined tickets allow travellers to hop from Metro to FGC to bus lines without leaving the station to pay again.

Tickets are as follows: *T-dia* and *T-mes* are for unlimited daily and monthly travel respectively; the *senzill* ticket, for one single journey, can be used on Metro, bus and FGC; the *T-10*, which can be shared and is the most useful for tourists, allows ten trips and combines journeys on Metro, bus and FGC in one trip (with a time limit of an hour and a half); the *T-50/30* is for 50 journeys in 30 days on Metro, bus and FGC.

Details of special tourist travel cards are on the inside back cover of this guide.

There are 2-, 3-, 4- and 5-day travelcards available, which offer unlimited journeys on the Metro, FGC and bus.

Using a Metro Ticket Machine

Insert tickets that don't work to make a duplicate.

Press to ask for information.

4 Collect your ticket and change due.

3 c Insert coins.

3 b Insert banknote(s).

3 a Insert credit card.

2 Select ticket: *senzill* (single trip), T-10 (10 trips), T-50/30 (50 trips in 30 days), then choose the area and quantity.

1 Select language: Catalan/Spanish, English, French.

Travelling by Car and Bus

Driving conditions in Catalonia vary enormously, from the dense road network and heavy traffic in and around Barcelona to almost empty country roads in the provinces, where villages – and in particular petrol (gas) stations – can be far apart. Toll highways *(autopistes)* are fast and free-flowing, but the ordinary main roads along the coast are usually very busy at all times of day. For tourists without private cars, joining an organized bus tour is a good way to visit well-known, but rather more remote, places of interest.

A toll motorway, a popular way of travelling across the region

Arriving by Car

Many people drive to Spain via the French motorways (highways). The most direct routes across the Pyrenees are the motorways through Hendaye in the west and La Jonquera in the east. Port Bou is on a scenic coastal route, while other routes snake over the top, entering Catalonia via the Vall d'Aran, Andorra and Puigcerdà in the Cerdanya. From the UK, car ferries run from Plymouth to Santander and from Portsmouth to Santander and Bilbao in northern Spain.

Car Rental

International car rental companies, such as **Hertz**, **Avis** and **Europcar**, as well as some Spanish ones, such as **Enterprise**, operate all over Catalonia. You are likely to get better deals with international companies if you arrange a car from home. A hire car is *un cotxe de lloguer*. Catalonia's three main airports *(see p182)* have car rental desks. However, those at Girona and Reus have irregular opening hours, so if you need a car there, it is best to book in advance and they will meet

your requirements. Avis offers deals in chauffeur-driven cars from major cities.

Logo of the National ATESA car-rental company

Taking your own Car

A green card from a car insurance company is advised to extend your comprehensive cover to Spain. In the UK, the RAC, AA and Europ Assistance have rescue and recovery policies with European cover. Vehicle registration, insurance documents and your driver's licence must be carried at all times. Non-EU citizens should obtain an international driver's licence; in the US, these are available through the AAA. You may also be asked to produce a passport or national-identity card as extra proof of identification. A country-of-origin sticker must be displayed on the rear of

foreign vehicles. All drivers must carry a red warning triangle, spare light bulbs, a visibility vest and a first-aid kit. Failure to do so will incur an on-the-spot fine.

Driving in Catalonia

At junctions, give way to the right unless directed otherwise. Left turns across the flow of traffic are indicated by a *canvi de sentit* sign.

Speed limits for cars without trailers are: 120 or 130 km h (75/80 mph) on *autopistes* and *autovies* (toll and non-toll motorways/highways); 90 km h (56 mph) on *carreteres nacionals* and *carreteras comarcals* (main and secondary roads); 80 km h (50 mph) on Barcelona's ring roads and 30 or 40 km h (19 or 25 mph) in urban areas. There are on-the-spot speeding fines of up to €520.

The blood-alcohol limit is 0.5 g per litre (0.25 mg per litre in a breath test) – tests are frequently given and drivers over the limit are fined. Front and rear seat belts must be worn; children under 1.35 m (4 ft 5 inches) must use a specially adapted car seat *(see p175)*. Ordinary unleaded fuel *(Súper 95)*, superior unleaded fuel *(Súper 98)* and diesel *(gas oil)* are sold by the litre.

Autopistes

On toll motorways *(auto-pistes)*, tolls are calculated per kilometre driven. Over some stretches near cities, a fixed toll is charged. You collect a ticket from the *peagte* (toll booth/plaza) when you join the *autopiste*, and pay when you leave. You must join one of three channels at the *peatge*: *Automàtic* has machines for credit cards; in *Manual* an attendant takes your ticket and money; for *Teletac* you need an electronic chip on your vehicle's windscreen (windshield).

Autopistes have emergency telephones every 2 km (1.25 miles) and service stations every 40 km (25 miles).

Parking

Central Barcelona has a pay-and-display system from 9am to 2pm and 4 to 8pm Monday to Friday and all day Saturday. You can park in blue spaces for about €2–3 per hour. Tickets are valid for 2 hours but can be renewed. Green spaces are reserved for residents but can be used, if available, at a higher rate and are free at off-peak hours.

At underground car parks (parking lots), *lliure* means there is space, *complet* means full. Most are attended, but in automatic ones, you pay before returning to your car. Do not park where the pavement edge is yellow or where there is a private exit *(gual)*. Blue and red signs saying "1–15" or "16–30" mean that you cannot park in the areas indicated on those dates of the month.

No parking at any time of day

Taxis

Barcelona's taxis are yellow and black, and display a green light when free. All taxis are metered and show a minimum fee at the start of a journey. Rates increase after 10pm and there is a €2 surcharge on Thursday–Sunday nights. The minimum fee stays the same. In unmetered taxis, such as in villages, it is best to negotiate a price before setting off. Supplements are charged for going to and from the airport and the port. **Radio Taxis** have cars adapted for disabled people, which need to be booked a day ahead. They also have some cars that will take up to seven people.

A busy taxi rank in Barcelona

An Alsa long-distance bus

Long-Distance Buses

Spain's largest inter-city bus company, **Alsa**, is an agent for **Eurolines**. This runs regular services from all over Europe to Sants bus station in Barcelona. Buses from towns and cities in Spain arrive at **Estació del Nord** and **Sants**.

Several companies run day trips or longer tours to places of interest in Catalonia. **Turisme de Catalunya** *(see p175)* has details of trips to Catalonia; in other towns, tourist offices can usually help with tours in their provinces.

Buses in Barcelona

The main city buses are white and red. You can buy a single ticket on the bus, or a *T-10* ten-trip ticket at Metro stations, valid for bus, Metro and FGC *(see p185)*. Other combined tickets are described inside the back cover. The *Nitbus* runs nightly from around 10pm to 5am, and the *Aerobus* offers a service between Plaça de Catalunya and El Prat airport. A good way to sightsee is by **Bus Turístic**. It runs all year on three routes from Plaça de Catalunya. A ticket, bought on board, is valid for all three routes and lets you get on and off as you please. **Julià Tours** and **Pullmantur** also offer tours of Barcelona.

DIRECTORY

Car Rental

Avis
Tel 902 18 08 54
(Barcelona airport).
Tel 902 18 08 54.
W avis.es

Enterprise
Tel 93 521 90 95.
(Barcelona airport).
Tel 902 100 101.
W atesa.es

Europcar
Tel 902 50 30 10.
W europcar.es

Hertz
Tel 902 402 405.
W hertz.es

Taxis

Radio Taxis
Tel 93 303 30 33.
Tel 93 225 00 00.
Tel 93 420 80 88 (taxis for the disabled).

Tour-Bus Operators

Alsa
Tel 90 242 22 42.

Bus Turístic
W barcelonabusturistic.cat

Eurolines
Tel 08717 81 81 81 in UK.
Tel 90 240 50 40 in Spain.

Julià Tours
Tel 93 402 69 51.

Pullmantur
Tel 90 224 00 70.

Bus Stations

Estació del Nord
Carrer d'Alí Bei 80.
Tel 90 226 06 06.
W barcelonanord.cat

Estació de Sants
Plaça del Països Catalans.
Tel 90 226 06 06/933 67 44 00.

BARCELONA STREET FINDER

The map references given with the sights, shops and entertainment venues described in the Barcelona section of the guide refer to the street maps on the following pages. Map references are also given for Barcelona's hotels (see pp136–39) and its restaurants, cafés and bars (see pp144–53). The schematic map below shows the areas of the city covered by the Street Finder. The symbols used on the Street Finder maps to indicate sights, features and services are explained in the key at the foot of the page.

0 kilometres   2

0 miles   1

Key to Street Finder

- Major sight
- Place of interest
- Other building
- Main train station
- Local (FGC) train station
- Metro station
- Main bus stop
- Cable car
- Funicular station
- Tramway stop

- Tourist information
- Hospital with A&E unit
- Police station
- Church
- Railway line (railroad)
- Pedestrianized street
- Funicular line
- Cable car line

Scale of Map Pages

0 metres   250

0 yards   250

Street Finder Index

A

Abaixadors, Carrer dels	5B3
Abdó Terradas, Carrer d'	3B2
Agullers, Carrer dels	5B3
Agustí Duran i Sanpere, Carrer d'	2F2
Alaba, Carrer d'	6F1
Alba, Carrer de l'	3C2
Albareda, Carrer d'	2E4
Alcalde de Móstoles, Carrer de l'	4E1
Alcanar, Carrer d'	5C5
Aldana, Carrer d'	2E3
Alí Bei, Passatge d'	6F1
Alí Bei, Carrer d'	5C1 & 6D1–6E1
Alió, Passatge d'	4D3
Allada, Carrer de l'	5C2
Almirall Aixada, Carrer de l'	5B5
Almirall Cervera, Carrer de l'	5B5
Almogàvers, Carrer dels	6D2
Alzina, Carrer d'	3C1
Amadeu Vives, Carrer d'	5B1
Amargós, Carrer de N'	5B1
Ample, Carrer	5A3
Amposta, Carrer d'	1A1
Andrea Dòria, Carrer d'	5C4
Àngel, Plaça de l'	5B2
Àngels, Carrer dels	2F2
Àngel Baixeras, Carrer d'	5A3
Anníbal, Carrer d'	1C3
Antic de Sant Joan, Carrer	5C3
Antiga de Mataró, Carretera	6E2
Antóni López, Plaça d'	5B3
Antóni Maura, Plaça d'	5B2
Aragó, Carrer d'	3A4
Arai, Carrer de N'	5A3
Arc de Sant Agustí, Carrer de l'	2F3
Arc del Teatre, Carrer de l'	2F4
Arcs, Carrer dels	5A2
Argenter, Carrer de l'	5B1
Argenteria, Carrer de l'	5B2
Argentona, Carrer d'	4D1
Aribau, Carrer d'	2F1
Armada, Plaça de l'	2D5
Arolas, Carrer d'en	5A2
Arq.Sert, Carrer de l'	6F2
Assaonadors, Carrer dels	5B2
Astúries, Carrer d'	3B1
Ataúlf, Carrer d'	5A3
Atlantida, Carrer de l'	5B5
Aulèstia i Pijoan, Carrer d'	3A1
Aurora, Carrer de l'	2E2
Ausiàs Marc, Carrer d'	5B1
Avinyó, Carrer d'	5A3

B

Badia, Carrer de	3B1
Bailèn, Carrer de	3C2
Baix, Carrer de	1C2
Balboa, Carrer de	5C4
Balears, Moll de les	5A5
Balmes, Carrer de	3A1–3A5
Baluard, Carrer del	5C4
Banyoles, Carrer de	3C2
Banys Nous, Carrer de	5A2
Banys Vells, Carrer de	5B2

Barceloneta, Moll de la	5B4
Barceloneta, Plaça de la	5B4
Barceloneta, Platja de la	6D5
Basea, Carrer de	5B3
Beates, Carrer de les	5B2
Benet Mercadé, Carrer de	3A1
Berenguer, Passatge de	4D3
Berga, Carrer de	3A1
Bergara, Carrer de	5A1
Bergnes de las Casas, Carrer	4E2
Bertrellans, Carrer de	5A1
Bisbe, Carrer del	5B2
Bisbe Laguarda, Carrer del	2E2
Blai, Carrer de	2D3
Blanqueria, Carrer de la	5C2
Blasco de Garay, Carrer de	2D3
Blesa, Carrer de	2D4
Bòbila, Carrer de	1C2
Bocabella, Passatge de	4D5
Bofill, Passatge de	4E4
Bogatell, Avinguda del	6E2
Bolívia, Carrer de	6F1
Boltres, Carrer d'En	5A3
Bonavista, Carrer de	3B2
Boné, Passatge de	4E1
Bonsuccés, Carrer del	5A1
Boquer, Carrer d'En	5B2
Boqueria, Carrer de la	5A2
Boqueria, Plaça de la	5A2
Bordeta, Carretera de la	1A1
Boria, Carrer de la	5B2
Bosch, Carrer de	3A2
Bot, Carrer d'En	5A2
Botella, Carrer d'En	2E2
Boters, Carrer dels	5A2
Bou de Sant Pere, Carrer del	5B1
Bous les Arenes, Plaça	1B1
Bretón de los Herros, Carrer de	3A1
Bruc, Carrer del	3B3
Brugada, Plaça de	5C5
Bruniquer, Carrer de	3C1
Buenaventura Muñoz, Carrer de	6D2

C

Ca l'Alegre de Dalt, Carrer de	4D1
Cabanes, Carrer de	2E4
Cadena, Passatge de la	5C4
Calàbria, Carrer de	2D1
Call, Carrer del	5A2
Camprodon, Carrer de	3C3
Camps Elisis, Passatge dels	3B4
Canadell, Passatge de	4F3
Canó, Carrer del	3B2
Canuda, Carrer de la	5A1
Canvis Nous, Carrer de	5B3
Capellans, Carrer dels	5A2
Carabassa, Carrer d'En	5A3
Cardenal Casañas, Carrer del	5A2
Carders, Carrer dels	5C2
Carles Buïgas, Plaça de	1B2
Carlos Ibáñez, Plaça de	2D4
Carme, Carrer del	2E2
Carrera, Carrer d	2E4
Carretes, Carrer de les	2E2

Carsi, Passatge de	4F3
Cartagena, Carrer de	4F1
Casanova, Carrer de	2E1
Cascades, Passeig de les	1A2
Cascades, Plaça de les	1B2
Casp, Carrer de	3B5
Castell, Avinguda del	1B4
Castella, Plaça de	2F1
Castillejos, Carrer de los	4F1
Catalunya, Plaça de	5A1
Catalunya, Rambla de	3A3
Catedral, Avinguda de la	5A2
Cendra, Carrer de la	2E2
Centelles, Passatge de	4F3
Cera, Carrer de la	2E2
Chopin, Carrer de	1A1
Cid, Carrer del	2F4
Cigne, Carrer de	3A1
Circumval.lació, Passeig de	5C3–6D4
Cirera, Carrer de la	5B2
Ciudad Real, Carrer de	3C2
Ciutat, Carrer de la	5A2
Clip, Passatge de	4E2
Còdols, Carrer dels	5A3
Colom, Passeig de	5A4
Colomines, Carrer de	5B2
Comerç, Carrer del	5C3
Comercial, Carrer del	5C2
Comercial, Plaça del	5C3
Comtal, Carrer de	5A1
Comte d'Urgell, Carrer de l'	2E1
Comte Borrell, Carrer de l'	2D1
Comte de Salvatierra, Carrer del	3A2
Comtes, Carrer dels	5B2
Concepció, Passatge de la	3A3
Concòrdia, Carrer de la	1C2
Congost, Carrer del	3C1
Conradí, Passatge	4D3
Consell de Cent, Carrer del	3A4
Consolat de Mar, Carrer del	5B2
Copons, Carrer d'En	5B2
Corders, Carrer dels	5B2
Còrsega, Carrer de	3A3
Cortines, Carrer d'En	5C2
Corts Catalanes, Gran Via de les	1A1
Cremat, Gran Carrer de	5B2
Creu dels Molers, Carrer de la	1C3–2D3
Cucurulla, Carrer de	5A2

D

Dàlia, Carrer de la	1A1
Dante, Plaça de	1C4
Diagonal, Avinguda de	3A2– 3C4 & 4D4–4F5
Diluvi, Carrer del	3B2
Diputació, Carrer de la	3A5
Doctor Aiguader, Carrer del	5B4
Doctor Joaquim Pou, Carrer del	2F2
Doctor Pons i Freixas, Plaça del	6D4
Doctor Rizal, Carrer del	3A2
Doctor Trueta, Carrer del	6E3

Domènech, Carrer de	3B2
Domingo, Passatge de	3A4
Don Carles, Carrer de	6D4
Drassana, Carrer de la	5B5
Drassanes, Avinguda de les	2F3
Duc de la Victòria, Carrer del	5A1
Duc de Medinaceli, Plaça del	5A3
Duran i Bas, Carrer de	5A1

E

Egipcíaques, Carrer d'	2F2
Elisabets, Carrer d'	2F2
Elkano, Carrer d	2D3
Enamorats, Carrer dels	4E4
Encarnació, Carrer de l'	4D1
Entença, Carrer d'	1C1
Erasme de Janer, Carrer d'	2E2
Escorial, Carrer de l'	4D2
Escudellers, Carrer dels	5A3
Escudellers, Passatge dels	5A3
Escudellers Blancs, Carrer dels	5A2
Escuder, Carrer d'	5B4
Espanya, Moll d'	5A4
Espanya, Plaça d'	1B1
Esparteria, Carrer de l'	5B3
Espaseria, Carrer de l'	5B3
Est, Carrer de l'	2F3
Estadi, Avinguda de l'	1A2
Estruc, Carrer d'	5B1
Exposició, Passeig de l'	1C3

F

Far, Camí del	1B5
Farell, Carrer del	1A1
Ferlandina, Carrer de	2E1
Ferran, Carrer de	5A2
Ferrer de Blanes, Carrer de	3B2
Flassaders, Carrer dels	5C2
Floridablanca, Carrer de	1C1
Flors, Carrer de les	2E3
Fonollar, Carrer del	5B2
Font, Carrer de la	2D4
Font, Passatge de	4E4
Font, Plaça de la	5C4
Font Florida, Carrer de la	1A1
Font Honrada, Carrer de la	1C2
Font-Trobada, Camí de la	2D4
Fontanella, Carrer de	5A1
Fontrodona, Carrer d'En	2D3
Franca Xica, Carrer de la	1C2
Francesc Cambó, Avinguda de	5B2
Francesc d'Aranda, Carrer de	6E2
Francesc Ferrer i Guàrdia, Avinguda de	1A1
Francisco Giner, Carrer de	3B2
Fraternitat, Carrer de la	3B2
Frederic Mompou, Carrer de	6F3
Freixures, Carrer de les	5B2
Fusina, Carrer de la	5C2
Fusta, Moll de la	5A4
Fusteria, Carrer de la	5B3

G

Gaiolà, Passatge de	4D4
Gal.la Placídia, Plaça de	3A1
Gaudí, Avinguda de	4E3
Gaudí, Plaça de	4E3
Gegants, Carrer dels	5A2
Gelí, Carrer de	5C5
General Álvarez de Castro, Carrer del	5B2
General Bassos, Passatge de	6F3
General Castaños, Carrer de	5B3
Gessamí, Carrer del	1A1
Gignàs, Carrer d'En	5A3
Gimbernat, Carrer dels	1B1
Ginebra, Carrer de	5B4
Giralt el Pellisser, Carrer d'En	5B2
Girona, Carrer de	3C3
Glòries Catalanes, Plaça de les	4F5
Gombau, Carrer de	5B2
Goya, Carrer de	3A2
Goya, Plaça de	2F1
Gràcia, Carrer de	3B2
Gràcia, Passeig de	3A2–3A5
Gràcia, Travessera de	3A2
Gran de Gràcia, Carrer	3A2
Granada del Penedès, Carrer de la	3A2
Grases, Carrer de	1C2
Grassot, Carrer d'En	4D2
Gravina, Carrer de	2F1
Gregal, Moll de	6F5
Guàrdia, Carrer de	2F3
Guàrdia Urbana, C de la	1B2
Guatla, Carrer de la	1A1
Guifré, Carrer de	2F2
Guilleries, Carrer de les	3B1
Guinardó, Ronda del	4E1
Guítert, Carrer de	5C5

H

Havana, Carrer de l'	5C5
Hipòlit Lázaro, Carrer d'	4D2
Hispanitat, Plaça de la	4E4
Hort de Sant Pau, Carrer de l'	2E3
Hortes, Carrer de les	2D3
Hospital, Carrer de l'	2E2

I

Icària, Avinguda d'	6E3
Igualada, Carrer d'	3C2
Indústria, Carrer de la	3C2
Isabel II, Passatge d'	5B3
Iscle Soler, Carrer d'	4D3

J

Jaén, Carrer de	3B1
Jaume Giralt, Carrer de	5C2
Jaume Fabra, Carrer de	1C2
Jaume I, Carrer de	5A2
Jesús, Carrer de	3B2
Joan Blanques, Carrer de	3C2
Joan Casas, Passatge de	4F5
Joan d'Austria, Carrer de	6E1
Joan de Borbó, P de	5B4
Joanic, Plaça d'En	3C1
Joaquim Blume, Carrer de	1B2
Joaquim Pou, Carrer de	5B2
Joaquim Renart Passeig de	6D2
Joaquim Ruyra, Carrer de	4D2

Joaquín Costa, Carrer de	2F2
Jonqueres, Carrer de les	5B1
Josep Anselm Clavé, Carrer de	5A3
Josep Carner, Passeig de	2E5
Josep Ciurana, Carrer de	4F1
Jovellanos, Carrer de	5A1
Judici, Carrer del	5B5
Julià, Carrer de	1C3
Julià, Passatge de	1C3
Julià Portet, Carrer de	5B1
Julian Romea, Carrer	3A2
Junta del Comerç, Carrer de	2F3

L

Laforja, Carrer de	3A1
Laietana, Via	5B1
Lancaster, Carrer de	2F3
Legalitat, Carrer de la	4D1
Leiva, Carrer de	1B1
Lepant, Carrer de	4E1
Lincoln, Carrer de	3A1
Llançà, Carrer de	1B1
Llàstics, Carrer d'En	5C2
Llavalloll, Passatge de	4D2
Lleialtat, Carrer de la	2E3
Lleida, Carrer de	1B2
Lleó, Carrer del	2F2
Lleona, Carrer de la	5A2
Llibertat, Carrer de la	3B2
Llibertat, Plaça de la	3A1
Llibreteria, Carrer de la	5A2
Llorens i Barba, Carrer de	4F1
Lluís Companys, Passeig de	5C2
Lluís Millet, Plaça de	5B1
Llull, Carrer de	6D2
Lluna, Carrer de la	2F2
Louis Braille, Carrer de	5A3
Luis Antúnez, Carrer de	3A2

M

Madrozo, Carrer dels	3A1
Magalhães, Carrer de	1C3
Magdalenes, Carrer de les	5B1
Maiol, Passatge de	4E4
Malcuinat, Carrer del	5B3
Mallorca, Carrer de	3A4
Manresa, Carrer de	5B3
Manso, Carrer de	2D2
Manuel Ribé, Platja de	5A2
Manufactures, Passatge de les	5B1
Maquinista, Carrer de la	5B4
Mar, Carrer del	5B5
Mar, Rambla de	5A4
Mare de Déu del Remei, Carrer de la	1C2
Mare de Déu dels Desemparats, Carrer de la	3B2
Margarit, Carrer de	1C3
Maria, Carrer de	3B2
Marià Cubí, Carrer de	3A1
Marina, Carrer de la	4E2–4E5 6E1–6E4
Marina, Moll de la	6E5
Marina, Passatge de la	4E1
Mariner, Passatge de	4D3
Mar i Terra, Passatge	2E4
Marítim de Nova Icária, Passeig	6E4

Marítim del Port Olímpic, Passeig	6E4
Marquès de Barberà, Carrer del	2F3
Marquès de Campo Sagrado, Carrer del	2D2
Marquès de l'Argentera, Avinguda del	5B3
Marquès de la Foronda, Plaça del	1B2
Marquesa, Carrer de la	5C3
Martí, Carrer de	4D1
Martínez de la Rosa, Carrer de	3B2
Martras, Passatge de	1C3
Mas Casanovas, Carrer del	4F1
Massanet, Carrer de	5B2
Massens, Carrer de	3C1
Mata, Carrer de	2E4
Mateu, Carrer de	3B1
Meer, Carrer de	5B5
Méndez Núñez, Carrer de	5C1
Méndez Vigo, Passatge de	3B4
Mercader, Passatge de	3A3
Mercaders, Carrer dels	5B2
Mercè, Carrer de la	5A3
Meridiana, Avinguda	6D2
Mestrança, Carrer de la	5B5
Metges, Carrer dels	5C2
Mèxic, Carrer de	1B1
Migdia, Passeig del	1A4
Milà i Fontanals, Carrer de	3C3
Milans, Carrer de	5A3
Milton, Carrer de	3A1
Minerva, Carrer de	3A2
Minici Natal, Passeig de	1A3
Mirador, Plaça del	1C5
Miralters, Carrer dels	5B3
Miramar, Avinguda de	1B3
Miramar, Carretera de	2D5
Miramar, Passeig de	2D4
Mistral, Avinguda de	1C1
Moianés, Carrer de	1A1
Moles, Carrer de les	5B1
Molí, Camí del	1A5
Molí Antic, Camí del	1A5
Mònec, Carrer d'En	5C1
Monistrol, Carrer de	3C2
Montalegre, Carrer de	2F2
Montanyans, Avinguda dels	1A2
Montcada, Carrer de	5B3
Montjuïc, Camí de	1C5
Montjuïc, Parc de	1C3
Montjuïc, Passeig de	2D4
Montmany, Carrer de	3C1
Montseny, Carrer del	3B1
Montserrat, Passatge de	2F4
Montsió, Carrer de	5A1
Morabos, Carrer dels	1A1
Moscou, Carrer de	6D4
Mosques, Carrer de les	5B3
Mossèn Jacint Verdaguer, Plaça de	3C3
Mozart, Carrer de	3B2
Muntaner, Carrer de	2F1
Murillo, Carrer de	2D3

N

Nacional, Passeig	5B5
Nàpols, Carrer de	4D2–4D5 6D1–6D2
Narcís Oller, Plaça de	3A2

Navas, Plaça de las	1C2
Neptú, Carrer de	3A2
Niça, Carrer de	4F1
Noguès, Passatge de	4E2
Nord, Carrer del	1A1
Notariat, Carrer del	2F2
Nou de la Rambla, Carrer	2D4
Nou Sant Francesc, Carrer	5A3
Nova, Plaça	5A2

O

Obradors, Carrer dels	5A3
Ocata, Carrer d'	5C3
Olímpic, Passeig	1A4
Olivera, Carrer de l'	1C2
Olles, Carrer de les	5B3
Om, Carrer de l'	2E3
Or, Carrer de l'	3B1
Oreneta, Carrer d'	3A1
Ortigosa, Carrer de	5B1

P

Pablo Neruda, Plaça de	4E4
Padilla, Carrer de	4F1
Pagès, Passatge de	4D5
Palau, Carrer del	5A3
Palaudàries, Carrer de	2E4
Palla, Carrer de la	5A2
Pallars, Carrer de	6E2
Palma, Carrer de la	1C3
Palma de Sant Just, Carrer de la	5B3
Paloma, Carrer de la	2E1
Pamplona, Carrer de	4F5 6F1–6F3
Paral.lel, Avinguda de	1B1 1C2 2D2–2F5
Parc, Carrer del	5A3
Pare Eusebi Millan, Plaça de	1A2
Pare Laínez, Carrer de	4D2
Parlament, Carrer de	2D2
Parlament, Passatge del	2D2
Patriarca, Passatge del	5A1
Pau, Passatge de la	5A3
Pau Claris, Carrer de	3B3
Pedreres, Carrer de les	1C2
Pedró, Plaça del	2E2
Pelai, Carrer de	2F1
Penedès, Carrer del	3B2
Pere Costa, Carrer de	4F1
Pere IV, Carrer de	6E2
Pere Serafí, Carrer del	3B1
Perill, Carrer del	3B2
Perla, Carrer de la	3B1
Permanyer, Passatge de	3B5
Pescadors, Carrer dels	5B5
Pescadors, Moll dels	5A5
Petons, Carrer dels	5C2
Petritxol, Carrer de	5A2
Peu de la Creu, Carrer del	2F2
Pi i Margall, Carrer de	4D1
Pi, Carrer del	5A2
Pi, Plaça del	5A2
Picasso, Passeig de	5C3
Pintor Fortuny, Carrer del	2F2
Piquer, Carrer de	2D3
Pizarro, Carrer de	5C4
Plata, Carrer de la	5A3
Poeta Boscà, Plaça de	5B4
Poeta Cabanyes, Carrer de	2D3
Polvorí, Camí del	1A1
Pompeu Gener, Plaça de	5C4
Portaferrissa, Carrer de la	5A2
Portal de l'Angel, Avinguda del	5A1

Portal de la Pau,
Plaça de **2F4**
Portal de Santa Madrona,
Carrer del **2F4**
Portal Nou, Carrer de **5C2**
Prat, Rambla del **3A1**
Princep d'Astúries,
Avinguda del **3A1**
Princep de Viana,
Carrer de **2E2**
Princesa, Carrer de la **5B2**
Progrés, Carrer del **3B2**
Provença, Carrer de **3A3**
Providència,
Carrer de la **4D1**
Prunera, Passatge de **1C2**
Puig i Xoriguer,
Carrer de **2E4**
Puigmartí, Carrer de **3B2**
Pujades, Carrer de **6F2**
Pujades, Passeig de **6D2**
Puríssima Concepció,
Carrer de la **1C3**

Q

Quevedo, Carrer de **3C2**

R

Rabí Rubén, Carrer del **1A1**
Radas, Carrer de **1C3**
Rambla, del **5A1**
Rambla del Raval, la **5A1**
Ramis, Carrer de **3C2**
Ramon Turró, Carrer de **6E3**
Ramon y Cajal,
Carrer de **3B2**
Raspall, Plaça del **3B2**
Ratés, Passatge de **6F1**
Rauric, Carrer d'En **5A2**
Rec, Carrer del **5C3**
Rec Comtal, Carrer de **5C2**
Rector Oliveras,
Passatge de **3B4**
Regàs, Carrer de **3A1**
Regomir, Carrer del **5A3**
Reial, Plaça **5A3**
Reig i Bonet, Carrer de **4D1**
Reina Amàlia,
Carrer de la **2E2**
Reina Cristina,
Carrer de la **5B3**
Reina Maria Cristina,
Avinguda de la **1B2**
Rellotge, Moll del **5B5**
Revolució de Setembre
de 1868, Plaça de la **3B1**
Ribera, Carrer de la **5C3**
Ribes, Carrer de **4E5 6D1**
Ricart, Carrer de **1C2**
Riera Alta, Carrer de la **2E2**
Riera Baixa, Carrer de la **2F2**
Riera de Sant Miquel,
Carrer de la **3A2**
Riereta, Carrer de la **2E2**
Ripoll, Carrer de **5B2**
Rius i Taulet,
Avinguda de **1B2**
Rius i Taulet, Plaça de **3B2**
Robador, Carrer d'En **2F3**
Robí, Carrer del **3B1**
Roca, Carrer d'En **5A2**
Rocafort, Carrer de **2D1**
Roger de Flor, Carrer de
4D2–D5 6D1–6D2
Roger de Flor,
Passatge de **4D3**

Roger de Llúria,
Carrer de **3B3**
Roig, Carrer d'En **2F2**
Romans, Carrer de **4D1**
Ros de Olano, Carrer de **3B1**
Rosa, Carrer de la **5A3**
Rosa Sensat, Carrer de **6F3**
Rosalía de Castro,
Carrer de **4F2**
Roser, Carrer del **2D3**
Rosselló, Carrer del **3A3**
Rull, Carrer d'En **5A3**

S

Sagrada Família,
Plaça de la **4D3**
Sagristans, Carrer dels **5B2**
Salamanca, Carrer de **5C5**
Salvà, Carrer de **2D3**
Salvador, Carrer del **2E2**
Salvador Espriu,
Carrer de **6E4**
Sancho de Ávila,
Carrer de **6E1**
Sant Agustí, Carrer de **3B3**
Sant Agustí, Plaça de **2F3**
Sant Agustí Vell,
Plaça de **5C2**
Sant Antoni, Ronda del **2E2**
Sant Antoni Abat,
Carrer de **2E2**
Sant Antoni Maria Claret,
Carrer de **4D2**
Sant Benet, Passatge de **5C1**
Sant Bertran, Carrer de **2E4**
Sant Carles, Carrer de **5B4**
Sant Climent, Carrer de **2E2**
Sant Cristòfol, Carrer de **3A1**
Sant Domènec,
Carrer de **3B2**
Sant Domènec del Call,
Carrer de **5A2**
Sant Elm, Carrer de **5B5**
Sant Erasme, Carrer de **2E2**
Sant Ferriol, Carrer de **1A1**
Sant Francesc de Paula,
Carrer de **5B1**
Sant Fructuós, Carrer de **1A1**
Sant Gabriel, Carrer de **3A1**
Sant Germà, Carrer de **1A1**
Sant Gil, Carrer de **2E2**
Sant Honorat, Carrer de **5B2**
Sant Isidre, Carrer de **1C3**
Sant Jaume, Plaça de **5A2**
Sant Jeroni, Carrer de **2F3**
Sant Joan, Passeig de **3C2–3C5**
5C1
Sant Joaquim,
Carrer de **3B2**
Sant Josep Oriol,
Carrer de **2F3**
Sant Lluís, Carrer de **3C1**
Sant Marc, Carrer de **3A1**
Sant Martí, Carrer de **2E3**
Sant Miquel, Baixada de **5A2**
Sant Miquel, Carrer de **5B5**
Sant Oleguer, Carrer de **2F3**
Sant Pacià, Carrer de **2E3**
Sant Pau, Carrer de **2E3**
Sant Pau, Ronda de **2E2**
Sant Paull de Nola,
Carrer de **1A1**
Sant Pere, Passatge de **4E1**
Sant Pere, Plaça de **5C1**
Sant Pere, Ronda de **5A1**
Sant Pere d'Abanto,
Carrer de **1A1**

Sant Pere Martir,
Carrer de **3B2**
Sant Pere Mes Alt,
Carrer de **5B1**
Sant Pere Mes Baix,
Carrer de **5B2**
Sant Pere Mitja,
Carrer de **5B1**
Sant Rafael, Carrer de **2F3**
Sant Ramon, Carrer de **2F3**
Sant Roc, Carrer de **1A1**
Sant Sebastià, Platja de **5B5**
Sant Sever, Carrer de **5A2**
Sant Vincenç, Carrer de **2E2**
Santa Anna, Carrer de **5A1**
Santa Carolina, Carrer de **4F2**
Santa Dorotea, Carrer de **1A1**
Santa Elena, Carrer de **2E3**
Santa Eugènia, Carrer de **3A1**
Santa Eulàlia, Carrer de **3C2**
Santa Madrona,
Carrer de **2E3**
Santa Madrona,
Passeig de **1B3**
Santa Magdalena,
Carrer de **3B1**
Santa Mònica, Carrer de **2F4**
Santa Rosa, Carrer de **3B1**
Santa Tecla, Carrer de **3B3**
Santa Teresa, Carrer de **3B3**
Saragossa, Carrer de **3A1**
Sardana, Plaça de la **2D4**
Sardenya, Carrer de **4E2–4E5**
6E1–6E2
Seca, Carrer de la **5B3**
Secretari Coloma,
Carrer del **4D1**
Sedata, Jardí de la **4D2**
Segons Jocs Mediterranis,
Carrer dels **1B2**
Seneca, Carrer de **3A2**
Sepúlveda, Carrer de **1C1**
Serra, Carrer d'En **5A3**
Sert, Passatge de **5C1**
Sevilla, Carrer de **5B5**
Sicília, Carrer de **4D2–4D5**
6D1
Sidé, Carrer de **5B2**
Sils, Carrer de **5A3**
Simó, Passatge de **4E3**
Simó Oller, Carrer de **5A3**
Siracusa, Carrer de **3B2**
Sitges, Carrer de les **5A1**
Sol, Carrer del **3B1**
Sol, Plaça del (Gràcia) **3B1**
Sol, Plaça del (Montjuïc) **1B3**
Sombrerers, Carrer dels **5B3**
Sòria, Carrer de **5C5**
Sortidor, Plaça del **2D3**
Sota Muralla, Pas de **5B3**
Sots-tinent Navarro,
Carrer de **5B2**

T

Tallers, Carrer dels **2F1**
Tamarit, Carrer de **1C2**
Tànger, Carrer de **6F1**
Tantarantana, Carrer d'En **5C2**
Tàpies, Carrer de les **2E3**
Tapineria, Carrer de la **5B2**
Tapioles, Carrer de **2D3**
Tarròs, Carrer d'En **5B2**
Tasso, Passatge de **4D5**
Taxdirt, Carrer de **4E1**
Templaris, Carrer dels **5A3**
Terol, Carrer de **3B1**
Tigre, Carrer del **2E1**
Til·lers, Passeig dels **5C2**

Iopazi, Carrer del **3B1**
Tordera, Carrer de **3B2**
Torrent de les Flors,
Carrer del **3C1**
Torrent de l'Olla,
Carrer del **3B3**
Torrent d'en Vidalet,
Carrer del **3C2**
Torres, Carrer de **3B2**
Torres, Passatge de les **4E3**
Torres i Amat, Carrer de **2F1**
Torrevella, Carrer de **6D4**
Torrijos, Carrer de **3C2**
Trafalgar, Carrer de **5C1**
Tragí, Carrer de **5B2**
Traginers, Plaça dels **5B3**
Trelawny, Carrer de **6D4**
Tres Pins, Carrer dels **1B4**
Tres Senyores,
Carrer de les **3C1**

U

Unió, Carrer de la **2F3**
Univers, Plaça de l' **1B1**
Universitat, Plaça de la **2F1**
Universitat, Ronda de la **2F1**
Utset, Passatge d' **4E4**

V

València, Carrer de **3A4**
Valldonzella, Carrer de **2F1**
Vallfogona, Carrer de **3B1**
Vallhonrat, Carrer de **1C2**
Ventalló, Carrer de **4D2**
Venus, Carrer de **3B2**
Verdaguer i Callís,
Carrer de **5B1**
Verdi, Carrer de **3B1**
Vermell, Carrer **5C2**
Verntallat, Carrer de **3C1**
Viada, Carrer de **3C1**
Vicenç Martorell, Plaça de **5A1**
Victòria, Carrer de la **5C1**
Vigatans, Carrer del **5B2**
Vila de Madrid,
Plaça de la **5A1**
Vila i Vilà, Carrer de **2E3**
Viladecols, Baixada de **5B2**
Viladomat, Carrer de **2D1**
Vilafranca, Carrer de **3C1**
Vilamarí, Carrer de **1C1**
Vilanova, Avinguda de **6D1**
Vilaret, Passatge de **4F3**
Villarroel, Carrer de **2E1**
Villena, Carrer de **6D3**
Vinaròs, Carrer de **5C5**
Vinyassa,
Passatge de la **6F2**
Vinyeta, Passatge de la **2D4**
Virtut, Carrer de la **3B1**
Vistalegre, Carrer de **2E2**
Voluntaris Olímpics,
Plaça dels **6E4**

W

Wellington, Carrer de **6D3**

X

Xaloc, Moll de **6F5**
Xiquets de Valls,
Carrer dels **3B2**
Xuclà, Carrer d'En **5A1**

Z

Zamora, Carrer de **6F1**

General Index

Page numbers in **bold** refer to main entries

A

Accessories shops 158–9
Addresses, Catalan 181
Adventure sports 170
Agila, King of the Visigoths 44
Air travel 182–3
Airborne activities 170
Albéniz, Isaac 21
Alfonso II, King of Aragón 128
   Monestir de Poblet 128
   Puigcerda 116
Almodóvar, Pedro 20, 21
Almogàvers 45
Amatller d'Art Hispanic 80
Ambulances 176, 177
Amposta 131
Amusement Park 163
Andorra **116**
Andorra la Vella 116
Anella Olimpica (Olympic Ring)
   93
Antiga Casa Figueres (Barcelona)
   28
Antiques shops 155, **160**, 161
Antoni Desvalls, Joan 100
Any Nou (New Year) 38
Aquàrium (Barcelona) 11, 13, **70**
Aqüeducte de les Ferreres
   (Tarragona) 131
Arc de Berà (Tarragona) 131
Arc del Triomf (Barcelona) **67**
Archaeological Museum
   (Barcelona) see Museu
   Arqueològic
Arché, Rafael 71
Architecture 26–7
   Gaudí and Modernisme 26–7
   Romanesque Art and
   Architecture 24–5
   La Ruta del Modernisme 28–9
Aribau, Bonaventura 47
Art 30–31
   Catalan Painting 30–31
   Romanesque Art and
   Architecture 24–5
   shops 155, **160**, 161
   see also Museums and galleries
Art Cristià workshops 30
Arties 114
Assumpció (Assumption Day) 38
ATMs 178
Augustus, Emperor 56
Autopistes (motorways/highways)
   186
Autumn in Catalonia 38

B

Bag shops **158**, 159
Bakeries 156–7
Balearic Islands
   sea travel 183
Bank notes 179

Banking 178
Banyoles 117
Baqueira-Beret **115**
Barcelona
   airport 182–3
   Eixample 72–85
   entertainment 162–71
   festes 36–9
   Further Afield 94–101
   hotels 136–7
   maps 16–17, 52–3
   Metro 185
   Montjuïc 86–93
   Old Town 54–71
   Quadrat d'Or 74–5
   restaurants 144–50
   shopping 154–61
   Streetfinder maps 188–97
   trains 184
Barcelona, Counts of 44
Barcelona Football Club **97**, 163
   Camp Nou Tour and Museum
   13, 96
Barceloneta 12, 13, **69**
Barri Gòtic (Barcelona) 10, 12, 13
   nightlife 168, 169
   Street-by-Street map 56–7
Barri Xinès (Barcelona) 64, 176
Barruera 115
Bars 140
   designer bars 163
Bartomeu, Mestre 30
Basílica de Santa Maria del Mar
   (Barcelona) 12, 13, **66**
Bassa, Ferrer 30, 97
Batlló i Casanovas, Josep 78
Beaches
   Costa Brava 123
   Costa Daurada 130
Beatus of Liébana, St 116
Bed and breakfast 135
Beget 117
Begur 123
Berga 117
   festes 36
Berga i Boix, Josep 30
Besalú **117**
Beuys, Joseph
   Chamber of Pain 97
Bicycling 170
Bird-watching 170
Black Virgin 125
Blai, Pere 59
Blanes **122**
Blay, Miquel
   Museu Comarcal de la Garrotxa
   (Olot) 117
   Palau de la Música Catalana
   (Barcelona) 65
Boats
   golondrinas (Barcelona) 11, 13,
   71
   Museu Marítim (Barcelona) 71
   sailing 171
   sea travel 183

Bofill, Guillem 118
Bofill, Ricard 101
Bonaparte, Joseph 47
Book shops 155, 160, 161
La Boqueria (Barcelona) 155
El Born 10, 12, 13
   A one-Hour walk around the
   Born 104–5
Borrassà, Lluís 30
Bossòst 114
Bourbon dynasty
   Carlist Wars 48
   Castell de Montjuïc (Barcelona)
   93
   War of the Spanish Succession
   46–7
Buigas, Carles 92
Buigas, Gaietà 71
Bureaux de change 178
Buses 187
Butterflies of the Vall d'Aran
   114

C

Caballé, Montserrat 21, 92
Cadaqués **122**
   Costa Brava 123
Cadí-Moixeró 116
Caesar, Julius 122
Cafés and Bars 163
CaixaForum (Barcelona) 11, **92**
Calder, Alexander 90
Caldes de Boí 115
Cambrils 130
Camp Nou stadium 13, 96
Camp sites 135
Camprodon 117
Canary Islands
   map 15
Cantada d'havaneres 37
Cardona 126
Cardona, Dukes of 126, 128
Carlist Wars (1833-9) 47, 48
Carnestoltes 39
Carnival 39
Carreras, Josep (José) 21, 166
Cars 186–7
Carthage 43
Casa de l'Ardiaca (Barcelona) 58
   Street-by-Street map 56
Casa Battló (Barcelona) 10, 12, 13,
   19, 26, 27, **78–9**, 80
Casa de la Ciutat (Barcelona) 12,
   59
   Street-by-Street map 56
Casa Lléo Morera (Barcelona) 28
Casa Milà (Barcelona) see La
   Pedrera
Casa-Museu Castell Gala Dalí
   (Figueres) 119
Casa-Museu Salvador Dalí
   (Cadaqués) 122
Casa Terrades (Barcelona) 81
   Street-by-Street map 75
Casa Vicens (Barcelona) 28

Casals, Pau 21
  Museu Pau Casals (Sant
  Salvador) 130
Casas, Ramon 31, 91
  *Procession outside Santa Maria
  del Mar* 30
Castell de Montjuïc (Barcelona)
  13, 52, **93**
  films 164
Castell dels Tres Dragons
  (Barcelona) 68
Casteller festivals 37, 127
Castles 126
  Cardona 126
  Castell de Montjuïc (Barcelona)
  13, 52, **93**
  Torre Bellesguard (Barcelona)
  100
Catalan language 20–21,
  174
Catalonia **110–31**
  Catalan painting 30–31
  history 42–9
  hotels 137–9
  maps 14–15, 17, 112–13
  Portrait of Catalonia 19–21
  restaurants 151–3
The Cathedral of the Poor (Mir)
  31
Cathedrals
  Barcelona 10, 12, 13, 53, 55, 56,
  60–61
  Girona 118–19
  Lleida 126
  La Seu d'Urgell 116
  Tarragona 131
  Vic 126
Cava Country 34–5
Centre de Cultura
  Contemporània de Barcelona
  (CCCB) 11, 64, 164
Cercle de Pessons 116
Cerdà i Sunyer, Ildefons 26
  Eixample (Barcelona) 73
Cerdanya 116
Cervantes, Miguel de 45
Charcuterie shops **156**, 157
Charlemagne, Emperor 44,
  118–19
Charles the Bald, King of the
  Franks 116
Charles Martel, King of the Franks
  44
Cheese shops **156**, 157
Cheques 141, 178
Children 175
Chillida, Eduardo 90
Chocolate and candy shops **156**,
  157
Christ in Majesty 91
Christmas 38, 39
Churches in Barcelona
  Basílica de Santa Maria del Mar
  12, 13, **66**
  opening hours 174–5

Churches in Barcelona (cont.)
  Sagrada Família 10–11, 12, 13,
  26, 53, 73, 80, **82–5**
  Temple Expiatori del Sagrat Cor
  95, 100
Cigar shops 157
Cinema **164**, 165
"Cistercian triangle" 127
Clavé, Josep Anselm 65
Climate 23, **36–9**
Climbing, safety 177
Clothes
  in restaurants 140
  shops 154, 155, 158–9
Cloud and Chair (Tàpies) 74
Clubs 163
Coins 179
Coll 115
Collegi de les Teresianes 27
Collet, Charles 125
Columbus, Christopher 46
  Barcelona Cathedral 60
  Dia de la Hispanitat 38
  Monument a Colom (Barcelona)
  11, 13, 52, 62, **71**
  Palau Reial Major (Barcelona) 58
Communications 180–81
Companys, Lluís
  arrest and imprisonment 48
  Castell de Montjuïc (Barcelona)
  93
  execution 49
Concert season (Barcelona) 37
Consulates 177
Convergència i Unió 19
Corpus Christi 36
CosmoCaixa **97**
Costa Brava 111, **123**
Costa Daurada 130
Credit cards 141, 178
Crime 176
Cruises 183
Currency 178–9
Cycling 170

D
Dalí, Salvador 21, 31, **119**
  Cadaqués 122
  Casa-Museu Castell Gala Dalí
  (Figueres) 119
  Casa-Museu Salvador Dalí
  (Cadaqués) 122
  Teatre-Museu Dalí (Figueres)
  119
Dalmau, Lluís 30
Dance 162, 163, **164–5**
  sardana 131
De Cajón! Flamenco Festival 39
Delicatessens 156, 157
Delta de l'Ebre **131**
Department stores **154**, 155
Desclot, Bernard 45
Dia de la Constitució 38
Dia de la Hispanitat 38
Diada de Catalunya 38

Dialling codes 180
Dijous Sant (Maundy Thursday)
  36
Dilluns de Pasqua (Easter
  Monday) 38
Disabled travellers 175
  in hotels 135
  in restaurants 141
Disseny Hub (DHUB) (Barcelona)
  100–101
Diumenge de Rams (Palm
  Sunday) 36
Divendres Sant (Good Friday) 38
Diving 171
Doctors 177
Dolça of Provence 44
Domènech i Montaner, Lluís
  Casa de l'Ardiaca (Barcelona) 58
  Casa Lleó Morera (Barcelona) 80
  Castell dels Tres Dragons
  (Barcelona) 68
  Fundació Antoni Tàpies
  (Barcelona) 74, 80
  Hospital de la Santa Creu i de
  Sant Pau (Barcelona) 12, 13, 73,
  81
  Modernisme 26
  Palau de la Música Catalana
  (Barcelona) 65
Domènech i Montaner, Pere 81
Dona i Ocell (Miró) 96
Drassanes (Barcelona) 71
Durro 115

E
Easter 36, 38
Ebre, Riu 131
Eco-Museu (Delta de L'Ebre) 131
Eixample (Barcelona) 17, **72–85**
  area map 73
  hotels 137
  nightlife 168, 169
  Quadrat d'Or: Street-by-Street
  map 74–5
  restaurants 148–9
  Sagrada Família 82–5
El Greco 30
El Prat airport (Barcelona) 182–3
El Raval (Barcelona) 13, **64**
  nightlife 168, 169
El Vendrell 130
Electrical adaptors 175
Elisenda de Montcada de Piños
  97
Emergencies 176
Empúries 43, **122**
Encants Vells (Barcelona) 155
Entertainment 162–9
Erill-la-Vall 115
L'Escala 123
Escunhau 114
Espace Lliure (Barcelona) 167
Estació de Sants 187
Estació del Nord (Barcelona) **101**,
  187

Estadi Olímpic Lluis Companys (Barcelona) **93**, 167
L'Estartit 123
Eulàlia, St 60, 61
European Union 49

F

Falqués, Pere 74, 101
Fashion shops 154, 155, **158**, 159
Faust, Karl 122
Felipe IV, King of Spain 46
Felipe V, King of Spain
    Castell de Montjuïc (Barcelona) 93
    Diada de Catalunya 38
    Parc de la Ciutadella (Barcelona) 67
    La Seu Vella (Lleida) 126
    War of the Spanish Succession 47
Felix, St 118
Feria de Abril (Barcelona) 36
Fernando II, King of Catalonia-Aragon 46, 58
Ferrer, Pere 59
Festa de Santa Eulàlia (Barcelona) 39
Festa del Treball 38
Festa major de Gràcia (Barcelona) 37
Festa major de Sants (Barcelona) 37
Festa major de Vilafranca del Penedès 37
Festes 36–9
Festes de Sarrià i de Les Corts (Barcelona) 38
Festival Internacional de Cinema de Catalunya 164
Festivals 36–9
    casteller 37, 127
Field sports 170
Fiestas *see* Festes
Figueres **119**
Film **164**, 165
Fira de Sant Ponç (Barcelona) 36
Fire Brigade 177
Fires, forest 177
Fishing 170
Fiveller, Joan 59
Flags
    Les Quatre Barres 116
Flame in Space and Naked Woman (Miró) 90
Flamenco 39, 169
Flor, Roger de 45
Flowers of the Matollar 22–3
Flying clubs 170
Foix, Counts of 116
Folguera, Francesc 124
Font de Canaletes (Barcelona) 63
Font i Carreras 93
Font Màgica (Barcelona) 13, 87, **92**
    Street-by-Street map 89
Fontseré, Josep
    Museu Martorell (Barcelona) 68

Fontseré, Josep (cont.)
    Parc de la Ciutadella (Barcelona) 67
Food and drink
    Cava Country 34–5
    The Flavours of Catalonia 32–3
    The Other Wines of Catalonia 34
    shopping 154, 155, 156–7
    What to Eat 142–3
    see also Restaurants
Football
    Barcelona Football Club **97**, 163
    Barcelona *v* Real Madrid 97
    Camp Nou Tour and Museum 13, 96
Forest fires 177
Forestier, Jean 64
Forment, Damià 129
Fortuny i Marsal, Marià 31, 65
Foster, Norman 97
Franco, General Francisco 48–9
Franks 44
Fundació Antoni Tàpies (Barcelona) 12, **80**
    Street-by-Street map 74
Fundació Joan Miró (Barcelona) 13, **90**
    Street-by-Street map 89

G

"Galeries" 154
Galleries *see* Museums and galleries
Galters, Charles 60, 61
Game hunting 170
Gandesa 113
Gardens *see* Parks and gardens
The Gardens at Aranjuez (Rusiñol) 30
Gargallo, Pau 65, 81
Garona, Riu 114
Garraf
    coast 111
Garran, Maurici 71
Gas (Petrol) 186
Gaudí, Antoni 20, 48, **80**
    Casa Battló (Barcelona) 10, 12, 13, 19, 26, 27, 78–9, 80
    Casa Vicens (Barcelona) 28
    Gaudí and Modernisme 26–7
    Museu Nacional d'Art de Catalunya (Barcelona) 91
    Palau Güell (Barcelona) 13, 26–7, 62, **64**
    Parc de la Ciutadella (Barcelona) 67
    Park Güell (Barcelona) 98–9
    La Pedrera (Barcelona) 10, 53, 75, **81**
    Plaça Reial (Barcelona) 63
    Sagrada Família (Barcelona) 10–11, 12, 13, 26, 53, 73, 80, **82–5**
    Torre Bellesguard (Barcelona) 100
Gay travellers 175

Generalitat 19
    Palau de la Generalitat (Barcelona) 59
George, St 36
Gift shops **160**, 161
Girona 111, **118–19**
    airport 182
    hotels 138
    map 118
    restaurants 151–2
Golf 170
Golondrinas (Barcelona) 11, 13, **71**
Gothic art 30
Goya, Francisco de 30
Gràcia
    A 90-minute walk through Gràcia 106–7
    nightlife 169
Gran Teatre del Liceu (Barcelona) 62
Granados, Enric 21
Grec Festival de Barcelona 37
Güell, Count Eusebi 48
    Park Güell (Barcelona) 27, 98–9
Guifré el Pelós (Wilfred the Hairy), Count of Barcelona 44
    Les Quatre Barres 116
    Ripoll 116
    Sant Joan de les Abadesses 117

H

Habsburg dynasty 46
Hamil Barca 43
Hannibal 43
Hat shops 159
Health 176
Herboristeria del Rei (Barcelona) 156, 157
Highways (Motorways) 186
Hiking 170–71
Hiring cars 186, 187
History 43–9
Holidays, public 38
Holy Week 36
Homar, Gaspar 28
Hospital de la Santa Creu i de Sant Pau (Barcelona) 12, 13, **81**
Hospitals 177
Hotels **134–9**
    Barcelona 136–7
    booking and check-in 134
    Catalonia 137–9
    disabled travellers 135
    grading and facilities 134
    Paradors 134
    prices and paying 134
    rural accommodation 135
Huguet, Jaume 59
    Palau Reial Major (Barcelona) 59
    St George and the Princess 30
Human towers 127
Hunting 170

I

Iberia 182
Iberians 43
Ice-skating 170

Illa de la Discòrdia (Barcelona) 12, **80**
　Street-by-Street map 74
Immaculada Concepció 38
Inquisition 58
Insurance
　holiday (vacation) 177
　motor 186
Interiors shops 161
International Exhibition (1929) 48
　Estadi Olímpic Lluís Companys (Barcelona) 93
　Montjuïc 87
　Museu Nacional d'Art de Catalunya (Barcelona) 91
　Pavelló Mies van der Rohe (Barcelona) 92
　Plaça d'Espanya (Barcelona) 93
　Poble Espanyol (Barcelona) 92
Internet 180–81
Isabel of Castile 46, 58
Isabel II, Queen 156
IVA see VAT

J

Jardí Botànic Marimurtra (Blanes) 122
Jaume I the Conqueror, King of Aragón 45, 59
Jaume II, King of Aragón 97
　Barcelona Cathedral 60, 61
　court painter 30
　Monestir de Santes Creus 127
Jazz **163**, 166–7
　Terrassa Jazz Festival 36
Jewellery shops **158**, 159
Jews 58
　Besalú 117
　expulsion of 46
　Museu d'Història dels Jueus (Girona) 118
Joan, Pere 131
Juan, Don of Austria 71
Juan II, King of Aragón 128
Juan Carlos, King of Spain 49
Jujol, Josep Maria 81
　Parc Güell (Barcelona) 98
　Plaça d'Espanya (Barcelona) 93

K

Kolbe, Georg 88

L

Language 20–21, **174**
Legal assistance 177
Lesbian travellers 175
Lichtenstein, Roy 70
Lingerie shops **160**, 161
Lithograph (Tàpies) 31
Llafranc 123
Lleida 111, **126–7**
Lliga de Catalunya 48
Llimona, Josep 67
Llívia 116
Lloret de Mar 123
　festes 37
La Llotja (Barcelona) **65**

Llull, Ramon 45
Llúria, Roger de 45
Lost property 176
Luke, St 125
Luminists 31
Luna, Bigas 21

M

Macià, Francesc 48
Magazines 181
Magic Fountain (Barcelona) see Font Màgica
Mancomunitat 48
Maps
　Barcelona 52–3
　Barcelona: City Centre 16–17
　Barcelona: Further Afield 95
　Barcelona: Quadrat d'Or 74–5
　Barcelona Streetfinder 188–97
　Barri Gòtic (Barcelona) 56–7
　Canary Islands 15
　Catalonia 17, 112–13
　Cava Country 34–5
　Eixample (Barcelona) 73
　Europe and North Africa 15
　Girona 118
　Montjuïc (Barcelona) 87, 88–9
　Old Town (Barcelona) 55
　La Rambla (Barcelona) 62–3
　La Ruta del Modernisme 28–9
　Spain 14–15
Maragall, Pasqual 49
Marès i Deulovol, Frederic **58**, 129
Maresme, coast 111
Mariscal, Javier 21
Maritime Museum (Barcelona) see Museu Marítim
Markets 155
　Mercat de San Josep (Barcelona) 62
Martí the Humanist 59, 100
Martín de Cermeño, Juan 69
Martorell, Bernat
　The Transfiguration 61
Martorell i Peña, Francesc 68
Martorell, Joanot 45, 46
Mas i Fontdevila, Arcadi 30, 31
Mateu, Pau 59
Matollar
　Flowers of the Matollar 22–3
　Wildlife of the Matollar 23
Medical treatment 177
Meier, Richard 62
Las Meninas (Picasso) 66
Menus 141, **142–3**
Mercat de Sant Josep (Barcelona) 62
La Mercè (Barcelona) 38
Mercury, Freddie 92
Metro 185
Mies van der Rohe, Ludwig
　Pavelló Mies van der Rohe (Barcelona) 92
Milà family 81
Mir, Joaquim
　The Cathedral of the Poor 31

Miró, Joan 20–21, 31
　Barcelona School of Fine Arts 65
　Dona i Ocell 96
　Flame in Space and Naked Woman 90
　Fundació Joan Miró (Barcelona) 13, 89, **90**
　Parc de Joan Miró (Barcelona) 96
　Plaça de la Boqueria (Barcelona) 63
Miró, Toni 21
Mitjans, Francesc 96
Modernisme 20–21
　Eixample (Barcelona) 73
　Gaudí and Modernisme 26–7
　La Ruta del Modernisme 28–9
　Mansana de la Discòrdia (Barcelona) 80
Moll d'Espanya 70
Mompou, Frederic 21
Monasteries
　"Cistercian triangle" 127
　Monestir de Montserrat **124–5**
　Monestir de Pedralbes (Barcelona) 11, 13, **97**
　Monestir de Poblet 128–9
　Monestir de Santa Maria (Ripoll) 24, 116
　Monestir de Santes Creus 127
　Sant Joan de les Abadesses 117
Money 178–9
Montblanc **127**
Montjuïc (Barcelona) 16, **86–93**
　area map 87
　Castell de Montjuïc 13, 52, **93**
　nightlife 169
　Street-by-Street map 88–9
Montserrat 124–5
Monturiol i Estarriol, Narcís 119
Monument a Colom (Barcelona) 11, 13, 52, 62, **71**
Moors 44, 46
　Tortosa 131
La Moreneta 125
Motor insurance 186
Motorways (highways) 186
Murals, Gothic art 30
Murillo, Bartolomé Esteban 30
Murt, Sita 158
Museums and galleries (general)
　admission charges 174
　opening hours 174
Museums and galleries (individual)
　Barcelona Cathedral 61
　CaixaForum 11, **92**
　Camp Nou Tour and Museum 13, 96
　Casa-Museu Castell Gala Dalí (Figueres) 119
　Casa-Museu Salvador Dalí (Cadaqués) 122
　Castell de Montjuïc (Barcelona) 93
　CosmoCaixa 97
　Disseny Hub (DHUB) (Barcelona) **100–101**

Museums and galleries
(individual) (cont.)
Eco-Museu (Delta de L'Ebre)
131
Fundació Antoni Tàpies
(Barcelona) 12, **80**
Fundació Joan Miró (Barcelona)
13, 89, **90**
Girona Cathedral 119
Monestir de Montserrat 124
Museu Arqueològic (Barcelona)
13, 89, **91**
Museu d'Art Contemporani
(Barcelona) 11, 13, **64**
Museu d'Art (Girona) 119
Museu d'Autòmats (Barcelona)
100
Museu Blau (Museu de Ciències
Naturals) 101
Museu Can Framis (Barcelona)
100
Museu Cau Ferrat (Sitges) 130
Museu de Cera (Barcelona) 63
Museu de Ciències Naturals -
Museu Blau (Barcelona) 101
Museu del Cinema (Girona) 119
Museu Comarcal de la Conca
de Barberà (Montblanc) 127
Museu Comarcal de la Garrotxa
(Olot) 117
Museu Diocesà i Comarcal
(Solsona) 126
Museu Diocesà (La Seu d'Urgell)
116
Museu Episcopal de Vic 25, 126
Museu Etnològic (Barcelona) 89
Museu d'Història de Barcelona -
Plaça del Rei (Barcelona) 10, 12,
13, 57, **58–9**
Museu d'Història de Catalunya
(Barcelona) 11, 70–71
Museu d'Història de Girona
(Girona) 119
Museu d'Història dels Jueus
(Girona) 118
Museu d'Idees i Invents (MIBA)
(Barcelona) **68**
Museu del Joguet (Figueres)
119
Museu Frederic Marès
(Barcelona) 10, 57, **58**
Museu Marítim (Barcelona) 13,
71
Museu Martorell (Barcelona) 68
Museu Municipal (Tossa de
Mar) 122
Museu Nacional Arqueològic
(Tarragona) 130, 131
Museu Nacional d'Art de
Catalunya (MNAC) (Barcelona)
11, 13, 88, **91**
Museu Olímpic i de l'Esport 93
Museu Pau Casals (Sant
Salvador) 130
Museu Picasso (Barcelona) 10,
12, 13, **66**
Museu de la Vall d'Aran (Vielha)
114

Museums and galleries
(individual) (cont.)
Museu de la Xocolata **67**
Poble Espanyol (Barcelona) 92
Sagrada Família (Barcelona)
83
Teatre-Museu Dalí (Figueres)
119
Vinseum (Vilafranca del
Penedès) 127
Music 166–7
classical music 37, **162**, 163,
166, 167
Palau de la Música Catalana
(Barcelona) 10, 13, **65**
rock, jazz and world music 163,
166–7
shops **160**, 161
Terrassa Jazz Festival 36

N

Nadal (Christmas) 38, 39
Nagel, Andrés 96
Napoleon I, Emperor 38, 47
Narcissus, St 118
National parks
hiking 170–71
Parc Nacional d'Aigüestortes
115, 171
negre nit 49
Newspapers 181
stores 155
Nightlife 168–9
Nonell, Isidre
Waiting for Soup 31

O

Old Town (Barcelona) 17, **54–71**
area map 55
Barcelona Cathedral 60–61
hotels 136–7
La Rambla 62–3
restaurants 144–8
Street-by-Street: Barri Gòtic
56–7
Oliva, Abbot 44, 126
Olot **117**
Olot School 30, 117
Olympic Games (1992) 49
Estadi Olímpic Lluís Companys
(Barcelona) **93**, 167
Montjuïc (Barcelona) 87
Port Olímpic (Barcelona) 69
Torre de Collserola (Barcelona)
97
Opening hours
banks 178
churches 174
museums 174
restaurants 140
Opera **166**, 167
Outdoor hazards 177

P

Painting, Catalan 30–31
Palamós 123
Palau Baró de Quadras
(Barcelona) 28, 75

Palau de la Generalitat
(Barcelona) 12, **59**
Street-by-Street map 56
Palau Güell (Barcelona) 13, 26–7,
62, **64**
Palau Moja (Barcelona) 63
Palau de la Música Catalana
(Barcelona) 10, 13, **65**
Palau Nacional (Barcelona) 52, 88
Palau Reial (Barcelona) 10, 57
Street-by-Street map 57
Palau Sant Jordi (Barcelona) 93,
167
Palau de la Virreina (Barcelona) 62
Pallarès Grau, Manuel 62
Palm Sunday 36
Parachute jumps 170
Paradors **134**, 135
Paragliding 170
Parc d'Atraccions (Barcelona) 100
Parc de la Ciutadella (Barcelona)
12, 53, **67**
Parc de l'Espanya Industrial
(Barcelona) 96
Park Güell (Barcelona) 13, **98–9**
Parc de Joan Miró (Barcelona) 96
Parc del Laberint d'Horta 100
Parc Nacional d'Aigüestortes **115**,
171
Parc Natural del Cadí-Moixeró
116
Parc Natural del Delta de L'Ebre
131
Parking 187
Parks and gardens
Fundació Joan Miró (Barcelona)
90
Jardí Botànic Marimurtra
(Blanes) 122
Parc de Joan Miró (Barcelona)
96
Parc de la Ciutadella (Barcelona)
12, 53, **67**
Parc de l'Espanya Industrial
(Barcelona) 96
Park Güell (Barcelona) 13,
98–9
Pasqua (Easter) 36
Passeig de Gràcia (Barcelona) 11,
12, 13
Street-by-Street map 74
Passports 174
Patisseries 156–7
Pavelló Mies van der Rohe
(Barcelona) **92**
Street-by-Street map 88
La Pedrera (Barcelona) 10, 12, 53,
81
Street-by-Street map 75
Pelegrí de Tossa (Tossa de Mar)
39
Peña Ganchegui, Luis 96
Peninsular War (War of
Independence, 1808-14) 47
Pepper, Beverley 101
Peratallada **122**
Pere IV the Ceremonious, King of
Aragon 45, 128

Perfume shops **160**, 161
Personal security 176–7
Peter, St 125
Petrol (gas) 186
Petronila of Aragon 44
Pharmacies 177
Picasso, Jacqueline 66
Picasso, Pablo 21, 31
  Barcelona School of Fine Arts 65
  Las Meninas 66
  Museu Picasso (Barcelona) 10, 12, 13, **66**
  Pablo Picasso in Barcelona 66
  Self-Portrait 66
Pilma (Barcelona) 155
Piscines Bernat Picornell (Barcelona) 93
Pla, Francesc 30
Plaça de la Boqueria (Barcelona) 63
Plaça d'Espanya (Barcelona) **93**
Plaça Reial (Barcelona) 63
Platja d'Aro 37, 123
  festes 39
Poble Espanyol (Barcelona) 92
  Street-by-Street map 88
Poble Sec
  nightlife 169
Poblenou **101**
  A Two-hour walk through Poblenou 108–9
Poblet *see* Monestir de Poblet
Police 176, 177
Port Aventura 130
Port Olímpic (Barcelona) **69**
  nightlife 168, 169
Port Vell (Barcelona) 12, 13, **70**
  nightlife 168, 169
Postal services 180
Pou de Gel (Solsona) 126
Primo de Rivera, Miguel 48
Procession outside Santa Maria del Mar (Casas) 30
Public conveniences 177
Public holidays 38
Puig i Cadafalch, Josep
  CaixaForum (Barcelona) 92, 97
  Casa Amatller (Barcelona) 80
  Casa Macaya (Barcelona) 29
  Casa Terrades (Barcelona) 75, **81**
  Font Màgica (Barcelona) 92
  Modernisme 26
  Palau Baró de Quadras (Barcelona) 28, 75
Puigcerdà **116**
Pujol, Jordi 19
Pyrenees 116

Q

Quadrat d'Or (Barcelona)
  Street-by-Street map 74–5
Les Quatre Barres 116

R

Radio 181
Rainfall 38
Rainy Taxi (Dalí) 119

La Rambla (Barcelona) 10, 12, 13, 20, 53, 62–3
Ramon Berenguer I, Count of Barcelona 44, 61
Ramon Berenguer III, Count of Barcelona 44
Ramon Berenguer IV, Count of Barcelona 44
  Monestir de Poblet 128
  Monestir de Santes Creus 127
Real Madrid Football Club 97
Rebull, Joan
  Three Gypsy Boys 56
Reccared, King of the Visigoths 43
Referendum (2014) 49
Reial Acadèmia de Ciències i Arts (Barcelona) 63
Reis Mags 38, 39
Renaixença 47–8
RENFE 184
Restaurants **140–53**
  Barcelona 144–50
  Catalonia 151–3
  eating hours 140
  how to dress 140
  prices and paying 141
  reading the menu 141
  smoking in 141
  What to Eat 142–3
  wheelchair access 141
  wine choices 141
  see also Food and drink
Reus 131
Reus airport 182
Revellón 39
Revetlla de Sant Joan 37
Ribera, José de 30
Rigalt, Lluís 28
Ripoll **116**
Road signs 186
Rock music **163**, 166–7
Roig i Soler, Joan 30, 69
Roman remains 43
  Barri Gòtic (Barcelona) 57
  Empúries 122
  Museu d'Història de Barcelona 59
  Tarragona 130–31
  Vic 126
Romanesque art and architecture 24–5
Romeu, Pere 91
Ros i Güell, Antoni 28
Roses 123
Rothko, Mark 90
Royal Palace *see* Palau Reial
Rural accommodation 135
Rusiñol, Santiago 31
  The Gardens at Aranjuez 30
  Sitges 130
La Ruta del Modernisme 28–9

S

Sabartes, Jaime 66
Safont, Marc 59
Sagnier, Enric 100
Sagrada Família (Barcelona) 53, 73, 80, **82–5**

Sagrada Família (Barcelona) (cont.)
  Gaudí and Modernisme 26
  Great Days in Barcelona 10–11, 12, 13
Sailing 171
St George and the Princess (Huguet) 30
Salardú 114
Salou 130
Sant Carles de la Ràpita 131
Sant Climent de Taüll 24, 115
Sant Cristòfol de Beget 25
Sant Jaume de Frontanyà 24, 116
Sant Joan 38
Sant Joan de les Abadesses **117**
Sant Jordi 36
Sant Josep 36
Sant Martí 116
Sant Medir (Barcelona) 36
Sant Miquel 38
Sant Pere de Besalú 25
Sant Pere de Camprodon 25
Sant Pere de Galligants 25
Sant Pere de Rodes 25, 119
Sant Sadurní d'Anoia
  cava 34–5
Santa Cristina (Lloret de Mar) 37
Santa Eulàlia (Barcelona) 39
Santa Maria (Ripoll) **24**, 115
Santa Maria (Taüll) 115
Santes Creus **127**
Sardana (dance) 131
Savall, Jordi 21
Science Museum *see* CosmoCaixa
Sea travel 183
Second-hand shops **158**, 159
Self-catering 135
Sert, Josep Lluís
  Fundació Joan Miró (Barcelona) 89, 90
Sert, Josep-Maria 31, 126
  Casa de la Ciutat (Barcelona) 59
  Cathedral (Vic) 126
Setmana Santa (Easter week) 36
La setmana tràgica (1909) 48
La Seu d'Urgell 112, **116**
Shoe shops 159
Shopping in Barcelona 154–61
  clothes and accessories 158–9
  food and drink 156–7
  speciality stores 160–61
Sitges 113, **130**
  festes 36, 39
  Luminists 31
Skating 170
Skiing 171
  Baqueira-Beret 115
Smoking, in restaurants 141
Solsona **126**
Spanish Civil War (1936–9) 48–9, 131
Speciality stores 154, 155, **160–61**
Speed limits 186
Sports **170–71**
Spring in Catalonia 36
Stationery shops **160**, 161

Student travellers 175
Subirachs, Josep Maria 82, 84
Summer in Catalonia 37
Sunshine 37
Swimming pools 170
Synagogues 58

T

Tàpies, Antòni 21, 31, 90
  Cloud and Chair 74
  Fundació Antoni Tàpies
    (Barcelona) 74, **80**
  Lithograph 31
Tarragona 111, **130–31**
Taxes
  in restaurants 141
  tax-free goods 174
Taxis 187
Teatre Grec (Barcelona) **90**
Teatre Lliure (Barcelona) 166, 167
  Street-by-Street map 89
Telephones 180
  emergencies 176
Television 181
Temperatures 39
Temple Expiatori del Sagrat Cor
  (Barcelona) 95, 100
Tennis 170
Terrassa Jazz Festival 36
Theatre 162, 163, **164–5**
Theft 176
Theme parks
  Port Aventura 130
Thirty Years War (1618-59) 46
Three Gypsy Boys (Rebull) 56
Tibidabo (Barcelona) 11, **100**
  amusement park 163
  nightlife 169
Time zone 175
Tipping 141
Toilets, public 177
Torre Bellesguard (Barcelona) 100
Torre de Collserola (Barcelona) 97
Tortosa **131**
Tossa de Mar 21, **122**, 123
  festes 39
Tots Sants (All Saints' Day) 38
Tourist offices 135, **174**, 175
Trains 184–5
The Transfiguration (Martorel) 61
Travel 182–7
  air travel 182–3
  buses 187

Travel (cont.)
  cars 186–7
  Catalonia 112
  cruises 183
  golondrinas (Barcelona) 11, 13,
    71
  Metro 185
  sea travel 182, 183
  taxis 187
  trains 184–5
Traveller's cheques 178
  in restaurants 141
Travellers with Special Needs 175
  in hotels 135
  in restaurants 141
Els Tres Tombs (Barcelona) 39
Tusquets, Oscar 21

U

Universal Exhibition (1888) 26, 48
  Arc del Triomf (Barcelona) 67
  Castell dels Tres Dragons
    (Barcelona) 68
  Monument a Colom (Barcelona)
    71
Usatges (Constitution) 44

V

Vall d'Aran **114**
  Butterflies of the Vall d'Aran
    114
Vall de Boí **115**
Vallmitjana, Agapit and Venanci
  125
Valls
  festes 37
Van Eyck, Jan 30
Van Gogh, Vincent 70
VAT
  in restaurants 141
  tax-free goods 174
Vayreda i Vila, Joaquim 30, 117
Velázquez, Diego de 30, 66
Verdaguer, Jacint 47
Verge del Carme (Barcelona) 37
Vespucci, Amerigo 71
Vic **126**
Vielha **114**
Viladomat, Antoni 30
Vilafranca del Penedès 35, **127**
  festes 37
Vilanova
  festes 39

Villar i Lozano, Francesc de Paula
  83
Vinçon (Barcelona) 11, 155
Vintage fashion shops 158, 159
Virgin of Montserrat 125
Visas 174
Visigoths 43–4

W

Waiting for Soup (Nonell) 31
Walking 102–9
  El Born 104–5
  Gràcia 106–7
  hiking 170–71
  Poblenou 108–9
  La Ruta del Modernisme 28–9
  safety 109
War of the Spanish Succession
  (1701-13) 46–7
Water sports 171
Waxwork museum (Barcelona)
  see Museu de Cera
Weather 23, **36–9**
Wheelchair access *see* Disabled
  travellers
Wi-Fi 180–81
Wildlife
  bird-watching 170
  Butterflies of the Vall d'Aran 114
  Parc Nacional d'Aigüestortes
    115
  Parc Natural del Delta de L'Ebre
    131
  Wildlife of the Matollar 23
Wine
  Cava Country 34–5
  in restaurants 141
  shops 157
  The Other Wines of Catalonia
    34
  Vinsmuseu (Vilafranca del
    Penedès) 127
Winter in Catalonia 39
Winter sports 171
Witiza, King of the Visigoths
  44
World music 163

Z

Zafón, Carlos Ruiz 21
Zoo de Barcelona (Barcelona)
  68–9
Zurbarán, Francisco de 30

Acknowledgments

Dorling Kindersley would like to thank the following people whose contributions and assistance have made the preparation of this book possible.

Main Contributor
Roger Williams contributed to the *Eyewitness Travel Guide to Spain* and has written Barcelona and Catalonia titles for Insight Guides. He was also the main contributor to the *Eyewitness Travel Guide to Provence*. *Lunch with Elizabeth David*, set around the Mediterranean, is his latest novel.

Additional Contributors
Mary Jane Aladren, Pepita Arias, Emma Dent Coad, Sally Davies, Rebecca Doulton, Josefina Fernández, , Mary-Ann Gallagher, Nick Rider, David Stone, Judy Thomson, Clara Villanueva, Suzanne Wales (Word on Spain).

Revisions Team
Louise Abbott, Amaia Allende, Queralt Amella Miró, Gillian Andrews, Imma Espuñes i Amorós, Shruti Bahl, Claire Baranowski, Kate Berens, Marta Bescos, Stuti Tiwari Bhatia, Rohan Bolton, Daniel Campi (Word on Spain), Paula Canal (Word on Spain), Anna Freiberger, Mary-Ann Gallagher, Alrica Green, Swati Gupta, Lydia Halliday, Christine Heilman, Jessica Hughes, Claire Jones, Zafar ul Islam Khan, Juliet Kenny, Elly King, Priya Kukadia, Rahul Kumar, Kathryn Lane, Alison McGill, Caroline Mead, Sam Merrell, Barbara Minton, Jason Mitchell, Sonal Modha, Casper Morris, Vikki Nousiainen, Susie Peachey, Marianne Petrou, Rada Radojicic, Mani Ramaswamy, Lucy Richards, Ellen Root, Collette Sadler, Alice Saggers, Azeem Siddiqui, Meredith Smith, Susie Smith, Vatsala Srivastava, Alícia Ribas Sos, Helen Townsend, Nikhil Verma, Alex Whittleton, Hugo Wilkinson, Lola Carbonell Zaragoza.

Proofreader
Stewart J Wild, Huw Hennessey.

Indexer
Hilary Bird.

Special Photography
Max Alexander, Departure Lounge/Ella Milroy, D. Murray/J. Selmes, Dave King, Ian O'Leary, Alessandra Santarelli, Susannah Sayler, Clive Streeter

Photography permissions
© Obispado de VIC; © Cabildo de la Catedral de Girona; Teatre Nacional de Catalunya (Barcelona); Institut Mpal. del Paisatge Urba i la Qualitat de Vida, Ajuntament de Barcelona.

Dorling Kindersley would like to thank all the churches, museums, restaurants, hotels, shops, galleries and other sights too numerous to thank individually.

Picture credits
Key: a= above; b = below/bottom; c = centre; f = far; l = left; r = right; t = top.

Works of art have been reproduced with the permission of the following copyright holders:

Salvador Dalí *Rainy Taxi* and *ceiling fresco in the Wind Palace Room, Teatre - Museu Dalí* © Kingdom of Spain, Gala - Salvador Dalí Foundation, DACS, London 2011; George Kolbe *Morning* © DACS, London 2011; IOC/ Olympic Museum Collections; Joan Miró *Dona i Ocell* 1983 and Tapestry of the Foundation Joan Miro 1975 © Succession Miró/ADAGP, Paris and DACS, London 2011.

The publisher would like to thank the following individuals, companies and picture libraries for their kind permission to reproduce their photographs:

ABaC Restaurant & Hotel: 140bl, 150tr; **Hotel Aiguaclara:** 134bc, 138bl; **Hotel Arts Barcelona:** 137tr; **AISA, Barcelona:** 16bl, 20br, 25bl, Jaume Huguet *San Jorge* 30cla, 46cb, 48cb, 48bl, 176bl; **Alamy Images:** Douglas Armand 99cr; Jon Arnold Images 78tr; John Barab 18; Andrew Bargery 64br, 78cb; Neil Barks 79tl; Peter Barritt 84tr; Oliver Bee 78crb, 79br; CW Images 50-1; Dalgleish Images 98cl; Danita Delimont 174cb; Iain Davidson Photographic 104cla, 105tl; Chad Ehlers 99tl; Mike Finn-Kelcey 185bc; Richard Foot 98tr; Kevin Foy 185tl; B J Gadie 64tc; Guido 186cla; Platinum GPics 1c; Terry Harris 17c; Chris I Iellier 102; Guillem Lopez 40-1; Stephen Saks Photography 70t; Neil Setchfield 62br; Sandro Vannini 84bc; Ruben Vicente 187bl; Ken Welsh 175tl; Alsa Group s.l.l.c: 187tr; **Aquila Photographics:** Adrian Hoskins 114cl; 114bl, 114clb; James Pearce 23bl; **National Atesa:** 186c; **El Atril:** 144br.

Balearia: 183cr; Basilica Sagrada Familia: Pep Daudé 83crb; **Mike Busselle:** 113br, 114tc.

Can Culleretes: 141tl; **El Celler de Can Roca** 152br; **El Celler de l'Aspic:** 151b; **Cinnamon:** 153tr; **Cinc Sentits:** 148 br; **Codorniu:** 35tl, 35ca; **Bruce Coleman Collection:** Erich Crichton 22tr; José Luis González Grande 23tr; Norbert Schwirtz 23tl; Colin Varwdell 23crb; **Comerc24:** 140cla; **Corbis:** 33tl, 33c, Archivio cla; Peter Aprahamian 107br; Carlos Dominguez 11clb; Owen Franken 32cla; Andrea Jemolo 84cla; Ken Kaminesky 76-7; Julian Martin/EPA 12bl; Jose Fuste Raga 11tl; Mark L. Stephenson 85cla; Vanni Archive 85br. **Cover**, Madrid: Pepe Franco 154cla; Matias Nieto 191b.

Dreamstime.com: Bayda127 12tr; Blitzkoenig 92tl; Alexandre Fagundes De Fagundes 93bl; Gurgenb 21t;

Hugera 96b; Mihai-bogdan Lazar 63cb; Lornet 91t; Marlee 110; Carlos Soler Martinez 13tc; Juan Moyano 81tl; Toxawww 10cl, 19b; Yuryz 182bl.

Hotel Empordà: 151tr; Espai Sucre: 146br; L'Estartit Tourist Office: 123cl; European Commission: 179.

Firo Foto: 71cl; Flickr.com: www.flickr.com/photos/del15xavii_xavo/4123975385/177tr; Frieixenet: 34cl, 35br; Fundacion Collection Thyssen-bornemisza: Fra Angelico Madonna of Humility 97t; Fundacio Joan Miro, Barcelona: Joan Miró Flama en l'espai i dona nua 1932 © Succession Miró/ ADAGP, Paris and DACS, London 2011 90tl.

Generalitat de Catalunya: 177cra; Getty Images: Peter Adams 120-1; Danbalboa Fotografo 94; Niko Guido 13br; Conor MacNeill 54; Nikada 172-3; JosÃ © Fuste Raga 2-3; Ferran Traite Soler 72; PHAS 8-9; Godo Photo: 126bl, 131t, José Luis Dorada 127t; Grupo Tragaluz: 149br.

Robert Harding Picture Library: 27tr, 61cra, 74cla, 93tr, 91b; La Huerta: 152tc.

The Illustrated London News Picture Library: 49t; Index, Barcelona: CJJ. 21br, 46tl, 49crb; Image Bank: 26bl, 75crb; Images Colour Library: 26clb; AGE Fotostock: 115br, 155tr, 155cl, 170cr; Nick Inman: 22b, 98br.

La Caixa: 178tr; Life File Photographic: Xabier Catalan 27crb; Emma Lee 27cra.

Marka, Milan: Sergio Pitamitz 64tl; Mas Salvanera: Ramón Ruscalleda 135tl; Milk Bar & Bistro: 145tr; Museu Arqueologic: 89cra; Museu de Ciencies Naturals de Barcelona: 68clb; Museu Nacional D'art De Catalunya: Ramon Marti Alsina La Compañia de Santa Barbara 1891 47tl; Museu Picasso: Pablo Ruiz Picasso Auto Retrato 1899–1900 © Succession Picasso/ DACS, London 2011 66bl.

Natural Science Photos: C Dani & I Jeske 170c; Naturpress, Madrid: Oriol Alamany 36cl, 39cra; Walter Kvaternik 39c, 177cra; Carlos Vegas 180tr; Jose A Martinez 111b.
Oronoz, Madrid: 43b, 44tr, 44cl, 47bl, 48tl.

Dos Palillos: 141bl, 147tr; Zoo de Barcelona: 68tr; Photographersdirect.com: Michael Dobson/Echo Imagery 109c, 109br; Fran Fernandez Photography 104bc, 107c, 108tl, 109tl; Jan van der Hoeven, 105br, 106cla, 108br. Francisco Fernandez Prieto:106bc; Prisma, Barcelona: 4tr, 20tl, 47crb, 48cra, 154br, 163c; Carles Aymerich 24bl, 38cra;; Jordi Cami 36br; Ramon Cases Carbo Procession outside Santa María del Mar c. 1898 30tr; Albert Heras 38bl; Kuwenal 45tr, 45clb; Mateu 37cra; Joaquim Mir Trinxet La Catedral de los Pobres 31bl; Isidro Nunell Monturiol Esperando la Sopa 1899 31tl; Santiago Rusiñol y Prats Jardines de Aranjuez 1907 30br; Antoni Tàpies Litografía 1948 © Foundation Tàpies, Barcelona/ADAGP, Paris & DACS, London 2011 31br.

Els Quatre Gats: 146t.

Raimat: 34cb; RENFE: 184cb; Rex Features: 119cb; Roca Moo, Hotel Omm: 149tl.

M Angeles Sanchez: 37bc; Sant Pau: 153bl; Sant Pere del Bosc Hotel & Spa: 139tr; Sauc Restaiurant: 148tl; Spectrum Colour Library: 26tr; Stockphotos, Madrid: 170bl; Campillo 171tl; Suculent: 147bl; Superstock: Age Fotostock 184cla; MIVA Stock 86.

TV3 Television de Catalunya: 181cra.

Wagakoro: 150bl.

Map Cover: Getty Images: Scott Barbour.

Jacket: Front and Spine - Getty Images: Vision of our Land.

Front End Paper:
Dreamstime.com: Marlee Rcr; Getty Images: Danbalboa Fotografo Rc; Conor MacNeill Lbr; Ferran Traite Soler Rtc; Superstock: MIVA Stock Lbl.

All other images © Dorling Kindersley. For further information see www.DKimages.com.

Special Editions of DK Travel Guides

English–Catalan Phrase Book

In Emergency

English	Catalan	Pronunciation
Help!	Auxili!	ow-**gzee**-lee
Stop!	Pareu!	**pah**-reh-oo
Call a doctor!	Telefoneu un metge!	teh-leh-fon-**eh**-oo oon **meh**-djuh
Call an ambulance!	Telefoneu una ambulància!	teh-leh-fon-**eh**-oo oo-nah ahm-boo-**lahn**-see-uh
Call the police!	Telefoneu la policia!	teh-leh-fon-**eh**-oo lah poh-lee-**see**-ah
Call the fire brigade!	Telefoneu els bombers!	teh-leh-fon-**eh**-oo uhlz boom-**behs**
Where is the nearest telephone?	On és el telèfon més proper?	on-ehs uhl tuh-leh-fon mehs proo-**peh**
Where is the nearest hospital?	On és l'hospital més proper?	on-ehs looss-pee tahl mehs proo-**peh**

Communication Essentials

English	Catalan	Pronunciation
Yes	Sí	see
No	No	noh
Please	Si us plau	sees plah-oo
Thank you	Gràcies	grah-see-uhs
Excuse me	Perdoni	puhr-**thoh**-nee
Hello	Hola	oh-lah
Goodbye	Adéu	ah-they-oo
Good night	Bona nit	bo-nah neet
Morning	El matí	uhl muh-**tee**
Afternoon	La tarda	lah tahr-thuh
Evening	El vespre	uhl vehs-pruh
Yesterday	Ahir	ah-ee
Today	Avui	uh-voo-ee
Tomorrow	Demà	duh-mah
Here	Aquí	uh-kee
There	Allà	uh-lyah
What?	Què?	keh
When?	Quan?	kwahn
Why?	Per què?	puhr keh
Where?	On?	ohn

Useful Phrases

How are you?	Com està?	kom uhs-**tah**
Very well, thank you	Molt bé, gràcies.	mol **beh** grah-see-uhs
Pleased to meet you.	Molt de gust.	mol duh **goost**
See you soon.	Fins aviat.	feenz uhv-**yat**
That's fine.	Està bé.	uhs-tah beh
Where is/are ...?	On és/són?	ohn ehs/sohn
How far is it to ...?	Quants metres/ kilòmetres hi ha d'aquí a ...?	kwahnz meh-truhs/ kee-**loh**-muh-truhs yah dah-**kee** uh
Which way to ...?	Per on es va a ...?	puhr on uhs bah ah
Do you speak English?	Parla anglès?	par-luh an-**glehs**
I don't understand	No l'entenc.	noh luhn-**teng**
Could you speak more slowly, please?	Pot parlar més a poc a poc, si us plau?	pot par-**lah** mehs pok uh pok sees plah-oo
I'm sorry.	Ho sento.	oo **sehn**-too

Useful Words

English	Catalan	Pronunciation
big	gran	gran
small	petit	puh-**teet**
hot	calent	kah-**len**
cold	fred	fred
good	bo	boh
bad	dolent	doo-**len**
enough	bastant	bahs-**tan**
well	bé	beh
open	obert	oo-**behr**
closed	tancat	tan-**kat**
left	esquerra	uhs-**kehr**-ruh
right	dreta	**dreh**-tuh
straight on	recte	**rehk**-tuh
near	a prop	uh **prop**
far	lluny	**lyoon**yuh
up/over	a dalt	uh **dahl**
down/under	a baix	uh **bah**-eeshh
early	aviat	uhv-**yat**
late	tard	tahrt
entrance	entrada	uhn-**trah**-thuh
exit	sortida	**soor**-tee-thuh
toilet	lavabos/ serveis	luh-**vah**-boos sehr-**beh**-ees

English	Catalan	Pronunciation
more	més	mess
less	menys	men**yees**

Shopping

English	Catalan	Pronunciation
How much does this cost?	Quant costa això?	kwahn kost ehs-**shoh**
I would like ...	M'agradaria ...	muh-arad-uh-**ree**-ah
Do you have?	Tenen?	tehn-un
I'm just looking, thank you	Només estic mirant, gràcies.	noo-mess ehs-**teek** mee-**rahn** grah-see-uhs
Do you take credit cards?	Accepten targes de crèdit?	ak **sehp** tuhn tahr-**zhuhs** duh **kreh**-deet
What time do you open?	A quina hora obren?	ah **keen** uh oh-ruh **oh**-bruhn
What time do you close?	A quina hora tanquen?	ah **keen** uh oh-ruh **tan**-kuhn
This one	Aquest	uh-**ket**
That one.	Aquell	ah-**kehl**
expensive	car	kahr
cheap	bé de preu/ barat	beh thuh preh-oo/ bah-**rat**
size (clothes)	talla/mida	tah-lyah/**mee**-thuh
size (shoes)	número	noo-**mehr**-oo
white	blanc	blang
black	negre	neh-gruh
red	vermell	vuhr-**mel**
yellow	groc	grok
green	verd	behrt
blue	blau	blah-oo
antique store	antiquari/botiga d'antiguitats	an-tee-**kwah**-ree/ boo-**tee**-gah/dan-tee-ghee-**tats**
bakery	el forn	uhl **forn**
bank	el banc	uhl **bang**
book store	la llibreria	lah lyee-bruh-**ree**-ah
butcher's	la carnisseria	lah kahr-nee-suh-**ree**-uh
pastry shop	la pastisseria	lah pahs-tee-suh-**ree**-uh
chemist's	la farmàcia	lah fuhr-**mah**-see-ah
fishmonger's	la peixateria	lah peh-shuh-tuh-**ree**-uh
greengrocer's	la fruiteria	lah froo-ee-tuh-**ree**-uh
grocer's	la botiga de quevlures	lah boo-**tee**-guh duh keh-vee-oo-ruhs
hairdresser's	la perruqueria	lah peh-roo-kuh-**ree**-uh
market	el mercat	uhl muhr-**kat**
newsagent's	el quiosc de premsa	uhl kee-**ohsk** duh **prem**-suh
post office	l'oficina de correus	loo-fee-**see**-nuh duh koo-**reh**-oos
shoe store	la sabateria	lah sah-bah-tuh-**ree**-uh
supermarket	el supermercat	uhl soo-puhr-muhr-**kat**
tobacconist's	l'estanc	luhs-**tang**
travel agency	l'agència de viatges	la-**jen**-see-uh duh vee-**ad**-juhs

Sightseeing

English	Catalan	Pronunciation
art gallery	la galeria d'art	lah gah-luh **ree**-yuh dart
cathedral	la catedral	lah kuh-tuh-**thrahl**
church	l'església la basílica	luhz-**gleh**-zee-uh lah buh-**zee**-lee-kuh
garden	el jardí	uhl zhahr-**dee**
library	la biblioteca	lah bee-blee-oo-**teh**-kuh
museum	el museu	uhl moo-**seh**-oo
tourist information office	l'oficina de turisme	loo-fee-**see**-nuh thuh too-**reez**-muh
town hall	l'ajuntament	luh-djoon-tuh-**men**
closed for holiday	tancat per vacances	tan-**kat** puh bah-**kan**-suhs
bus station	l'estació d'autobusos	luhs-tah-see-**oh** dow-toh-**boo**-zoos
railway station	l'estació de tren	luhs-tah-see-**oh** thuh **tren**

Staying in a Hotel

Do you have a vacant room?	¿Tenen una habitació lliure?	teh-nuhn oo-nuh ah-bee-tuh-see-oh lyuh-ruh
double room with double bed	habitació doble amb llit de matrimoni	ah-bee-tuh-see-oh doh-bluh am lyeet duh mah-tree-moh-nee
twin room	habitació amb dos llits/ amb llits individuals	ah-bee-tuh-see-oh am dohs lyeets/ am lyeets in-thee-vee-thoo-ahls
single room	habitació individual	ah-bee-tuh-see-oh een-dee-vee-thoo-ahl
room with a bath	habitació amb bany	ah-bee-tuh-see-oh am bah-nyuh
shower	dutxa	doo-chuh
porter	el grum	uhl groom
key	la clau	lah klah-oo
I have a reservation	Tinc una habitació reservada	ting oo-nuh ah-bee-tuh-see-oh reh-sehr-vah-thah

Eating Out

Have you got a table for…	Tenen taula per…?	teh-nuhn tow-luh puhr
I would like to reserve a table	Voldria reservar una taula.	vool-dree-uh reh-sehr-vahr oo-nuh tow-luh
The bill please	El compte, si us plau	uhl kohm-tuh sees plah-oo
I am a vegetarian	Sóc vegetarià/ vegetariana	sok buh-zhuh-tuh-ree-ah/buh-zhuh-tuh-ree-ah-nah
waitress	cambrera	kam-breh-ruh
waiter	cambrer	kam-breh
menu	la carta	lah kahr-tuh
fixed-price menu	menú del dia	muh-noo thuhl dee-uh
wine list	la carta de vins	uh lah kahr-tuh thuh veens
glass of water	un got d'aigua	oon got dah-ee-gwah
glass of wine	una copa de vi	oo-nuh ko-pah thuh vee
bottle	una ampolla	oo-nuh am-pol-yuh
knife	un ganivet	oon gun-ee-veht
fork	una forquilla	oo-nuh for-keel-yuh
spoon	una cullera	oo-nuh kool-yeh-ruh
breakfast	l'esmorzar	les-moor-sah
lunch	el dinar	uhl dee-nah
dinner	el sopar	uhl soo-pah
main course	el primer plat	uhl pree-meh plat
starters	els entrants	uhlz ehn-tranz
dish of the day	el plat del dia	uhl plat duhl dee-uh
coffee	el cafè	uhl kah-feh
rare	poc fet	pok fet
medium	al punt	ahl poon
well done	molt fet	mol fet

Menu Decoder *(see also pp32–33 & 142–3)*

l'aigua mineral	lah-ee-gwuh mee-nuh-rahl	mineral water
sense gas/ amb gas	sen-zuh gas/ am gas	still/ sparkling
al forn	ahl forn	baked
l'all	lahlyuh	garlic
l'arròs	lahr-roz	rice
les botifarres	lahs boo-tee-fah-rahs	sausages
la carn	lah karn	meat
la ceba	lah seh-buh	onion
la cervesa	lah-sehr-ve-sah	beer
l'embotit	lum-boo-teet	cold meat
el filet	uhl fee-let	sirloin
el formatge	uhl for-mah-djuh	cheese
fregit	freh-zheet	fried
la fruita	lah froo-ee-tah	fruit
els fruits secs	uhlz froo-eets seks	nuts
les gambes	lahs gam-bus	prawns
el gelat	uhl djuh-lat	ice cream
la llagosta	lah lyah-gos-tah	lobster
la llet	lah lyet	milk
la llimona	lah lyee-moh-nah	lemon
la llimonada	lah lyee-moh-nah-thuh	lemonade
la mantega	lah mahn-teh-gah	butter
el marisc	uhl mah-reesk	seafood
la menestra	lah muh-nehs-truh	vegetable stew
l'oli	loll-ee	oil
les olives	luhs oo-lee-vuhs	olives
l'ou	loh-oo	egg
el pa	uhl pah	bread

el pastís	uhl pahs-tees	pie/cake
les patates	lahs pah-tah-tuhs	potatoes
el pebre	uhl peh-bruh	pepper
el peix	uhl pehsh	fish
el pernil salat serrà	uhl puhr-neel suh-lat sehr-rah	cured ham
el plàtan	uhl plah-tun	banana
el pollastre	uhl poo-lyah-struh	chicken
la poma	la poh-mah	apple
el porc	uhl pohr	pork
les postres	lahs pohs-truhs	dessert
rostit	rohs-teet	roast
la sal	lah sahl	salt
la salsa	lah sahl-suh	sauce
les salsitxes	lahs sahl-see-chuhs	sausages
sec	sehk	dry
la sopa	lah soh-puh	soup
el sucre	uhl-soo-kruh	sugar
la taronja	lah tuh-rohn-djuh	orange
el te	uhl teh	tea
les torrades	lahs too-rah-thuhs	toast
la vedella	lah veh-theh-lyuh	beef
el vi blanc	uhl bee blang	white wine
el vi negre	uhl bee neh-gruh	red wine
el vi rosat	uhl bee roo-zaht	rosé wine
el vinagre	uhl bee-nah-gruh	vinegar
el xai/el be	uhl shahee/uhl beh	lamb
el xerès	uhl shuh-rehs	sherry
la xocolata	lah shoo-koo-lah-tuh	chocolate
el xoriç	uhl shoo-rees	red sausage

Numbers

0	zero	seh-roo
1	un (masc)/una (fem)	oon/oon-uh
2	dos (masc)/dues (fem)	dohs/doo-uhs
3	tres	trehs
4	quatre	kwa-truh
5	cinc	seeng
6	sis	sees
7	set	set
8	vuit	voo-eet
9	nou	noh-oo
10	deu	deh-oo
11	onze	on-zuh
12	doce	doh-dzuh
13	tretze	treh-dzuh
14	catorze	kah-tohr-dzuh
15	quinze	keen-zuh
16	setze	set-zuh
17	disset	dee-set
18	divuit	dee-voo-eet
19	dinou	dee-noh-oo
20	vint	been
21	vint-i-un	been-tee-oon
22	vint-i-dos	been-tee-dohs
30	trenta	tren-tah
31	trenta-un	tren-tah oon
40	quaranta	kwuh-ran-tuh
50	cinquanta	seen-kwahn-tah
60	seixanta	seh-ee-shan-tah
70	setanta	seh-tan-tah
80	vuitanta	voo-ee-tan-tah
90	noranta	noh-ran-tah
100	cent	sen
101	cent un	sent oon
102	cent dos	sen dohs
200	dos-cents (masc)	dohs-sens
	dues-centes (fem)	doo-uhs sen-tuhs
300	tres-cents	trehs-sens
400	quatre-cents	kwah-truh-senz
500	cinc-cents	seeng-senz
600	sis-cents	sees-senz
700	set-cents	set-senz
800	vuit-cents	voo-eet-senz
900	nou-cents	noh-oo-cenz
1,000	mil	meel
1,001	mil un	meel oon

Time

one minute	un minut	oon mee-noot
one hour	una hora	oo-nuh oh-ruh
half an hour	mitja hora	mee-juh oh-ruh
Monday	dilluns	dee-lyoonz
Tuesday	dimarts	dee-marts
Wednesday	dimecres	dee-meh-kruhs
Thursday	dijous	dee-zhoh-oos
Friday	divendres	dee-ven-druhs
Saturday	dissabte	dee-sab-tuh
Sunday	diumenge	dee-oo-men-juh

Rail Transport Maps

The main map shows the whole of Barcelona's Metro system, which has nine lines. It also shows the city's FGC suburban lines, funiculars and tram *(see pp184–5)*. Public transport in Barcelona is modern and efficient, and the integrated transport system allows for interchanging between different modes of transport if you have a multi-journey (for example a *T-10*) card. A special ticket for tourists is the *Barcelona Card*, available in one-day to five-day values, which offers unlimited travel on Metro and bus, and discounts at leading sights and museums. The inset map shows Catalonia's mainline rail network, which is run by RENFE, the Spanish state system. The stations selected for inclusion here are those closest to sights described in this guide.

Key

- **L1**　Metro line
- ◯　Interchange station
- ┄　Tram line
- ┿┿　Funicular
- ▬▬　FGC line
- ▬▬　RENFE line